Awaken the "Gree

The magical system of *Glamoury* is based on an Irish Celtic tradition that has been practiced successfully for uncounted years. Apply the marvelous stories, magical concepts, practical techniques, and spiritual wisdom in this book to your life and experience a profoundly "Green" change in your world.

Like all ancient peoples, the Celts lived in harmony with natural cycles. From this acceptance of the ebb and flow of life, they began to understand how these cycles are deeply related to individual growth. As time passed, they couched their wisdom in a huge body of legends, many of which have been passed down to us through the generations. These legends, which cradle the wisdom of the great Celtic magical tradition, have survived the centuries because humans have always instinctively recognized their essential truth and validity.

Today, we have moved so far away from these natural cycles that we've all but forgotten the truths that our ancient ancestors knew. *Glamoury* was written to help you rediscover these lost truths and to restore a sense of unity with life's cycles.

Glamoury describes a practical application of the wisdom from Celtic myths that is relevant to spiritual seekers today. As you submerge yourself in the transformative power of these magical myths, they will spontaneously interact with your subconscious to activate personal change at the deepest levels, enabling you to internalize them and act from a glowing core of timeless, fundamental truth.

The visualisation exercises in these pages are a proven means of accomplishing inner growth. They will enable you to journey to the realm of the Celtic Otherworld, where you will meet mythical beings who reflect aspects of yourself—beings you can question to gain a deeper understanding of yourself, the world, and how to effect a more perfect harmony between the two.

About the Author

Steve Blamires was born in Ayr, Scotland, in 1955, and currently lives on the west coast of the United States. At the age of nineteen, he began his studies with Gareth Knight and the legendary Company of Hawkwood. After studying the Western Mystery Tradition for twelve years, his interest moved to his Celtic roots. Ever since, he has concentrated on promoting all facets of this ancient tradition.

In 1986, Mr. Blamires founded the Celtic Research and Folklore Society (CRFS) as a way of helping others along the Celtic path. He has produced many magazine articles for several publications in the U.K. and the U.S.A.; writes and edits the CRFS journal, Seanchas; and carries out research on behalf of other authors and groups. He gives talks throughout the U.K. and U.S.A. on Celtic spirituality and magic, as well as carrying on the ancient tradition of storytelling. In Chicago, Mr. Blamires represented the interests of the indigenous Celtic peoples at the Council for a Parliament of the World's Religions. He has most recently been working with Tibetan Buddhist monks to make Holy Isle, Scotland, a place of spiritual retreat for people of all beliefs.

To Write to the Author

If you wish to contact the author or would like more information about this book, please write to the author in care of Llewellyn Worldwide, and we will forward your request. Both the author and publisher appreciate hearing from you and learning of your enjoyment of this book. Llewellyn Worldwide cannot guarantee that every letter written to the author will be answered, but all will be forwarded. Please write to:

Steve Blamires
℅ Llewellyn Worldwide
P.O. Box 64383, Dept. K069-8, St. Paul, MN 55164-0383, U.S.A.

Please enclose a self-addressed stamped envelope for reply, or $1.00 to cover costs.
If outside U.S.A., enclose international postal reply coupon.

Free Catalog from Llewellyn Worldwide

For more than 90 years, Llewellyn has brought its readers knowledge in the fields of metaphysics and human potential. Learn about the newest books in spiritual guidance, natural healing, astrology, occult philosophy, and more. To get your free copy of *Llewellyn's New Worlds of Mind and Spirit,* send your name and address to:

Llewellyn's New Worlds of Mind and Spirit
P.O. Box 64383, Dept. K069-8, St. Paul, MN 55164-0383, U.S.A.

Llewellyn's Celtic Wisdom Series

GLAMOURY

MAGIC OF THE CELTIC GREEN WORLD

STEVE BLAMIRES

1997
Llewellyn Publications
St. Paul, Minnesota 55164-0383

Excerpts from *The Tain,* by Thomas Kinsella (copyright 1986 by Oxford University Press) are reprinted by permission of the Author. Excerpts from *Cath Maige Tuired,* by E.A. Gray, (copyright 1983), *Lebor Gabala Erenn* by R.A.S. MacAllister (copyright 1938), and *Keatings History of Ireland* by P.S. Dinneen (copyright 1902) are reprinted by permission of the Irish Texts Society.

FIRST EDITION
Second Printing, 1997

Cover Art: Carrie Westfall
Cover Design: Lynne Menturweck and Tom Grewe
Illustrations: Nicola Jane Swinton
Book Design and Layout: Designed To Sell

Library of Congress Cataloging-in-Publication Data
Blamires, Steve
      Glamoury: Magic of the Celtic Green World / Steve Blamires.
         p. cm. — (Llewellyn's Celtic Wisdom Series)
      Includes bibliographical references and index.
      ISBN 1-56718-069-8 (trade pbk.)
      1. Magic, Celtic. 2. Mythology, Celtic. 3. Goddess religion.
4. Ritual. I. Title. II. Series.
BF1622.C45B57 1995
299'.16—dc20   95-39750
                                            CIP

Llewellyn Publications
A Division of Llewellyn Worldwide, Ltd.
St. Paul, Minnesota 55164-0383, U.S.A.

Llewellyn's Celtic Wisdom Series

Can it be said that we are all Celts? Certainly Western civilization owes as much, if not more, to our Celtic heritage as to Greek and Roman influences.

While the origins of the Celtic peoples are shrouded in the mists of time, they seem to have come from a civilization centered around Greece and the Aegean Sea in the third and fourth millennia B.C., moving out across Europe and occupying areas from Russia to Spain and finally, Scotland and Ireland in 1472 B.C. The Celtic tribes were politically independent, and—in contrast to the Roman Empire— never truly united under a single ruler. That same independence brought Europeans to the New World, then pulled them westward across the continent through a continuous need to create a "new order for the ages"—and a nation of people free of social, religious, political, and economic oppression. Today, the same Celtic spirit asserts itself as peoples everywhere struggle for a new political reality.

Celtic art, music, magic, and myth are unique, and are enjoying a renaissance today. Of particular interest is the Grail legend, which Carl Jung called the most recent of the great myths to surface from the collective unconscious, constituting the primary myth of Western civilization. The Grail legend offers us the means to find our way to the Otherworld and come back again—richer, wiser, healed and whole, having gained the knowledge and power to live consciously and fully. Basic to the Celtic tradition is the acceptance of personal responsibility and realization that all of us constantly shape and affect the land on which we live. Intrinsic to this notion is the Celtic interrelationship with the Otherworld and its inhabitants. The Celtic world view is a magical one, in which everything has a physical, mental, and spiritual aspect and its own proper purpose, and where our every act affects both worlds.

It is true that we are all Celts—for even the most humble of us must face the challenges of Arthur and Guinevere, of Merlin and Morgan le Fay in our own lives. And like the Knights of the Round Table, we all seek the Holy Grail in some shape or form. Like all great myths, the Grail legend is the model for the life we must live to bring this world and the Otherworld together, and thus to restore the wholeness we were all meant to possess.

The books of the Celtic Wisdom Series comprise a magical curriculum embracing ideas and techniques that awaken the soul to the myths and legends, the psychological and spiritual truths and the inner power each of us can tap to meet the challenges of our times.

Other Books by the Author

Irish Celtic Magical Tradition (Aquarian Press)

Seanchas: Journal of the Celtic Research and Folklore Society. Published quarterly since 1986.

Forthcoming

Celtic Tree Mysteries

For the good people of Eamhain Abhlach,
known and unknown, seen and unseen;
but, especially, for my Queen of Enchantment
and Passion, Eilidh of the Golden Hair.

Irish Celtic Magical Sites

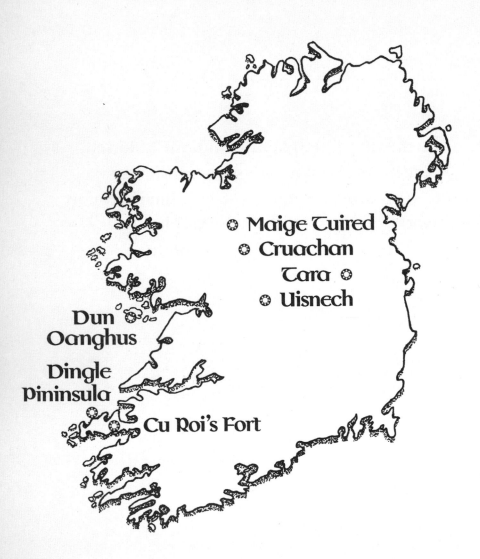

Maige Tuired
Cruachan
Tara
Uisnech

Dun Oanghus

Dingle Pininsula

Cu Roi's Fort

IRELAND

Contents

Section One
Setting the Scene

Chapter One

An examination of the vague and mysterious beginnings of the Celtic people, their spread throughout Europe, and their very early appearances in Great Britain.

Chapter Two

A comparison of the archaeological evidence with literary sources from both Europe and Great Britain.

Section Two
Preparation for the Practical Work

Chapter Three

Magic is a Natural Process; Techniques for Practical Work: Posture and Physical Location, Diet, Drugs, and Alcohol, Visualisation and Imagination, and Magical Ritual; The Proper Attitude: Understanding the Otherworld, Keeping a Magical Diary, and The Importance of Purpose.

Chapter Four

The Three Levels; The Concept of Time; Everything Is Equal; What Happens after Physical Death; Involvement in the Physical World; Humour and Fun.

Section Three
The Irish Tradition

Chapter Five

Cessair; Partholon; Neimheadh; The Fir Bolg; The Tuatha De Danann.

The importance of reading, studying, listening, and learning about Irish Celtic mythology for the practice of the Celtic magical tradition.

Chapter Six

The Mythological Cycle; The Ulster Cycle; The Fenian Cycle; and The Historical Cycle.

Using visualisation to understand the four Cycles, how they affected the land of Ireland, and how you are also affected in your growth and development.

Chapter Seven

The story of the five fifths of Ireland and the provincial attributes: West: Connacht, Knowledge; North: Ulster, Battle; East: Leinster, Prosperity; South: Munster, Music; and Centre: Meath, Kingship.

Assuming the position of Celtic warrior in each of the five provinces, in order to experience and develop the provincial attributes within yourself.

Section Four
A Who's Who of the Otherworld

Chapter Eight

Getting to know and understand the beings of the Otherworld. A comprehensive listing of gods and goddesses to consider as contacts and guides in Otherworld journeys.

Creating an Otherworld Working area in which to meet contacts and experience events in Celtic mythology.

Chapter Nine

The Otherworld beings who will provide personal advice, laws, and principles. A comprehensive listing of satirists, warriors, and kings.

Using visualisation, Celtic legends, your Otherworld landscape, and provincial attributes to facilitate contact with Otherworld deities and characters.

Section Five
The Four Festivals

Chapter Ten

The origins of the four main festivals of the ancient Irish Celts, Samhain, Imbolg, Bealtaine, and Lughnassadh.

Learn to understand the meaning behind the Irish Celtic legends by becoming an active participant.

Chapter Eleven

The Celtic festival celebrating the end of one year and the beginning of the next, involving personal reflection and preparation for the dark period.

Chapter Twelve

A personal, family celebration of the coming of spring, this festival is performed largely by the women of the group or clan.

Chapter Thirteen

A daytime festival during which men accept their personal High Kingship, and women celebrate their connection to the Earth.

Chapter Fourteen

A celebration of the harvest, involving sacrifice of the High King, recognition of the work of the four elements, and the sovereignty of the Land.

Section Six
Magical Weapons and Working Areas

Chapter Fifteen

Finding Your Magical Weapons; Cleansing and Consecrating Your Weapons.

Chapter Sixteen

How to set up a magical Working area within the home, if an outdoor area is either impractical or unavailable.

Illustrations

Acknowledgements

I would like to express my thanks to various people for helping me make the idea of this book a reality. Many of these important people are people who have made a chance remark, or whose conversations I have overheard, and which have led me to a new way of thinking and understanding. To these unknown and anonymous people I owe a debt of gratitude. I would also like to express my sincere thanks to Thomas Kinsella for allowing me to quote from his fine rendering of *The Tain,* and to the Irish Texts Society for allowing me to quote from several of their excellent translations of Irish Celtic legends. To all of these people I owe a great debt. My thanks are also extended to Nicola Jane Swinton for providing the illustrations which far outweigh my feeble attempts to describe things in words. Finally, I must acknowledge my deep gratitude to Eilidh for giving me the life experiences I need to truly understand what this world is all about.

Introduction

This book is not intended to provide a thorough definition of the lengthy, in-depth, and complicated subject of Irish Celtic magic. Instead, it is a reference, providing a basic grounding in the subject, to give you the information you need to decide whether to further pursue this system or to look for other means of self-development. While each section can be read independently as a quick guide to the topic covered, I would recommend that you start at the beginning, and work your way through to the end, going back as necessary to sections which may have been difficult to grasp.

The Practical and Ritual Work given throughout the book will help you understand the points raised in the text, and will help you to develop, by simulating learning experiences which you might otherwise never have. By speeding your learning process to help you consciously and subconsciously reconstruct your world-view, these practical techniques and your attempts to adopt the changes in mental attitude described in the text will put you in a position to experience more of life than would otherwise be the case. That, in a nutshell, is the purpose of this book.

Because the system I describe is based on Irish Celtic mythology, it will be necessary for you to become familiar with Irish mythology, who the Irish Celts were, and how they saw the world. A Bibliography has been provided for those of you who wish to research further into this fascinating subject. This book will give you enough of a grounding to be able to start the practical techniques with confidence, and with a solid mental base upon which to build. I urge you to study the sections which set the scene as far as Irish Celtic mythology is concerned, if you plan to attempt any Practical Work. These sections give your mind—conscious and sub-conscious— very important symbols to be used later in Practical Work as the foundation upon which all else will eventually rest.

The first two sections of the book are the most important for readers coming new to this subject. They give critical advice on matters which are basic to the Irish Celtic magical tradition and to your ability to practice it. The concepts they discuss must become a part of not only your magical Workings, but your daily life. Magic should be the most important factor in your life—twenty-four hours a day, seven days a week. To effectively practice the Celtic system, you will need to understand and accept some concepts which may be totally foreign to your experience so far, and which may be difficult to assimilate. Study these sections well, and be sure you have a good grasp of these attitudes and ideas before you attempt the Practical Work.

Although I have included several full magical rituals in the Practical Work, it is not necessary for you to carry these out to understand the learning process described in the rest of the book. Not everyone is suited to ritual, and there is no point in forcing yourself to do something which you intuitively dislike.

Some of you will find this system appealing, but will never bother to go any further. Some will find it to be a lot of rubbish, and of no practical use. Others will find the subject to be exactly what they have been looking for, and will want to find out more. This book and the additional references I provide will allow you to make considerable progress. To help you along the way, I intend to publish all I know about this very useful and extremely practical system, in books addressing very specific subjects such as the Celtic Tree Alphabet. For now, all that I ask is that you read this book with an open mind and heart, and have a good try at this system.

Section One

Setting
the
Scene

Chapter One

The Origins of the Celts

T he origins of the Celts are vague and mysterious. We really do not know much about their roots, but many different theories have been advanced to explain who the Celts were and where they came from. Some are ridiculous, like the theory that claims they were the original inhabitants of Greenland, who paddled down to Ireland in their kayaks and then spread out across Europe. Others are more plausible, being based on archaeological evidence and the testimonies of ancient Greek and Roman writers, travellers, and historians. We will take a more detailed look at some of these theories in Chapter Two.

It is known that there was a race of people called the Keltoi or Galatae by the Greeks. These names are still in use today. We do not know if this race of people used the Greek, Roman, or similar names themselves. They may not have had a racial or group name at all, preferring instead to identify themselves by tribal name. Even the all-embracing term still used today—the Celts—may be wrong.

What we can say with a degree of confidence, and based on archaeological evidence, is that there was a civilisation centered near Greece and the Aegean Sea in the third and fourth millennia B.C. This may have been the people who later moved out across Europe and became the Celtic tribes, which we can identify during the last millennium B.C. It helps to note that both the archaeological evidence and later legends indicate that the British and Irish Celts had a strong contact with Greece.

There were people living in Ireland and Britain long before this time who can be regarded as the indigenous population of these islands. Exactly who these people were we cannot say. Examination of ancient pollen deposits taken from the peat on Machrie Moor, Isle of Arran, Scotland, has shown that as early as 6550 B.C., humankind was leaving its mark on the landscape and cultivating the native vegetation. It is very unlikely that these ancient people were of Celtic origin. During the period 2000-1500 B.C., many different groups of people arrived in Britain, mainly from the Baltic regions, who to a great extent mixed peaceably with the native peoples. Virtually all of these incomers remained in what is now southern England, and it is doubtful that they came farther north in any great numbers, or that they crossed over to Ireland. The great mythological history of Ireland and the Irish Celts, known as *The Book of Invasions of Ireland*, states specifically that Celtic peoples came to Ireland in 1472 B.C. This date is remarkably close to the dates suggested by the archaeological evidence, and was determined by Celtic scribes who compared the events in Ireland with contemporary events described in the Bible. Many of their dates have proven to be very accurate.

About 800 B.C., an intrepid Carthaginian, called Himilcon, made a daring sea voyage of discovery which took him to the British Isles, and perhaps even as far as Iceland. He noted that the two main islands comprising the British Isles were called Albion and Ierne by the native people—names which are still used today. Unfortunately, Himilcon did not say anything about the inhabitants of these islands or what they called themselves. A Greek explorer, Pytheas the Massaliote, refers to Ireland as being Celtic in the fourth century B.C., but again does not go into any detail concerning the people or where they came from.

There is a reference to the Celts attributed to Hecataeus, which has been dated to about the sixth century B.C.; however, the dating is not very accurate, and his wording implies he was referring to a previous period, and not to his personal knowledge of these people. Livy (born 59 B.C.-died A.D. 17) records the Celts as having been in Italy in 534 B.C., but again, this was written centuries later. The earliest known *contemporary* written reference, which specifically mentions the Celts as an identifiable people, is from 450 B.C. by the Greek, Herodotus. Even though he still tells us nothing of the people themselves, he says:

> The Istrar has its source in the *Celtic* lands of the Pyrenees and crosses Europe, cutting it in half. (emphasis added)

From this brief mention of a Celtic land, we can deduce that the Celts were a recognised and identifiable people in ancient Europe. Because Herodotus does not bother to explain who the Celts were, we can infer that the name was already familiar to his readers at that time. It also implies that they were quite numerous and spread over a large area. Other written references and archaeological finds indicate that, from this period onward, Celtic tribes covered a vast area stretching from Portugal to Russia and from Southern Spain to Northern Scotland. Evidence of this is found today in many place names: London, Milan, Paris, and Dublin, and the literally thousands of towns, villages, rivers, and mountains throughout Europe with names of Celtic origin.

Many European personal and family names similarly derive from ancient Celtic words. There are some oblique references by Southern Greek travellers to people who could be Celtic dating from the sixth century B.C. This implies that the Celts were already very numerous in the region of the Danube. Even the Danube River is named for the Celtic goddess Danu. It seems safe to assume that they must indeed have been an influential people in this region.

One of the earliest archaeological finds relating to Celtic peoples is a series of inscriptions in the old Lepontic Celtic language, written in Etruscan characters dating from the sixth century B.C., which were found in Northern Italy. Slightly farther north there is a good deal of evidence for Celtic peoples inhabiting modern Austria and Switzerland. In an area called Halstatt in the Salzkammergut district of Austria, there are some very ancient salt mines which have been dated to 1000 B.C., and which seem to have been worked more or less continuously until about the first century A.D. In this area, a huge cemetery was discovered in 1846 which contained not only a large number of bodies, but also a large quantity of grave goods. All of these artifacts bore a very distinctive, but previously unknown design style. This early Celtic art has come to be known as Halstatt Style, which has been dated to between the seventh and fifth centuries B.C. This era has consequently become known as the Halstatt Period.

Another significant find was made last century in the waters of Lake Neuchatel in Switzerland. Many different artifacts again all bore very distinctive and similar designs, but were different from the Halstatt art. This new series was given the name, La Tene Style, after the area in which it was discovered; and the period to which these artifacts were dated—about 400 B.C. to about 100 B.C.—is now called La Tene Period. These two finds indicate that not only was Central Europe heavily populated with Celts, but also that the Celts of these regions were wealthy, had an aristocracy, and a very high standard of living. These are the social conditions necessary for a people to start to evolve an appreciation of the arts, and to develop the spiritual side of their nature. This is borne out by subsequent archaeological finds, contemporary written references from foreign observers, and the later writings of the Celtic peoples themselves.

The sixth century through the second century B.C. in Europe has been split into several phases with various names. (There is a good deal of overlapping of periods, so these should not be considered hard-and-fast dividing lines.) The sixth century has been called the Age of the Princes, due to the many rich and elaborate burial sites which have been discovered throughout Europe—especially in the Rhineland and Austria—all dating to this period. One find in Germany was positively dated to 577 B.C., and was a burial on a truly lavish scale. The word, "Princes," used to denote this period, should not necessarily be given its modern connotation. It is more

likely that these individuals were local chieftains or local aristocracy, than members of a particular royal bloodline.

The fifth century is referred to as the La Tene period due to the
profusion of La Tene Style artifacts. The fourth century is the period
of the First Expansion, a time when there is a good deal of evidence
for movements of large numbers of Celtic people all over Europe—
particularly in Brittany and Switzerland. This movement may have
been an ongoing thing that did not start during the fourth century;
it is only because we find the first archaeological evidence for this
movement during this time that it has been given this name. It
should also be stressed that there is no evidence of large-scale movements of people either coming to Ireland or within Ireland itself at
this time. We shall look at this more closely later.

The third century has been classified as the Age of the Warriors,
again from archaeological finds and contemporary written accounts
of the exploits of the Continental Celtic warriors—particularly in
Italy and Austria. The second century was a time of fragmentation,
when the previously large and powerful Celtic tribes started to break
up, and the Celtic heyday in Europe came to a close. There were still
many Celtic people living and moving throughout Europe after the
second century B.C., but evidence indicates that these movements
and advances were on a much smaller scale. The Celts became a
more settled people who had stopped making war on others, but
who, nevertheless, still fought constantly among themselves—a Celtic
trait which, sad to say, persists to this day.

Some people erroneously assume that the Celtic peoples died
out, or were absorbed into the races and cultures of the lands in
which they found themselves; but the Celts were a definite racial
group with distinct language, culture, art, and beliefs as late as the
seventeenth century A.D. It can be argued that in some areas they are
still an identifiable people with their own languages, culture, music,
and beliefs (it is estimated that there are some two million people in
Europe who still speak a Celtic language). Writers tend to refer to the
Celts in the past tense, as usually they are referring to the ancient

Celts; but you should remember that we are still around, despite the suppressions of successive invaders, conquerors, and governments.

We know a great deal about the European Celts from the fourth century B.C. onward, thanks to the records of Greek and Roman writers, travellers, and explorers. We know that during the Age of the Warriors, many foreign armies used Celtic mercenaries in their ranks. Celts fought in Greece, Macedonia, Corsica, Sardinia, and North Africa. In Sicily, there were some three thousand Celtic mercenaries. In Egypt, four thousand Celts helped Ptolemy II, then stayed on to fight with Ptolemy III and Ptolemy IV. It is recorded that, in 369 B.C., two thousand Celts joined the beleaguered Spartans who successfully sacked Rome in 387 B.C., and Delphi, Greece, in 279 B.C., under the command of the warrior Brennos. Treasure found in a lake near Toulouse, France, may have come from this particular raid. These Celtic mercenaries were particularly favoured because of their fierceness in battle, their devotion to their leaders, and the fact that they brought their own weapons with them, and insisted on using them.

The fierceness of these Celtic warriors is described by the Asiatic Greek writer, Flavius Arrianus, in an account of a meeting between a group of Celtic warriors and Alexander the Great in 335 B.C., in a region near the Danube. Alexander had heard of these brave warriors, and probably had some Celtic mercenaries in his own ranks, and he knew that they certainly would have heard of him. Convinced that they would be in awe of him, he asked them what it was they feared most. He was rather put out when they replied that the only thing they feared was that someday the sky would fall on them. This example shows not only their total lack of fear of Alexander, but also a good deal of humour and bardic allusion, as they clearly understood that such a thing would never happen.

One unwanted side-effect of employing Celtic mercenaries was that their wives and children followed them around from country to country and battle to battle. Once the fighting was over, they tended to remain, and settle wherever they happened to be. They quarrelled with each other frequently, forcing their previous employers to try to keep the peace among them.

An Etruscan quote from this period calls them "Outlandish warriors with strange weapons," yet Cato the Elder recorded that the Celts of Gaul pursued two things: valour in combat and talking common sense. This was the first hint that they were not the brutal savages other writers depicted them to be.

The wealth of material available on the European Celts in the forms of archaeological evidence, oral evidence, and written evidence is massive. From these various sources it has been possible for archaeologists and historians to put together a very complete picture of these independent Continental tribes. Unfortunately, the same cannot be said for the Celts of Britain and Ireland, where the evidence is sparse indeed. The commonly held notion that there were several large-scale movements of Celtic people into Britain, who went on to populate Ireland, is just not supported by the material evidence that remains.

In the case of Ireland, it appears that the indigenous Bronze-Age people started to be influenced by La Tene culture during the Iron Age, and for a period of time afterwards. Gradually they adopted more of the Continental Celtic influences which they encountered. Already by the La Tene period, these people were speaking a definite Celtic language, which implies that their original tongue may have been very similar. This raises the question: where did these apparently isolated people learn a Celtic root language? Unfortunately, we do not know the answer to this. There is also very little evidence for an incoming influence of the Halstatt style. A few artifacts have been found which might be classed as Halstatt, but they are inferior copies of either earlier bronze or Continental artifacts, and cannot be regarded as indicating a flourishing Halstatt culture or people in Ireland contemporary with the Halstatt culture in Europe.

The isolation of these strange Celtic people is highlighted by the fact that there appears to have been an almost total collapse of societal living in Ireland between 500 and 300 B.C., despite their Continental cousins doing so well for themselves at the time. It is very difficult to piece together a clear picture of what was going on in Ireland. Many theories have been put forward, based on such diverse reasons as weather, social disintegration, and politics, but the fact is we just do not know. Ancient Irish legends, which linguistically, in some cases, go back to the second or third century B.C., indicate a large population with a sophisticated way of life; however, no site has ever been positively identified in Ireland as a place of large-scale human habitation. There are many known secular and ritualistic sites, such as Tara and Eamhain Macha, but these were not residential. This lack of Celtic villages, and an almost total absence of mundane artifacts from the Iron Age, including such basic items as pottery, has greatly hampered our understanding of the Celtic Iron Age in Ireland.

Paradoxically, some archaeological discoveries seem to indicate that there was a large, *mobile* population in Ireland at this time, despite the bulk of the discoveries which suggest otherwise. I am referring in particular to the many large sections of sophisticated roadways which have been unearthed, mainly in Irish peat bogs. These roadways were constructed from thousands of sections of tree trunks, laid one next to the other, the spaces between them carefully filled with twigs and dirt to form a smooth surface. These roads were clearly intended for use by high-speed chariots, which must have been travelling from one town or village to another, but the habitation sites they must have connected have yet to be found. One possible explanation for this could be inferred from Julius Caesar's comments on the Helvetii's practice of moving *en masse* and burning their towns behind them. Did the Irish Celts follow this practice as well? If so, this would also help to explain one of the strange classes of old Irish legends known as Togail, which basically describes the burning of buildings.

There have been several finds in Ireland of artifacts such as gold torcs, horse trappings, swords, spearheads, and axes, all of very high quality. Their scarcity, and their association with warriors rather than the ordinary folk, however, only serves to frustrate the completion of the picture. Yet even here is a paradox: Many of the Continental references to Celtic warriors mention that the male fighters always wore torcs around their necks. Although many highly ornate torcs have been found in Ireland, none has ever been found in association with a grave. All have been chance finds in isolated locations. Artifacts from other lands and races, such as Greek, Roman, and Egyptian, have been found in Celtic archaeological sites, but no pieces of Celtic manufacture, whether weapons, jewelry, or domestic goods, have ever been found in areas not settled by the Celts. It is almost as if the people of the Irish Iron Age deliberately removed all evidence of their presence. If this was the case, it is surprising that none of the known Irish Celtic legends refers to this fact. Some legends have been dated, by linguistic means, to this period, but none of them sheds any light on why there is such a lack of knowledge of the period.

Many of the artifacts which do exist bear a striking resemblance in style to artifacts made by the Parisii tribe, in what is now Yorkshire. This tribe was, no doubt, linked to the tribe of the same name in central Gaul, who gave their name to the city of Paris. It may well be that there was an Irish-Continental link which we do not yet fully understand. A link between Ireland and central England is also indicated in another curious way in the legend of Cu Chulainn, the great hero of the Ulster Cycle. In his early boyhood, Cu Chulainn was known as Setanta. Directly across the Irish Sea from where he was supposed to have been born, in what is now Lancashire, there was a large and powerful Celtic tribe called the Setantii. These two names are so close that there must have been a common root. Add to this the fact that Blackpool, in Lancashire, is almost due east of Dublin (which means "black pool"), and we start to get hints that there was more of a link between Ireland, Britain, and the Continent than the archaeological evidence suggests.

Archaeological evidence sadly tells us very little about the Irish Celts in comparison to what is found on the Continent. Where Ireland is at a great advantage though, is in the wealth of oral and literary evidence which has remained. It is these legends and pseudo-histories which tell us many important things the archaeological evidence cannot, such as what Irish Celtic society was like, how they saw and understood the world around them, and more importantly from our point of view, what they believed and practised on a magical and spiritual level.

Chapter Two

The Literary Sources

By comparing archaeological data with available written material, it is possible to build a fairly complete picture of what the Irish Celts were like, how they thought, how they lived, and what they believed. There are problems, however, when it comes to reconciling the two records, because both are incomplete, and quite often one seems to contradict the other.

The problem with the archaeological evidence is that it tells us nothing of the economic, social, or ideological way of life of the Celts who populated any given site. It does shed a good deal of light on the technological ability of the people, the climate they enjoyed (or endured!), the crops they grew, the animals they reared, and hence, their diet. It is also possible to tell a lot about their general physique and health from bone and dental remains. All of these things are very important, but they are all of a physical nature, and, do not reveal anything of a more abstract nature.

Conversely, the written records and oral tradition tell us virtually nothing about technological abilities, but they do provide a good deal of information relating to Celtic political, social, and ideological values. We have to be careful when studying this material, because it can be contradictory and misleading. Because of this, archaeologists rarely pay much attention to the thousands of extant manuscripts. Similarly, the student of the old manuscripts does not very often read up on the latest developments in the archaeological fields. To my mind, it is vital to keep up to date with both disciplines, and to be familiar with data from both sources, in order to be able to put together as complete a picture as possible. The combining of these two disciplines worked extremely well in the case of the famous Lindow Man, the Celtic body which was found in the Lindow Marshes of England. A forensic scientist, Don Robins, examined the physical remains, and came up with a great deal of information about the dead Celtic druid; however, there were several things he could not understand. Dr. Anne Ross, the eminent Celtic scholar, was able to explain most of these factors by referring to known Celtic practices and beliefs. Their book, *The Life and Death of a Druid Prince*, tells an amazing story, and shows just how much knowledge can be gleaned from one source if all available channels are investigated and utilised. Such techniques can also be used successfully by the student of Irish Celtic magic.

From the archaeological point of view, there are two types of sites to investigate, which we call deliberate sites and accidental sites. The deliberate sites are places such as burial mounds, impressive tombs, standing stones, stone circles, fortified hills, and earth works, where changes to the landscape were made intentionally to impress both contemporary viewers and those to come. Deliberate sites contain artifacts such as grave goods, votive offerings of jewelry, weapons, or animal bones and human remains, which very often yield a great deal of information. Accidental sites are mainly habitation sites, which today are no more than ruined or rotted remains, and which clearly were never meant to be seen like this. There are also the rarer accidental sites such as battlefields. Many of these were discovered purely by chance; but today there are more and more investigators reading the old legends, deciding where such and such a battle was supposed to have taken place, and then going out to look for it. A surprising number of sites have been located this way, the most important probably being the ongoing work at Navan

Fort in Ulster. This backs up my argument for the need for the two disciplines to be familiar with each other's work.

Accidental sites can provide a lot of artifacts, such as jewelry, household goods, and weapons, which were either lost, thrown away, or abandoned, and which were never intended to be found at the site. These, too, can tell us a great deal, but because their location is not always deliberate, they can also sometimes lead to a great deal of confusion and speculation.

As the written evidence is clearly deliberate, and its whole function is to inform and educate, it tells us much more than the anonymous and ambiguous evidence from archaeological sites. It has a great advantage over archaeological investigation, which by its very nature is destructive, in that it is possible to go back over the same written sources and study them afresh and from differing points of view. The literary historian rarely expects any significant, previously unknown manuscripts or books to suddenly appear for investigation, but tends to examine and re-examine the same sources until, by luck, some unexpected new manuscript should happen upon the scene. The archaeologist definitely *does* expect new sites to be discovered on a regular basis, and actively goes out to find them. The whole approach to each of the two disciplines is completely different, and the modern-day student of the Irish Celtic magical tradition must learn the techniques of both.[1]

As discussed earlier, there is a great deal of information available concerning the Continental Celts from both archaeological sites and the few written accounts of mainly non-Celtic contemporaries, who recorded what they saw and what they believed. It is an error, however, to assume that what applied to the Celts in Gaul must similarly apply to all other Celts. Ireland does not have the same body of archaeological evidence to study, but it is almost unique in that it has a vast body of literature dating back as early as the sixth century A.D., based

---

[1] For an excellent discussion of this subject see Bernard Wailes' article entitled "The Irish 'Royal Sites' in History And Archaeology" in the *Cambridge* (now *Cambrian*) *Mediaeval Celtic Studies Journal,* Number Three (1982). See Bibliography.

on accounts going back as far as the third century B.C. These ancient writings were compiled by Celtic scholars and scribes and cover every imaginable subject. They tell us an enormous amount about the whole Irish Celtic way of life, religious beliefs, magical practices, and philosophical outlook. The problems encountered when trying to compare writings about the Continental Celts with those about their Irish cousins can be seen if we take a look at what we know about the druids. While common to all the Celtic peoples, the druids in Gaul differed greatly in their beliefs and practices from druids in Ireland. The main difference in the written materials available for study is that the accounts of the Continental druids were written at the time they were being studied and discussed, but there are no such contemporary records in Ireland, although there are many references to druids in legends. Despite the hundreds of books which have been written on the druids over the centuries, it surprises most people to learn that there are only thirty-four known contemporary references to druids, none of which refer to Irish druids, and that even these may not be all that accurate. The lengthiest of them are by Caesar, who was in the middle of a great war against the Gaulish Celts, and was not terribly favoured toward them. His writings make the Gaulish druids out to be little more than judges and supervisors in legal and religious matters, whereas the Irish legends often describe them as magicians and powerful miracle workers. It is clear that the Irish druids had quite a different philosophy from their Continental, and even Welsh, cousins.

Their name comes from the old Celtic word *druid,* which means "very knowledgeable." Other commentators suggest that it is derived from the Gaulish word *dru,* or the Irish *dair,* both of which mean "oak." As only the Continental druids paid particular reverence to the oak, it is unlikely that this interpretation would apply in the case of the Irish druids, who revered the yew and the ash rather than the oak.

Nearly all of the contemporary references to druids are Roman, from the period after the Roman invasion of Gaul. Most of these only mention the druids in passing, implying that they were not all that important—at least to the Romans. The few comments which do give any specific details about them tend to be repeated by later writers. So, what we know about them is very limited, and even this may be tainted by the views of the conqueror. One of the few Greek references to the druids is by Diogenes Laertius who, writing in the third century A.D., and referring to two books believed to have existed about 200 B.C., says:

> Some say that the study of philosophy was of barbarian origin. For the Persians had their "Magi," the Babylonians or Assyrians the "Chaldeans," the Indians their "Gymnosophists," while the Celts and the Galatae had seers called "Druids" and "semnotheoi," or so Aristotle says in the "Magic," and Sotion in the twenty-third book of his "succession of Philosophers." Those who think that philosophy is an invention of the barbarians explain the systems prevailing among each people. They say that the Gymnosophists and Druids make their pronouncements by means of riddles and dark sayings, teaching that the gods must be worshipped, and no evil done, and manly behaviour maintained.[2]

The fact that this reference can be dated back to the second century B.C. shows that, even at this early date, the druids were known to the great philosophers and thinkers of Greece. They must have been recognised as a people whose teachings were worthy of mention and learning.

The main source of commentary specifically about the druids, their beliefs, and practices, is Caesar's volumes entitled *The Gallic War*. He is one of the few commentators who had first-hand knowledge of the druids. In Book Six, he says:

> Throughout Gaul there are two classes of persons of definite account and dignity...one consists of druids, the other of knights.

---

[2] From *The Druids* by T.D. Kendrick, Banton Press, 1990.

The former are concerned with divine worship, the due performance of sacrifices, public and private, and the interpretation of ritual questions; a great number of young men gather about them for the sake of instruction and hold them in great honour. In fact, it is they who decide in all disputes, public and private; and if any crime has been committed, or murder done, or there is any dispute about succession or boundaries, they also decide it, determining rewards and penalties; if any person or people does not abide by their decision, they ban such from sacrifice, which is their heaviest penalty. Those that are so banned are reckoned as impious and criminal; all men move out of their path and shun their approach and conversation, from fear they may get some harm from their contact, and no justice is done if they seek it, no distinction falls to their share. Of all these druids one is chief, who has the highest authority among them. At his death, either any other that is pre-eminent in position succeeds, or, if there be several of equal standing, they strive for the primacy by vote of the druids, or sometimes even with armed force. These druids, at a certain time of the year, meet within the borders of the Carnutes, whose territory is reckoned as the centre of Gaul, and sit in conclave in a consecrated spot. There assemble from every side all that have disputes, and they obey the decisions and judgements of the druids. It is believed that their rule of life was discovered in Britain and transferred thence to Gaul; and today those who would study the subject more accurately journey, as a rule, to Britain to learn it.[3]

The practice of excommunication by the druids seems to have been recognised in Ireland, and was, as suggested by Caesar, literally a fate worse than death for the victim. The institution of a "head" or "arch" druid was not recognised by the Irish Celts. Under their system, all druids and druidesses were held to be of equal status, although some earned fame by virtue of their wisdom and wise

---

[3] Caesar's writings are excerpted from *The Druids* by T.D. Kendrick, published by Banton Press, 1990.

counsel. There is no indication under the Irish system that the druids held great assemblies or gatherings with each other for any reason. Caesar goes on to say:

> The druids usually hold aloof from war and do not pay war taxes with the rest; they are excused from military service and exempt from all liabilities. Tempted by these rewards, many young men assemble of their own motion to receive their training; many are sent by parents and relatives. Report says that in the schools of the druids they learn by heart a great number of verses, and therefore some persons remain twenty years under training. And they do not think it proper to commit these utterances to writing, although in almost all other matters, and in their public and private accounts, they make use of Greek letters. I believe that they have adopted the practice for two reasons—that they do not wish the rule to become common property, nor those who learn the rule to rely on writing and so neglect the cultivation of the memory. The cardinal doctrine which they seek to teach is that souls do not die, but after death pass from one to another; and this belief, as the fear of death is cast aside, they hold to be the greatest incentive to valour. Besides this, they have many discussions as touching the stars and their movements, the size of the universe and of the earth, the order of nature, the strength and the powers of the immortal gods, and hand down their lore to their young men.

It may have been the case that the Gaulish druids were exempt from military service and deliberately kept away from war, but this was not the case in Ireland, where the most famous of druids, Cathbhadh, has a name which means "battle-slayer." It is unlikely that in a warrior-based society, which the Irish Celtic society clearly was, young men or parents interested in their children's welfare would deliberately try to use the priesthood as a means of avoiding military service. The prohibition on writing does not seem to have existed in Ireland either. In fact, it is believed that the Irish druids had vast libraries of written works dealing with all manner of subjects, including the classical legends of Greece and Rome. They did recognise the importance of memory, however, and the trainee druids of Ireland underwent the same lengthy memory training as their Continental cousins. The impression given by the rest of this passage, concerning the actual druidic lore and methods, is that Caesar was not actually all that sure about it, and was relying on second-hand information.

The next quote from Caesar introduces the topic which has most caught hold of the popular imagination, and which once more highlights great differences between the Gaulish and the Irish druids:

> The whole nation of the Gauls is greatly devoted to ritual observances, and for that reason those who are smitten with the more grievous maladies and who are engaged in the perils of battle either sacrifice human victims or vow so to do, employing the druids as ministers for such sacrifices. They believe, in effect, that, unless for a man's life a man's life be paid, the majesty of the immortal gods may not be appeased; and in public, as in private life they observe an ordinance of sacrifices of the same kind. Others use figures of immense size whose limbs, woven out of twigs, they fill with living men and set on fire, and the men perish in a sheet of flame. They believe that the execution of those who have been caught in the act of theft or robbery or some crime is more pleasing to the immortal gods; but when the supply of such fails they resort to the execution even of the innocent.

This short quote from what is, in total, a huge work, is the one which has caused the general public, and many practising magicians of both Celtic and other systems, to assume that all druids used human sacrifice. If we study what is actually being said by Caesar, however, we will see that this is not the case. From the first sentence, it is clear that he is talking about the practices of the laity in general, and not the druidic caste specifically. Earlier it was said that the druids were exempt from military service, yet in this section he specifically states it was "those who are engaged in the perils of battle" who perform human sacrifice. This clearly could not be the military-exempt druids. He then goes on to confirm this by adding, "employing the druids as ministers for such sacrifices," which suggests the druids were acting on behalf of the ordinary people, and were not carrying out sacrifices themselves or for their own ends. This is exactly the situation which existed in the United Kingdom until recently, and which still exists in many American states today, where "the people" can sentence a man to death for murder while a minister of the church is in attendance. There is no evidence of human sacrifice ever having taken place in Ireland at any time, and from the ancient Brehon Laws, it would seem that such practices would have been illegal anyway.

Many of the later Greek commentators seem to have relied heavily on Caesar's comments, and do not contribute very much to our knowledge of Gaulish druids. The exception to this are the strange descriptions given by Pliny the Elder, in A.D. 77, in his book *Natural History:*

> Here we must mention the awe felt for this plant [mistletoe] by the Gauls. The druids—for so their magicians are called—held nothing more sacred than the mistletoe and the tree that bears it, always supposing that tree to be the oak. But they choose groves formed of oaks for the sake of the tree alone, and they never perform any of their rites except in the presence of a branch of it; so that it seems probable that the priests themselves may derive their name from the Greek word for that tree. In fact, they think that everything that grows on it has been sent from heaven and is proof that the tree was chosen by the god himself. The mistletoe, however, is found but rarely on the oak, and when found is gathered with due religious ceremony, if possible on the sixth day of the moon (for it is by the moon that they measure their months and years, and also their ages of thirty years). They choose this day because the moon, though not yet in the middle of her course, has already considerable influence. They call the mistletoe by a name meaning in their language the all-healing. Having made preparation for sacrifice and a banquet beneath the

trees, they bring thither two white bulls, whose horns are bound then for the first time. Clad in a white robe, the priest ascends the tree and cuts the mistletoe with a golden sickle, and it is received by others in a white cloak. Then they will kill the victims, praying that god will render this gift of his propitious to those to whom he has granted it. They believe that the mistletoe, taken in drink, imparts fecundity to barren animals, and that it is an antidote for all poisons. Such are the religious feelings that are entertained towards trifling things by many peoples.[4]

This quote has caught the imagination of both the general public and scholars of the Celts, and has inspired numerous paintings and engravings depicting this scene. Archaeological evidence does not support this account, though, and it is likely that Pliny was relating second-hand information. It is doubtful that the Irish druids participated in this particular ritual if, in fact, any druids did. Mistletoe was unknown to the Irish druids—it was not introduced to Ireland until the nineteenth century—and we know that the Irish druids did not pay as much reverence to the oak as Pliny suggests the Gaulish druids did. It also seems highly unlikely that any druid would attempt to cut the tough stalks of the mistletoe with a sickle made of gold, a metal which does not take an edge. No gold sickles have ever been found in Britain, Ireland, or on the Continent.

At any rate, none of Pliny's references sheds any light on the Irish druids. What few references we do have are of a very different nature. The only existing contemporary account of the British druids comes from Tacitus, who described the attack on Anglesey, the stronghold of Welsh druidism, by Suetonius Paulinus in A.D. 60. Once again, we have the version of the conqueror, which is clearly biased, and trots out the same old stuff about sacrifice and cutting up victims. Tacitus wrote:

---

[4] From *The Druids* by T.D. Kendrick, Banton Press, 1990.

On the shore stood the opposing army with its dense array of armed warriors, while between the ranks dashed women in black attire like the Furies, with hair disheveled, waving brands. All around, the druids, lifting up their hands to heaven and pouring forth dreadful imprecations, scared our soldiers by the unfamiliar sight, so that, as if their limbs were paralysed, they stood motionless and exposed to wounds. Then urged by their general's appeal and mutual encouragements not to quail before a troop of frenzied women, they bore the standards onwards, smote down all resistance, and wrapped the foe in the flames of his own brands. A force was next set over the conquered, and their groves, devoted to inhuman superstitions, were destroyed. They deemed it, indeed, a duty to cover their altars with the blood of captives and to consult their deities through human entrails.[5]

All this British account really tells us is that there had been a druidic presence on Anglesey, that the Romans killed all the druids and druidesses and destroyed their sacred groves. None of this refers to Ireland, where no such attempt at suppressing and destroying the druids took place until the arrival of St. Patrick in the fifth century.

The deficit of contemporary Irish accounts of the druids is more than made up by the many references to them in stories, legends, and annals, in which they often play a significant part. The overall image we get from these references gives quite a different picture from the one painted by Caesar of the Continental druids. The Irish druid was much more concerned with and involved in the practice of magic than was his Gaulish counterpart; however, references to this in the legends give away just as little as the Gaulish references do. One druidic ritual which is mentioned in several manuscripts is the one used for determining the identity of the next High King. The success of this ritual was of the utmost importance. The name given to it was Tarbh Fheis (tarv faysh) which means "bull-feast." The ritual consisted of slaying a white bull, drinking a broth made from its flesh,

---

[5] From *The Druids* by T.D. Kendrick, Banton Press, 1990.

and then entering into a magical sleep or trance while wrapped in the bull's hide. As the sleeper was lying in his or her magical trance, other druids would set up a rhythmic chant, known as Or Firindi (awr feer-indi) "truthful speech," which aided the sleeper to dream the dream which would reveal the identity of the future High King.

We also know of a curious druidic ritual designed to make people insane, which was called Dlui Fulla (dloo foolah), and centred on magical wisps of straw. The druid would utter a magical incantation over the straw and then fling it in the face of the person to be cursed. Just as the straw danced and was blown about by the wind, so, too, would the victim start to leap and dance uncontrollably like a madman. Other known druidic rituals and forms of magic are Imbas Forasnai (eembas forash-nie), Teinm Laida (chaynim loyda), Dichetel Do Chenaid (dih-aytal doh haynah), Briarmon Smetrach (bree-armon smay-trah), and Glam Dichenn (glam dee-hin). A few of these are described in *Cormac's Glossary*, which was compiled by Archbishop Cormac MacCullenan, King of Cashel, before he died in 908. Unfortunately, not enough information is given to fully reconstruct these rituals. The passage concerning the first of these reads:

> Imbas Forasnai, that is "Manifestation that Enlightens" [or perhaps "Illumination between the Hands"], discovers what thing soever the poet likes and which he desires to reveal. The manner of it is that the poet chews the red meat of a pig, dog, or cat and then places it by the door on the flags. He chants an incantation over it and makes an offering of it to the gods. He puts his two palms over his face and sleeps, asking the gods not to be disturbed. What he desires to know will be revealed to him after three days and nights.[6]

---

[6] From *Keating's History of Ireland* by P.S. Dinneen, Irish Texts Society.

This curious ritual of chewing raw meat, and the hands being put next to or over the face, is very similar to the stories concerning Fionn Mac Cumhaill and how he gained his great knowledge. One version of the story says that he was cooking the Salmon of Knowledge, not for himself but for another, when three drops of its juice spurted out of its skin and landed on his thumb. Instinctively he stuck his thumb in his mouth to cool it and found he knew all that there was to know. These were the three drops which contained all the knowledge in the world. There is a connection between covering the face with the hands and the use of darkness. It is known that the poets and druids used darkness to still their minds and compose poetry, or sought divine inspiration while cut off from daylight. Note that in Cormac's description of this ritual, he says it was carried out by poets, and not by druids.

The ritual or magical practice of Teinm Laida, which may mean something like "Enlightenment by Song," is more obscure, and seems to have been a spontaneous and intuitive verse composed by the poet to determine a person's nature or a forthcoming event. It may have involved the use of a magic wand to touch the person in question before the verse was uttered; but the main part of it seems to have been the poet's, or druid's, ability to clear his or her mind sufficiently to allow the Inner, intuitive part to speak freely.

Dichetel Do Chenaid was another method of composing spontaneous verse, which would answer a question the poet or druid had in mind. This method does not seem to have involved the use of any Magical Weapons, although it may have been performed while the poet or druid was chewing hazelnuts. Hazelnuts were, symbolically, the fruit which contained all knowledge, and may have been a ritualistic aid to the composing poet or druid. The meaning of Dichetel Do Chenaid may be something like "Inspired Verse from the Finger Tips (or Bones)."

Briarmon Smetrach is mentioned in *Cormac's Glossary,* where he says, "Briarmon Smetrach—the name of an operation which poets perform on a person who refuses them. He grinds the person's ear lobe between his two fingers and that person dies." This may seem like a highly improbable way of killing someone, but this is not what

it means. Briarmon Smetrach is what we would call satire or slan-
der. It is a verse or verses composed to point out the individual's
weaknesses or faults, which, to the ancient Celt, was the worst possible thing that could happen—to lose face in front of family, com-
rades, or clan. The death referred to by Cormac is not physical death,
but the death of a personality, who would never again be accepted
by the people the way he or she had been up until that point. This,
of course, still happens today when an accusation, rightly or wrongly,
is made against a person. That person is tainted with the accusation,
which, in some cases, can have a devastating effect on the individual concerned.

It is interesting to note that, under our current legal system, if
a person feels an accusation has been made unjustly or inaccurately,
there is recourse to the courts. Under the ancient Irish system, the
Brehon Laws, there was no such recourse, despite the fact that the
Brehon Laws covered every other imaginable set of circumstances.
There was no right of appeal or even defense against a Briarmon
Smetrach, which, once it had been made, was irrevocable. This helps
to explain in the latter, corrupt days, why the satirists were held in
such fear, until eventually they were outlawed altogether.

Another form of satire was the Glam Dichenn, which caused
three great blisters to erupt on the face of the person against whom
it was made. To have been satirised and then to have to go about
with the very obvious evidence of it on your face would have been
too much to bear. This blemishing was used several times against
unjust kings to force them to abdicate. A king who was blemished in
any way could not hold the throne. The fact that a satire had been
made against such a king, assuming the satire was justified in the
first place, indicates that the king was not fit anyway, and the blem-
ishes were more or less confirmation of this.

While most druid rituals consisted of words, some Magical
Weapons and tools were also used. There are references to the druids
possessing a magical cloak, known as a Celtar, which rendered the
wearer invisible. They also practised a ritual called Fe Fiada (fay fee-
ada), which likewise had the effect of producing invisibility, but by

the use of incantation and a magical fog, as opposed to a garment. This same magical fog was believed to surround every fairy mound, and was what prevented ordinary people from gazing upon the comings and goings of the Sidhe. The druids' ability to control the elements and to create violent storms out of otherwise perfectly calm weather conditions is also frequently suggested. Druids were masters of illusion, and could create hallucinations so lifelike that the viewer believed them to be real. Unfortunately, we do not know exactly how they did these things, which makes research into the druids and their practices so frustrating. Study of both the written material and other available corroborative material will improve the chances of creating a more informative picture.

Most references to the Irish druids are buried in books dealing with a whole host of subjects. A few of these are written in Old Irish, which was in use until the tenth century; some are in Middle Irish, which was in use from the tenth to the fifteenth century; and the later manuscripts, dealing mainly with the Fenian Cycle and the many different histories and pseudo-histories of Ireland, are all in Modern Irish, which dates from the fifteenth century, and is still in use to this day. Many of the Old Irish manuscripts contain what are known as glosses, which often tell us more than the original manuscripts do. Glosses were inserted between the lines of the original manuscript, or often in the marginal areas, and are short explanations of archaic words or ideas which the Middle Irish writers came across as they studied these ancient documents. Eventually the glosses on some manuscripts became so numerous, as each new writer and student added his or her comments, that some of the original texts became almost impossible to read. Luckily for us, these scribblings are a great source of information on both the contents of the original manuscript and the people making them.

From glosses, it has been possible to virtually recreate the previously lost grammar of Old Irish. This has lead to still further examinations of the oldest known documents, thereby extracting even more knowledge. So important are these glosses that even as far back as the ninth and tenth centuries, scholars of the day were putting together books specifically on this subject. *Cormac's Glossary* is the most famous and the most important of these. Others are those by Michael O'Clery, Duald MacFirbis, and O'Davoren. Some other Irish history books also contain ancient grammars within them. The most important of these ancient books have been preserved, at least in part, and some are available from specialist outlets in translation or partial translation. (See the Bibliography for details of these editions.) Even with our glossaries and ancient grammars, though, there are still passages within the books which defy translation.

Although we have been referring to these sources as books, they are really no more than collections of manuscripts which have been copied into one volume by the mediaeval scribes. Each contains diverse material such as very ancient legends, stories which the compilers would have considered to be contemporary, lengthy genealogies, histories and pseudo-histories, glosses, and a whole range of instructive and practical matters. The oldest such compilation is the *Lebar-na-hUidhre* (yower no hoodra), commonly known in English as the *Book of the Dun Cow*. It was written by Mailmuri Mac Kelleher, in the great Monastery of Clonmacnoise, where he died in 1106. It is very heavily glossed, and there is a part, in Mac Kelleher's own handwriting, commenting on the fact that he copied much of it from even older works—which, sadly, have been lost. Today all that is left are 134 pages, a mere fragment of the original. It contains sixty-five stories and legends, plus a few historical pieces, and gets its curious name because it allegedly was written on vellum made from the hide of St. Kieran's pet cow.

The *Lebar Laigen* (yower lie-in), the *Book of Leinster*, was written in 1160 by Finn MacGorma, Bishop of Kildare, and Aed Mac Criffan. Today it consists of 410 pages and covers over a thousand different stories, legends, poems, and histories, and is a very important source for students on all aspects of the Celts and Celtic culture. One of the fullest versions of the great Ulster Cycle epic, the Tain Bo Cuailnge (the Cattle Raid of Cooley), is to be found in the *Book of Leinster*.

The *Lebar Brecc* (yower brek), the *Speckled Book*, probably from the same period as the *Book of Leinster,* is 280 pages long, and deals almost exclusively with religious and secular matters. These can be of value to students of the pre-Christian Celts, as these tracts still give away valuable bits and pieces of Celtic society and attitudes, all of which help to build a more complete picture.

The important *Book of Ballymote* consists of 501 pages, and was written by several hands in Ballymote, Co. Sligo, in 1391. It contains some of the most important versions of well-known legends, as well as treatises on things such as the ancient history of Ireland and the Ogham script. Also written in Co. Sligo, at Lecan, was the *Yellow Book of Lecan.* This was compiled by Donagh Mac Firbis and Gilla Isa Mac Firbis around 1390, and today about 500 pages of it remain. As with the others, it contains a vast selection of stories, legends, and historical accounts. The *Book of Lecan,* not to be confused with the *Yellow Book of Lecan,* was written by Gilla Isa Mor Mac Firbis in 1416, and closely resembles the *Book of Ballymote* in content. All of these books derive from much older sources, and the language used in some of them, especially in passages of direct speech and poetry, can sometimes be dated back to the third century B.C. There are also literally thousands of individual manuscripts extant, some dealing with only one subject or legend, some with several, some complete, some incomplete. These, likewise, yield a huge amount of information which is of use to anyone studying the Celts of Ireland.

Perversely, there are more Irish manuscripts existing today on the Continent than there are remaining in Ireland. This is a result of the Viking raids of the seventh to ninth centuries, when many monks fled Ireland and took sanctuary with their secular brothers in France, Belgium, and, especially, Switzerland. The only things they took with them were their books and manuscripts, which shows the very high value they placed on them. The illiterate Vikings seemed to regard books and written material as dangerous and magical, and whenever they came across them, they would destroy them by "drowning" in a river or lake.

It is worth pointing out at this stage that, although we know the titles of some 335 different legends (as opposed to histories, factual works, and lives of saints), only a fraction of the actual stories have survived, and most of these are incomplete. We also find several different versions of the same stories, which shows the vast repertoire the ancient Irish storyteller had at his or her disposal. It must be kept in mind that, to the ancient Celt, these legends were factual and accurate, and were not considered to be fiction in any way. So important were they that The Brehon Laws cover their telling, and split them into two groups. These are Prim Scela and Fo Scela—main tales and secondary tales—with only certain clearly defined grades of storytellers allowed to tell the Prim Scela, and only certain other grades allowed to tell the Fo Scela. Many of these Prim and Fo Scela also have Rim Scela, shorter, secondary tales which explain how things came to be the way they are when the main tale opens. For a full discussion of the Scela, see Proinsias MacCana's book, *The Learned Tales of Mediaeval Ireland.*

If you add these Prim, Fo, and Rim Scela to the many annals which exist, and couple these with the many Irish versions of classical Greek and Roman stories, plus the factual manuscripts dealing with subjects like cookery, medicine, astronomy, botany, and secular life, it soon becomes clear just what a vast repository of knowledge and information lies within the Irish Celtic writings. If you wish to read further into this aspect of Celtic history, the Bibliography lists not only books containing good translations of the legends, but also books dealing with the manuscripts themselves.

The other great source of information is, of course, the oral tradition; but this by its very nature is much harder to study. At the end of the ninteenth century, a few writers and researchers realised the value of the oral tradition, which was beginning to die out. Recording what they heard in poems and stories were people such as W. B. Yeats, Fiona Macleod, Lady Gregory, and that great compiler of Gaelic lore and tradition, Alexander Carmichael. Reading these works is not only highly entertaining, but can also be very informative. In Ireland and Scotland, it is still possible to hear some of the few traditional storytellers left, who continue to tell these ancient tales along with a few more contemporary ones as they travel the countryside. They may be the only true descendants of the early Celts left in these lands. Should you ever have the opportunity to hear a traditional storyteller at work, I would advise you to make the effort to go and hear what he or she has to say. With a little bit of deeper knowledge as to the hidden meanings of the legends, it can be a very enlightening experience.

The study of the oral and written traditions must be balanced with Practical Work to gain any real understanding of Irish Celtic magic. By learning how to handle this wealth of material in a practical way, we learn to make sense of the contradictions, omissions, errors, and unintelligible passages which we come across in the legends. What this Practical Work involves is the subject of the following sections of this book. With a basic understanding of this, it will be time to have a closer look at the mythological history and structure of Ireland in Celtic times.

Section Two

Preparation
for the
Practical
Work

Chapter Three

Techniques
and Attitudes

To get the most from physical exercise, it is important to concentrate on what your body is doing. In other words, there must be a mental-level input. Similarly, there must be the true desire to do the exercises in the first place—a spiritual-level input. Physical exercise, therefore, demands input from all three levels, and so, too, do magical exercises, if you are to achieve maximum benefit from them. Before you begin, I would advise you to read the following points concerning the Otherworld and magical Working under the Irish system, as success is dependent entirely upon the mental attitude and spiritual awareness with which you approach this Work.

The Irish tradition is very much one of involvement, with emphasis on personal responsibility for your own progress, and on doing things, as opposed to merely reading or thinking about them. To this end, I have incorporated a series of Practical Exercises into this book, which build one upon the other to give you some experience of the Otherworld and the techniques needed to operate fully within nonphysical realms. These exercises are by no means the sum total of such techniques under this system, nor are they the most important ones. They will, however, help to give you a basic familiarity with the life forces of the Green World, a deeper understanding of the mechanics of both this world and the Otherworld, and an understanding of how we all constantly shape and affect the land on which we live. They will give you guidance to find your way around the Otherworld, and, most important of all, make conscious contact with the inhabitants of the Otherworld in order to learn from them.

Some of you may already be familiar with the magical techniques of other disciplines; however, the attitudes and techniques which I suggest are necessary to work the Irish Celtic system successfully will differ from those with which you are familiar. If you have no prior knowledge of or experience with magic, then you may find that some of what follows is, at first, difficult to accept. This is understandable, and all I ask is that you accept what is written here for the duration of your studies, and try the exercises with an open mind and heart. Once you have done this, you will have the knowledge and experience to make a decision as to whether or not this is the correct system for you. You might also ask yourself: Am I prepared to adapt, even temporarily, to the belief system presented here, in order to give these exercises and techniques a fair trial? If so, put aside your doubts and fears and venture forward.

Magic is a Natural Process

Probably the most important point to heed is never to force the Practical Work, no matter how difficult that may seem. Everything we do under this ancient Irish system complies with natural Green World laws. Nothing is ever forced or put under unnecessary pressure to grow or develop in the Green World, and similarly, you should not feel that you must push yourself to the limit to make a success of your Working. Dedication and commitment are needed, but dedication and commitment should not be confused with the useless stress and strain suffered by those who concentrate so hard during meditation that their brows knit and their heads ache. This is unnatural, unnecessary, and gets you nowhere. Perhaps the emphasis in modern society is to get everything completed as quickly as possible, but this is not the case in the Green World, and it is not the case with Irish magic. Take your time, tune in to the natural pace of the Green World around you, and let everything else go hurtling by.

On the other hand, do not become lazy or inconsistent with your Practical Work. Regular practical sessions, even of short duration, are preferable and more beneficial than lengthy, irregular sessions performed on a spontaneous basis. Ideally, you should set aside some time each day, and at the same time each day, to go over your Practical Work, and to do something practical about the Irish system. Results may seem slow at first, and while this may test your patience, you will eventually realise and understand that everything has its own cycle of development and growth, and these things cannot be forced or changed. Once you have established your regular Practical Work routine, you should begin to get a feel for your own growth rate as well. Resist the temptation when progress seems slow to assure yourself that you have found the growth rate which is applicable to you. Your conscious mind may resist that which it does not want to do. Anyone who is out of condition physically knows how much resistance there is from the body to starting physical exercise, and how clever the mind can be in thinking up excuses not to do the exercises anyway. As you come to understand the Irish system, you will see that the physical level and the spiritual level are interlinked, and that there may be a certain amount of devious resistance to these magical exercises from your mental and spiritual levels. The exercises in this book will make your mind do things it does not normally do. They will make it consider things it has not considered before. They will challenge deeply entrenched ideas and beliefs and they will cause a good deal of activity in areas of your brain which have probably been grossly underworked. Expect resistance, but do not give in to it.

Once you have successfully recognised your natural rate of growth, you will then discover that your learning and progress will go in cycles of growth and stagnation, despite the fact that you perform the exercises diligently and correctly. In the Green World, we recognise this process as the changing of the seasons. There are growth periods, periods when nothing seems to happen, and periods when things seem to die away. It is a good thing to be aware that these cycles exist, for sooner or later they will play an important part in your magical life.

It will also be necessary to make sure you have a good supply of nourishment to help your mind and spirit grow as you practice the exercises. This nourishment should be in the form of books, tapes, films, talks, and lectures dealing with Irish mythology. A Bibliography at the back of this book will help you identify useful resources to give your mind more information to work on and digest. Filling your memory and visual imagination with symbols and images now, will be the building blocks of Otherworld communication in the months and years to come. Equally important is contact with people of a like mind. Having close friends in whom you can confide, and with whom you can talk about your magical progress, is invaluable. Take care, though; you may well be surprised by the reactions of people to what you are doing. Friends and family you thought were open-minded and understanding may suddenly warn you of the "dangers of occult dabbling," and start to shy away from you. Conversely, you may be surprised that friends and family who have never voiced an opinion on such matters turn out to be understanding and supportive. These reactions emphasise the point behind the much-voiced, but little understood, subject of occult secrecy. Because you may expect surprise or even open hostility, it makes sense to discuss what you are doing only with those you know to be sympathetic or to have a genuinely open mind on such matters. On a more positive note, the study of magic tends to bring together people of a like mind, which will put you in contact with people you can trust, and with whom you can talk openly and freely about your beliefs and experiences. Follow up these new contacts, and nourish your magical self through exchange with them.

Techniques for Practical Work
Posture and Physical Location

The best posture for meditation and Otherworld journeying is seated on a hard-backed chair with both feet on the ground and hands resting on your lap. Some people assume that it is necessary to adopt a special posture for meditation or Otherworld journeying, but this is not the case. The yoga postures of the Eastern traditions, for example, have nothing to do with the Irish system, and it is not a good idea to mix the two, especially during Practical Work. The Irish system specifically, and Western systems generally, stress becoming absorbed in *this* world and what is happening within it and within yourself. The ways of the East tend to put the emphasis on detachment from this physical world, and "rising above" the pleasures and temptations of the flesh. Such notions are embodied in the physical exercises developed by Eastern systems, and should not be mixed with a system which encourages the opposite approach to life.

If possible, Practical Work should be performed outdoors among the Green World life forms and life forces. This will make you more aware of the Green World around you, while it helps to test areas of your character and make-up which indoor Working does not. For example, it will test your dedication to the Work, in that you will have to make more of an effort in performing your Practical Work than you would indoors. A common experience people have while meditating outdoors with eyes closed is a strong feeling that they may be discovered and interrupted at any moment. The slightest sound or change of light causes them to open their eyes with a start, usually for no more reason than their built-in apprehension about being exposed to the unfamiliar forces of the Green World. By overcoming these feelings, you will enhance your understanding of the Green World, and start to learn a lot more than you would otherwise. You may also find that you encounter more guides and helpers when Working outdoors than indoors. This is because your contact with the Green World and the Otherworld is so much stronger when you are in their midst than when you are sitting in a human-made building surrounded by electro-magnetic fields and forces. Try to experience both indoor and outdoor Working, and see if you notice any differences, and which feels better for you.

Later in your Practical Work, you will be given some experience of ritual Working. Some people become very stiff and awkward during rituals, and feel that they should be moving and speaking in ways that are somehow different from the way they move or speak normally. This is completely wrong, and misses the basic point of ritual Working. While it is true that the purpose of ritual is outside of your day-to-day routine, and while it must be approached with the correct mental and spiritual attitude, you should not force unnatural or uncomfortable ways of moving or speaking.

Diet, Drugs, and Alcohol

There is no need to fast or to follow any special diet while undertaking the Practical Work. The exercises given in this book should be seen as an extension of your day-to-day activities, requiring no changes in your diet or other physical habits to make them more powerful or viable. Vegetarianism, for example, which is encouraged a great deal under many Eastern systems, has no place under the Irish system, unless followed purely as a matter of taste, or as a conscious objection to unnatural forms of modern farming and livestock rearing. If you are already a committed vegetarian or vegan when you start this course of study, then by all means carry on with your dietary habits.

To refrain from eating meat in an attempt to purify the body and mind, or to obviate or negate so-called Karmic influences, is a concept which is alien to the Irish system, which teaches that all things in this world and in the Otherworld are of equal status and importance. To kill and eat animals for food is exactly the same as killing and eating plants for food, and, ultimately, we are all eaten by the very Earth Herself when we die. It is a good thing to keep in mind that we, too, are an integral part of the food chain, and as liable to be eaten as any plant or animal. No matter how superior we like to consider ourselves to be, there are some things we simply cannot rise above.

You will notice, when reading the Celtic legends, that one of the favourite pastimes was feasting and banqueting. The favourite food of the Celts during these feasts was pork, and there are several legends in which pigs are clearly considered to be Otherworld creatures. There are also legends which describe heroes being killed by wild boars and other animals, and which together show the importance of partaking of the whole food chain, as well as accepting the fact that we are all a part of it.

Some diets tend to heighten the psychic awareness, and can cause problems later in the Practical Work when you will be introduced to fairly powerful sources. Probably, any negative effects would be limited to feelings of uneasiness, lack of sleep, tiredness, or irritability, and none of these is of any great danger, but they will certainly upset your concentration and make progress difficult. Should you experience adverse physical or mental reactions, you are advised to stop the Practical Work immediately and give your body time to rest and recover. Any diet being followed for medical reasons, including weight-loss or weight-gain diets, can be continued, but again, should you find that you are experiencing difficulties with the Practical Work, I would advise you to stop your Work until your system has had a chance to return to normal, and your psychic centres are once more operating at their usual levels.

Whether or not you are following a special diet, it is best not to carry out any of the exercises immediately following a meal. Try to wait at least two hours before going ahead with magical Work, and you will find yourself to be more relaxed and alert. There is a minor magical aspect to this suggestion, too, in that while the body is carrying on involuntary tasks such as digestion, the psychic centres tend to close down, and your Otherworld perceptions become dulled. For the same reason, it is recommended that soon after you have completed a Practical Work session, you should have a light snack and hot drink to deliberately close down these psychic centres. It may not always be apparent, but the effect of the exercises on these centres is quite powerful, and to attempt to go about your normal business while in a heightened state of awareness is not a good thing.

No Practical Work should ever be undertaken if you are on a course of prescribed drugs or medication. The reasons for this are based on sound principles of how drugs and medicine affect your body, and of how magical Working can affect your body—the two do not normally go together. Some forms of homoeopathic medicine may be compatible, but again, should you experience any difficulties, lay aside your magical Work and give your system a rest until such time as it tells you you are ready to resume your Work.

I must also make it absolutely clear that if you take illegal drugs, you would be well to leave this book now and forget all about the Celts and the Celtic way of life and belief. As long as your drug-taking persists, you will never be compatible with Celtic ideals. The crux of the Irish Celtic system is a total involvement in *this* world, which includes facing up to all the stresses and strains which modern life brings. Anyone who feels the need to resort to drugs to relieve this pressure, or as a way of escaping from it altogether, is obviously not capable of even this, and will be unable to face up to the greater stresses imposed by Working in the Otherworld. Similarly, the inhabitants of the Otherworld have no time for people of this world who spend their time in drug-induced daydreams or fantasies. Remember, too, that the Celts were one of the first races to introduce a lengthy, complex, and extremely thorough civil and criminal law system. As a matter of honour, all Celts adhered to it strictly. If you are genuinely trying to understand the Celtic magical system, then you must try to achieve the same frame of mind, and adopt the same world view. This includes an acceptance of the laws of the land in which you live. Anyone who knowingly takes illegal drugs is not worthy of the title Celt, even if he or she should be so by accident of birth.

These strong words apply equally to those who abuse legal drugs, including alcohol. Certainly there is nothing wrong with taking alcohol in moderation, but to use it as a means of escape from the pressures of this world is to become as useless as the junkie with his heroin. This is a magical fact which people ignore at their peril. Every genuine magical system has built-in safeguards, one of which is that anyone incapable of Working it properly will never be able to advance to the stage where they gain real power or knowledge. Drug abusers who ignore these warnings will spend a lot of time getting absolutely nowhere.

Visualisation and Imagination

The visual imagination is the most powerful tool anybody, magician or otherwise, will ever own. Like all good tools, it must be looked after, maintained, and used properly to gain its full advantage. All of the progress humankind has made has been as a result of the imagination. If we did not have imagination, we would never have crawled out of the primordial swamp and progressed to where we are today. All of our great inventions have come about by someone having a glimpse of how something could be improved or changed, or by the steady effort of someone with an idea which they knew would work, who spent perhaps a lifetime proving it. On the mental and emotional levels, moments of clear visualisation can result in the dreamer producing beautiful paintings, poetry, or music. On the spiritual level, individuals throughout history have had moments of vision in which they instantly knew and understood some great truth about themselves, humankind, or the workings of the universe. These initial sparks of imagination later mushroomed into what are now worldwide religions and philosophies. This same visual imagination is within all of us, and its potential is just as vast.

Some people can use their visual imagination very effectively, yet others find it hard even to visualise their own living room, once they close their eyes. Most of us fall somewhere between these two extremes. It does not matter where you feel you fit, as long as you carry out the exercises as described, and let them build up in your imagination as best you can. The important point to remember about any of these Otherworld journeys is that they are absolutely real, and must be treated as such, whether you can see things clearly or not.

If you find clear visualisation difficult, do not try to force it to come, for it will not. Just as everyone has his or her own growth rate, so, too, does everyone have his or her own degree of visualisation. This does not mean, however, that some people are at an advantage over others. The importance of visualisation lies not in what your visual imagination is seeing, but in what your intuition tells you about it.

If you are unfamiliar with the techniques of visualisation, try the following simple exercise. Close your eyes and calm your mind, putting aside any mundane thoughts. When you feel relaxed and ready to begin, imagine the scene in front of you exactly as it was before you closed your eyes. You will find it helpful to do this exercise in a room with which you are very familiar, and facing some object or objects which you know well. Imagine that you have opened your eyes and are taking a good look at the room. Once you feel sure you can see it clearly, and that you know exactly where everything is, what colour everything is, and how near or how far from you each object is, open your eyes and see if you were correct. Do this as often as necessary, until you can visualise the room exactly as it is.

Next, imagine that you are standing up and leaving the room. See what is on the other side of the door, go into the next room or corridor, and examine closely everything which you know to be there. Extend this to exploring your entire home by going through every room and every cupboard, looking closely at objects which have become so familiar to you that you no longer notice them during your day-to-day life. You may even find that you come across objects you had thought to be lost. Look out of the windows. What do you see?

An important point to note here, which applies to all Otherworld Work, is that you must always see the scene before you *through your own eyes.* Do not sit and watch yourself doing things as if it were being shown on some inner television screen. That is not the way you see things in this world, and it certainly should not be how you see things in the Otherworld. Always see the Otherworld through your own Inner eyes, just as you see this world through your own physical eyes.

Once you have mastered looking around your room and your home, extend your visualisation by leaving the house and going down the street. This will be more of a challenge, for not only will you need to observe how the street and the buildings look, but you will now need to visualise other people being in the street with you, cars and vehicles passing by you, perhaps airplanes overhead. What is the weather like? Does it feel warm or cold? Are you dressed for this sort of weather? Indeed, are you dressed at all?

This simple but useful exercise should help you start to appreciate your natural level of visualisation. If, after repeating the exercise several times, you still find you cannot visualise clearly, do not despair; eventually, you will find that your lack of clear visualisation will be compensated for by an increased Otherworld awareness and intuition. Blind people, in this world, often find that their other senses increase to compensate for the loss of their sight. So, too, in the Otherworld; and in a way, this is actually more useful than having twenty-twenty Otherworld vision, for it is what the visual image is conveying, what it symbolises, which is important, and not simply how it looks. Most of the Practical Work given in this book uses visualisation as a basis for Otherworld travel. When you feel ready to start the Work, go ahead, whether or not you are completely satisfied with your visualisation capabilities.

At first, each exercise of the Practical Work should be repeated several times exactly as it has been laid out in the text, until you become familiar with its feel, imagery, and general content, and are quite conversant with the more obvious symbolism being employed. To help you with this, it may be a good idea to tape-record each exercise to play back during your meditations, rather than trying to read from the book. Thinking about the exercises when you are not Working will allow their imagery to sink deeply into your conscious and subconscious mind, where it will reveal itself more fully during successive Practical Work sessions.

A very important element of visualisation and Otherworld Working is a certain amount of spontaneity. Once you are sure you can recall the scenes from memory, stop using the tape recorder, or referring to the book, and learn to use your visual imagination on its own. The first time you do this, go into the Working as if it were the first time, trying to recapture the excitement and nervousness of that very first occasion. The Working will probably seem no different, but should you find that it starts to go in a slightly different direction, go with it. Listen to your intuition and feelings. If it suddenly seems right to go off in a totally different direction from usual, then do that. If someone appears spontaneously during the Working where there was nobody before, accept that this person is real and listen to what he or she has to tell you, or look at what he or she may wish to show you.

If this is no more than daydreaming or a lack of concentration, the Working will probably go nowhere, and will degenerate to the point where it becomes obvious that the proper thread has been lost. In such cases, consciously make a mental note that the Working has ceased, open your eyes, note in your Magical Diary what happened, and finish off with a hot drink or snack to close down your psychic centres. I suggest you record this in your Magical Diary because there is a lesson to be learned here: Losing the thread of the Working is not as negative as it may seem. It could be that you ended up in a daydream because of something to do with yourself or your mood. Perhaps you were tired, or perhaps it was something outside of yourself such as the weather, the time of year, or even the time of day or night. All of these things should be noted, as a pattern may eventually emerge which could indicate why you are losing concentration and lapsing into daydreams.

If, on the other hand, the Working goes off on its own and you find it has taken on a stronger feel and more powerful or vivid visual imagery than before, go with it, and follow up any leads you are given. This is using Otherworld journeys to their fullest. When the images take on an apparent life of their own, you may not believe that they are real, but the more you learn to trust your intuition, the sooner you will be able to know when things are real and when they are imaginary. Intuition is the decision-maker in the Otherworld, as opposed to logic, which is the decision-maker of this world.

It is very common for parts of the Working to verify themselves in your day-to-day life by apparent coincidences which reproduce images seen during your Otherworld journey. These incidents are usually referred to as signs-following, and are the Otherworld's way of letting you know you are on the right path. There is nothing particularly wondrous or magical about this; such signs-following always occur in perfectly natural and normal ways. You will not receive a visit from some mysterious stranger bearing a book which will reveal all to you. Nor will you suddenly receive, out of the blue, a letter from the magus of some high-powered lodge inviting you to join, as some of the more sensational writers on magical matters would have you believe. You may, however, come across a book in a bookshop or library which helps to clarify confusing points in a previous Working. You may overhear a conversation between total strangers which echoes thoughts or feelings you have had. Magic is wonderful and quite amazing, but mostly it is simply a matter of recognising the magical in the mundane, which is what makes the magician different from his or her non-magical neighbours.

Magical Ritual

A magical ritual is a means of heightening your perception, awareness, and intuition, by the use of movement, objects, sound, and concentration. This change of state helps Otherworld powers, forces, and dynamics to come into the ritual Working area and be directed by the magician for whatever purposes the ritual has been designed.

All of us have experienced ritual in one form or another, although many people would not look upon it that way. Any religious ceremony, such as the giving of a name, a wedding, a funeral, or a thanksgiving, is a ritual. Some religions use very powerful symbolism combined with robes, incense, chalices, and other symbolic objects, all of which have a very strong effect on the participants. Rituals are employed not only by religions, but also by organisations such as the Freemasons and some types of Friendly Societies. Some places of employment still put new recruits through elaborate initiations—often seen as no more than practical jokes—which are, nonetheless, rituals. You may be surprised at just how many rituals you have already performed throughout your life which have nothing to do with magic. Magical ritual has a specific purpose behind it, and summons up the energy necessary to achieve that purpose. Social ritual does not necessarily have an important purpose, and rarely summons up any energy other than, perhaps, on a very basic emotional level.

Rituals do not have to be elaborate, nor do they need to involve several people. A perfectly valid ritual can be performed in a relatively short time, using almost no props, by a single practitioner. It is true that some rituals have deliberately been designed to be lengthy and complicated, involving a lot of magical paraphernalia and several participants or officers. Such rituals are normally carried out by a well-established magical group, who has built up good Working relationships both among the members of the group and with their Otherworld contacts. It is highly unlikely that newcomers to magic will soon find themselves being introduced to such complicated rituals.

The rituals given in this book are designed to give you practical experience of ritual Working itself, the movements, the use of Magical Weapons, the use of words, and the use of your intuition to tell you what is happening. They will also have results, at a later stage, on all three levels, which should be the ultimate point of every ritual. It is as important to study the structure of the ritual itself as it is to await the result.

I made reference earlier to the Working area as an important part of any ritual. You must always clearly define, both in your mind and on the physical level, the area in which you are going to perform the ritual. This serves to contain the flows of energies which you may generate, and helps to concentrate your mind on that immediate area—stopping it from wandering too much. This defining of the Working area, which is one of the first acts in any ritual, is usually performed by drawing your Sword or Wand along the ground, and literally tracing out the area—usually a circle—in which you will remain for the duration of the Working. As you are carrying out this physical act, you should be restricting your thoughts to what remains in the area with you, and visualising a mental barrier going up between what is within the circle and what is outside its boundaries. It is important to remember, on closing, to reverse this process.

Once the Working area has been defined, you should not step outside its limits until the full ritual is complete. Always ensure that you have everything you are going to need within the proposed area before you begin, and always emphasise this point to any others who may be Working with you. For the same reasons, it is advisable to ensure, as far as possible, that you are not going to be disturbed in your Working area by some third party innocently stumbling upon what you are doing. Interruptions not only ruin concentration and the flow of the Working, but can also break the defined Working area, causing a total disruption of the flows and energies being invoked. This is not dangerous, but you may well find yourself feeling upset and agitated about the interruption for some time following.

The old idea of demons and angels being evoked into magical triangles which held them prisoner while the magician forced them to do his or her bidding is absolute rubbish, as is the notion of the magical circle being broken and these same demons and angels escaping and running riot in the physical world. The magical circle is no more than another aspect of the all-important magical "hygiene." Before a surgeon performs an operation, he or she ensures that the working area is clearly defined, sealed, and safe from cont-amination and interruptions. This is not only to aid concentration, but also to prevent unwanted persons from entering the area, and perhaps bringing infections with them which could jeopardise the health of the patient. So, too, in magical operations, you must always take care in preparing your Working area and its security to ensure the success and safety of the ritual.

Using the medical analogy again, note that surgeons only use instruments which have been sterilised and cleansed for hygienic reasons. This should also be the case with the magician. It is for this reason that Magical Weapons should always be treated with respect, kept out of view when not being used, and never dis-played as curiosities or objects of power. If an object is not looked after and treated with respect, it will become contaminated on the mental and spiritual levels, making it just as dangerous to use during a magical ritual as would be a dirty scalpel during a surgical operation.

One of the most important principles of any magical ritual is a sense of balance. During the ritual, certain powers are brought into play, some directly at the will of the magician, and others incidental to things which are happening during the Working. It is important to understand this, to be aware of the in-flow of energy, and to be able to direct it effectively to avoid a buildup in one area which may cause imbalance in another. Most rituals have a central focal point (usually an altar of some kind), and this should be seen as the pivot around which everything and everyone moves. If you are Working in a group, it is good practice to situate men and women opposite each other within the Working area in order to maintain a balance of Polarity. If the main celebrant of the ritual is a man, it is a good idea to have a woman at the opposite side of the altar, handing him the Magical Weapons as they are needed. Similarly, the weapons should be handed back to the woman after use by the man. The opposite applies, of course, if the main celebrant is a woman. This maintains a balance and a nice flow between the sexes.

This situation arises often in rituals where the formal Opening of the Quarters is performed. This is normally done by taking the Magical Weapon from the central altar to each Quarter, presenting it to its appropriate Quarter with the relevant words to invoke the power of that Quarter, and then either leaving it in place or returning it to the altar. To have a man opening the Quarters with a woman assisting, or vice versa, aids in the smooth flow of the ritual, and helps maintain the necessary balance of Polarity. In some rituals, the Opening of the Quarters is carried out by participants sitting in each Quarter, who verbally and visually open it while they remain seated. If this is the type of Working you are undertaking, then again it is good practice to have men and women sitting in opposing Quarters.

If you are Working alone, as will most often be the case, it is not possible to achieve a physical balance of officers and energies. It is possible, however, to keep your actions centred on the altar while energies and forces flow, invisibly, within your Working area. The main focus of balance in these circumstances will not be horizontal, as in the group situation, but on a vertical plane, where the magician sees him or herself as the balancing point between that which is above and that which is below. This is why, in some rituals, I recommend you visualise a cone of light extending up into the sky and down into the Earth. This makes your balancing aspect all the more evident, and helps to seal and define your Working area on the vertical axis, just as you will have done earlier on the horizontal axis, by drawing your circle with your Wand or Sword.

Although it is natural to concentrate your energies on any ritual once it actually starts to take place, it should be realised that the real Working begins as soon as you formulate the idea of holding a ritual in the first place. From that point on, the seed which you have planted in your mind will be growing and making itself known in the Otherworld, where it will be picked up by those who will eventually help you in making the ritual a success. It should be thought about carefully, and with dignity and respect at all times. The physical part of the ritual can be said to start as soon as you begin to gather together the various bits and pieces you are going to need for it. Similarly, the ritual does not fully finish until everything is cleaned up, you have returned home if Working outdoors, your Magical Weapons have been put away, and your Magical Diary duly noted. During these closing procedures you should maintain the same mental state you had during the Working of the ritual itself. Always do these things properly and thoroughly, as soon as possible after the Working. Adopting these habits and attitudes of mind right from the beginning of your magical career will stand you in good stead with your Otherworld contacts, as well as help you develop good magical discipline and practice.

A good ritual should flow smoothly, allowing the mind and higher senses to open up and become totally immersed in the symbolism and powers being invoked. A lot of time in rituals is spent sitting, and the guidelines given earlier on posture during meditation apply here. When you are moving around the Working area, a steady, but slightly slower than normal speed of movement is all that is required. Any signs which are made in the air should be made with dignity and emphasis, so all present see what is being done, and their attention is directed not to the person making the movements, but to the movements themselves. Any objects which are picked up and carried around the Working area should be held slightly farther than normal in front of the body, thereby placing the emphasis on the object, rather than the bearer. Take care with objects, especially chalices filled with wine or lighted candles and tapers, so they are not dropped or spilled, which will not only ruin the ritual, but may be hazardous as well.

A great deal of skillful magical ability relies on good intuition and an ability to react to what is happening at any given moment. This should be the main factor in what you say during ritual. Say what feels right at that exact point in the ritual, and not what you have been desperately trying to memorise for days prior specifically for that moment. You will need to be very familiar with what each stage in the ritual represents to be able to spontaneously sum it up for the benefit of all participants. For example, if you are Opening the Quarters, you must know and fully understand what Earth, Water, Fire, and Air really represent in order to be able to put this into words to help you and your fellow participants visualise the appropriate symbolism. There is nothing wrong with using words composed by someone else, from a book of magic or even an appropriate piece of prose or poetry, if you genuinely and intuitively feel that those second-hand words or lines express how you feel about that particular force, Weapon, or symbol. If, though, you are going to spend the whole of the ritual up to that point reciting the lines over and over in your head so that you do not fluff them at the critical point, then that is worse than useless, as all it will serve to do is distract you completely from the rest of the ritual. Keep it simple. There is no need for elaboration or flamboyance just for effect.

There has always been a great debate in magical circles over the issue of Working robed or naked. I always Work in robes for several reasons: The main one is nothing but practical, as anyone who has experienced the Western Isles of Scotland, or the rural areas of Ireland in summer will know the folly of going around naked when the air is thick with thousands of tiny little winged insects known as midges, whose bite causes the intensest of itching. Similarly, the outdoor temperature in these regions during the dark period of the year would defy even the hardiest of naturists to remain unclothed. Putting aside these basic but important considerations, a robe helps to make the wearer feel he or she has taken on a different personality or aspect to his or her being. Because robes should only be worn during ritual, they have a psychological effect of preparing you for Working as soon as you don them. Robes can also be used as a means of displaying symbols or devices, by sewing them into the fabric. Careful use of colour in each robe can be effective from a magical point of view. All of this adds to the combined effect of the ritual itself. If you are Working in a group situation, then uniform robes can be a useful way of making everyone aware of the fact that they are all equal.

Some advocates of Working naked claim that, by being naked, all are shown to be equal. I have found being naked highlights the physical differences among the group, and that this, during ritual, can be subconsciously related to the higher levels, producing an overall feeling of imbalance and inequality. The choice, however, is yours. There is no right or wrong way of Working as far as robes are concerned, although if you are going to be Working outdoors, there may be locations where it may be illegal to perform naked. Also, if you are going to be Working with others, you should consider whether they feel comfortable appearing with no clothes on, even though you may.

Finally, rituals should always have a definite purpose. It is not a good idea to perform a ritual because you can think of nothing else to do at that moment, or as a means of showing off your new Sword. To do so will result in the loss of established Otherworld contacts, as such contacts have no time for egocentrics or show offs. The purpose does not have to be some grand, cosmic scheme, but during the acting-out of the ritual, you should have, in the back of your mind, a specific reason for doing it in the first place. This reason may be as simple as gaining experience, which is the purpose behind the

Practical Work in this book, or an act of celebration and recognition of the Green World and its phases, as in the case of the rituals for the Four Festivals in Section Five.

As your Work progresses and you become more experienced and knowledgeable, your ritual Workings will start to take on a more serious and important aspect, which will be guided by the Otherworld contacts you build up over your years of training and learning. The purpose behind ritual at that stage will be determined mainly by those Otherworld contacts. For now try to understand the purpose behind the movements and objects used in the rituals given in this book. Try to devise simple rituals of your own along these same principles. There is never any harm in experimenting; and don't be afraid of failure, because, as in everything, it is by your mistakes that you will learn.

The Proper Attitude
Understanding the Otherworld

Some people treat Otherworld journeys with the attitude that they are no more than fanciful daydreams or an elaborate form of mental role play. Consequently, they get results deserving of these misconceptions—none! If you accept that these journeys are absolutely real, and if you can enter the Otherworld with the same attitude that you would adopt when entering a foreign country of this world, then you will surely meet the inhabitants of the Otherworld, get to know them, and learn from them. If you are prepared to visit some new location in this world, and accept without question that it and its inhabitants are real, then it is only right that you should adopt the same outlook when venturing into new locations in the Otherworld.

When people meet and interact socially in this world, there are certain courtesies each expects from the other. As long as these are followed, things go well and beneficially for both parties. So, too, in the Otherworld. The ancient Irish Celts were renowned for their hospitality and courtesy to strangers. You will be shown such hospitality and courtesy when you enter the Otherworld, and you should respond by extending courtesy and good manners to your new non-physical acquaintances. You should also extend such courtesy to strangers you meet in this world, and offer to them the same hospitality that you would to a dear friend. Remember that what you do on one level should always manifest on the others as well.

Many of the guides you will encounter and Work with may give you information which will be of great use and help to you in both your magical Workings and ordinary life. It is only right that thanks should be given where and when appropriate, and offers of help should be given back to such guides and way-showers. Your Otherworld contacts can learn from you just as much as you can learn from them, and, on occasion, they may ask you to be their physical arms and legs to carry out some task in the physical world which they cannot do. When this happens, you will know that you have a true Working relationship with the Otherworld, and as you get deeper into this Irish system of magic, you will find that the inhabitants of the Otherworld will rely on you more and more. To a great extent, this is what practical magic is all about.

The people of the Otherworld are not all-knowing and do not always have the answers to your questions. In the Irish legends, there are many examples of people travelling to the Otherworld, finding a guide or helper, and asking some specific question, only to be told that they will have to go to someone else. This may come as a surprise to followers of other belief systems which teach that the inhabitants of the Otherworld, however they may be known, are all-knowing and full of wisdom. The Irish concept considers the Otherworld to be no more than an extension of this world. We are not all-knowing in this world; why should we expect everyone in the Otherworld to be so? There are also as many deceivers and tricksters in the Otherworld as there are in this world, as the legends reveal. You should be as wary and cautious while journeying in the Otherworld as you would be when journeying through unknown lands of this world.

It is worth mentioning at this stage that the Otherworld beings known as the Sidhe (shee)—or as the fairies under other systems—are not the gossamer-winged, friendly little sprites often described in other apparently serious books on magic. If you wander around the Otherworld looking for nice little fairies as portrayed in children's books, you will certainly meet them, but they will be nothing more than the product of your own imagination. If you come across the real thing, be prepared for a certain amount of hostility. The Sidhe are powerful and independent beings, who have taken a dislike to humans, and may show open aggression toward us. This is mainly because of the great damage we are doing to the planet, which is as much in their care as it should be in ours. If your motives are genuine and honest, it is possible to meet members of the Sidhe, gain their confidence, and thereby gain a trusty ally; but it will take your convincing them that your reasons for being there are valid, and that you wish to help them in repairing the damage the rest of your kind is doing. As always, the most important thing to keep in mind is your attitude toward them. If you are successful in striking up a trusting friendship with a member of the Sidhe, you will find you have a true ally and a real friend to both guide you and protect you while journeying in the Otherworld. This is a very rewarding experience for both parties.

Keeping a Magical Diary

Recording your Otherworld journeys and magical rituals in a diary kept specifically for this purpose has the advantage of being a permanent record of your progress, while it serves a more important magical function in "earthing" the realisations obtained during an Otherworld journey, or the powers invoked during a ritual. As such, it serves to formally finalise a particular Working. It will also be a useful tool later in your progress, when things which may have seemed odd or unimportant earlier in your studies suddenly take on a much deeper and more important meaning.

It is vital that you record as much detail in your diary as possible, even if it seems irrelevant at the time. It is also a good idea to note the time you commenced your Working, how long it took, how you felt physically before you began, and the climatic conditions. From this information, you will be able to identify any patterns which start to emerge about how your health, or, as a lot of people discover, the weather affects your magical Workings. This information can be put to good use later, when you start to plan ahead for important Workings. It will also show your own seasonal cycles of learning and progress, as mentioned earlier. You can also record in your Magical Diary any of the signs-following which may have occurred, as these, too, can sometimes take on a distinctive pattern.

As with your Magical Weapons and robe, your Magical Diary is personal to you, will become a powerful magical tool in its own right, and accordingly, should not be left lying around for anyone who happens by to read. Nor should it be used for mundane purposes such as jotting down telephone numbers or making shopping lists. Over the years, it will become a very accurate mirror of your magical persona, and this should always be treated with due respect and care.

The Importance of Purpose

No magical Work, whether a solitary Otherworld journey, or a full ceremonial ritual involving several people, should ever be undertaken just for the fun of it. There must always be a purpose behind any magical Working, and that purpose should be kept clearly in mind when the Working is actually taking place. There is a certain danger, especially for those new to such things, of getting caught up in the glamour of rituals and the Otherworld, and carrying them out at a moment's notice for no good reason. This is not good practice and will only serve to hinder your development. In the early stages, the purpose behind all the Workings is simply to learn. As you become more confident and adept, you will be able to work out journeys and rituals of your own for specific purposes, and this shows true progress is being made. The main thing to be learned during these formative stages is not so much what magic is, but rather when it should be used. Magic should only be used as a last resort. If there is a "normal" way to deal with a situation, then that is the way to choose. The normal abilities we all have, whether physical, mental, or spiritual, are just as magical as any abilities heightened by ritual Working. It is only once you have mastered your everyday magical abilities that you will be capable of mastering your extra magical abilities. Your initial learning period should give you a clarity of vision and an ability to see what is really happening in your life, as well as how to deal with problematic situations. The practical lessons at the start of any magical career are concerned with recognising normal ways of dealing with life's many trials. This is what I meant when I said that the Irish system centres on a total involvement in this world, and is completely different in practice from systems which teach detachment from the events of this world. Magic will not provide you an easy way out. You are going to have to face up to all the same trials, tests, difficulties, and failures as everyone else. After all, if you cannot master the basic, day-to-day forces of this world, which most people learn by instinct and trial and error, how can you ever expect to master the forces of the Otherworld?

You will also come to realise that the popular image of the magician being in total control of his or her own circumstances, emotions, and destiny, is very far from the truth. If anything, most Working magicians find they have more than their fair share of life's problems and crises, and that things rarely go as planned. This is one inevitable side-effect of stirring things up in the Otherworld, and is perfectly natural. If you can understand and accept this, then the problems are not really problems at all, but are merely situations to be dealt with. Some people put these interruptions and distractions down to psychic attack or interference from some anonymous dark forces, but this is very rarely the case. As a trainee magician, you are really not worth the time and effort involved in mounting such an attack. Being a beginner at least has that advantage.

In the early days of your training, it is advisable to adopt a regular routine of magical Working and study to program your body clock to expect a Working at a specific time. It also helps those who are looking after your interest from the Otherworld to tune in to what you are doing. Be aware of your feelings and readiness to Work, however, so that your Work has purpose. If you perform a Working simply because it is Tuesday and you always do a Working on Tuesday, or it is the full Moon and you always Work at the full Moon, then you are in danger of making your magical Workings no more than a habit, which by nature has no purpose.

As you progress you will find, at some point, that your Working pattern has to be changed. When this occurs, simply go with the feeling, and make the necessary changes. Do not make the mistake of thinking that, just because a regular pattern has been established over a period of months or years, it should not be broken. Once you start thinking in a rut, you will stay in that rut, and spend the rest of your magical career doing nothing of value either for yourself or for others.

It is often said that the path of the magician is a difficult and a lonely one. The Irish system in particular is a hard one, and you are advised to seriously consider your motives for taking it up, as well as your ability to do so. There is no shame in recognising that you are not fully ready for such magical training. It is far better to accept this, go away and learn a bit more about life and yourself, and then come back and face the challenge when you are truly ready for it, than to foolishly rush into it knowing within yourself that you are not ready for what is going to happen to you. There is no rush; there never is.

Chapter Four

Concepts and Beliefs

Magic is a twenty-four-hour-a-day, seven-day-a-week affair, and it cannot be switched on and off at the whim of the magician. So much of successful magic depends not only on your powers of visual imagination, or on being able to perform elaborate rituals without mistake or pause, but also on your understanding of the workings and machinery of this world and the Otherworld, and your attitudes toward them. Some of the concepts of the Irish system will be completely new you, or you may think you know them already. Be careful, though, as this may not be the case.

Try to approach the concepts put forward in this next section with an open mind, and without preconceptions or assumptions. While you may already practice a system which someone has designated as Celtic, your system may not necessarily comply with what I will tell you. There are many different types of Celts, and many different types of Celtic magic; and although they may superficially seem the same, they nonetheless have many subtle differences embodied in their deeper teachings.

I do not wish to imply that any one system is better than any other. It is true that some people will be more suited to one system than another, and that particular system is therefore the best for them, but this does not mean that the other systems are inferior in any way. We are all different and have different needs, and this applies equally to magic.

If you start this system, progress through the various levels, and then decide it is not the one for you, stop your studies and look for something more suited to your needs. This is using your intuition at its best, and it is a wise person who can do it. Many do not pay attention to what their intuition is telling them because they feel they have gone far into a system, and do not want to give up. This is both foolish and dangerous. Always pay attention to how you feel about things, and do not constantly try to rationalise your feelings.

Study the ideas that follow as a further preparation for the Practical Work given in the later sections. Some of this may seem superfluous to a study of magic, but I would stress again the need for the successful magician to have a sound understanding of the energies and powers of this world before attempting to handle the very different energies and powers of the Otherworld. Most of what follows is on a mental or abstract level. It is at this level we formulate our understanding of this world and what is happening to us and around us. If you can come to your own understanding of what follows then you will be on a sure footing as far as your magical studies are concerned.

The Three Levels

The most important concept you will come across under this system is that of the three levels of existence. This is an extremely simple concept which states that everything has a physical aspect, a mental aspect, and a spiritual aspect to its being. Like most simple concepts, though, once its full implications are considered, you will begin to realise that it demands a radical change in your current view and understanding of the world. Meditating over this concept will bring up apparent anomalies which may at first cause you to doubt the validity of this basic idea. For example, if everything has a mental and spiritual aspect, as well as the more evident physical aspect, then rocks, trees, plants, and old bits of dirty and useless rubbish must likewise have mental and spiritual aspects to them. Can this be so? Where are the mental and spiritual parts of a broken-down refrigerator or a worn out and discarded car tire? Similarly, if everything has a physical and mental aspect, then the Otherworld, the spiritual realms, must also have a physical and mental reality. Where is this physical aspect of the Otherworld? How does the Otherworld think, if it has a mental aspect? Likewise, if everything has a physical and spiritual manifestation, then our very thoughts and emotions must share these two others aspects as well. Where are they? Why can I not touch them, if they are physical?

To people raised under the very materialistic, logic-based philosophies of the Western world, this may seem to be a lot of nonsense. What you must learn to do is listen to your intuition, not your logic. In a sense, what I am asking for is an act of faith. Faith, by its very nature, supersedes logic. It simply is. That is the state you must achieve in order to progress. This tradition is still worked, believed, and lived by many people in the Celtic lands. It is an ancient tradition with ancient teachings which we have learned not to question, and which have been proven over countless generations. This is not to imply that we discourage an inquiring mind; far from it. It does show that we can accept that things are simply beyond our range of comprehension. It had never even occurred to me to question the concept of the three levels until I started to write this book. It was only when I had to break down into components the things which make up my belief system that I realised others would want answers to such questions. I cannot give you those answers. All I can do is ask that you try to see things as I describe them, try to live by these methods and standards for a while, and take note of how they feel to you. Temporarily lay aside your preconceptions of this world and the Otherworld while you study them. If you can clear your mind sufficiently, the truth of the three levels will make itself known to you, and you will realise that this is the only way to make sense of this world, and the only way to understand the Otherworld.

Once you accept the concept of the three levels in your magical Workings, it is necessary to start to look upon your daily life with this same understanding. When you do this, you will begin to see so much more in what is going on around you. Your feelings toward people, events, and inanimate objects will all change for the better. You must make these things real for yourself. That is one of the fundamentals of magic: no one can do it for you. Your success is entirely up to you; there are no priests, priestesses, gurus, or teachers to blame if you fail.

For now, mull over this idea of the three levels and see how it feels to you. Look at yourself and your life, and try to see the three levels in operation. You will already be most aware of your physical and mental (or emotional) levels of existence, but can you see where your spiritual level comes in? Can you identify how, where, and when the three levels work in conjunction and harmony? Most of the time one level will be more dominant than the other two, such as when the physical level is the most dominant during physical exercise. When you are trying hard to solve a problem, it is the mental level which is doing the bulk of the work. When you are deep in prayer or contemplation, it is the spiritual level which holds the reins. Try to see and understand what parts the other levels are playing during these different times. Try to identify moments in your life when all three come into play at the same time.

Next, consider your friends and family, and how you relate to them on the three levels. Look at the Green World with all its different life forms, and see the three levels manifesting in the ways plants and animals behave and interact. When you start to get a grasp of this vital concept, turn to the Irish legends, and look for the ways the three levels are written into these apparently simple and straightforward tales of battles and heroic deeds. It is in the ability to read the legends in the way they were written down which allows previously lost or ignored aspects of the system to be recovered.

I do not expect the newcomer to grasp the significance of this—nevermind actually do it—but it is a good thing to be aware of such high possibilities from the start, as a spur to Working hard and achieving these ideals.

The Concept of Time

Most of us in the West consider time to flow steadily in one direction, as if drawing some invisible straight line with where we stand right now as the present, what is ahead as the future, and what lies behind as the past. Under the Irish system, we believe that time does not flow along some imaginary line, but that it simply is. Everything that ever was, is, or will be, exists right now in a great amalgam of past, present, and future. Recognising this helps in understanding something most people find odd about Irish legends: They make almost no references to time. Everything is described in the present tense with only rare references to the past or the future. To the Celts, everything is the present. This same concept of time is now being considered seriously by scientists working in the field of sub-atomics, especially with the new theory of "super strings," as they slowly begin to realise that this is the only way to make sense of what they are discovering about the internal workings of the universe.

As with the concept of the three levels, this at first seems deceptively simple and straightforward, but it does not reflect the way we see and understand the events of this world. It will, therefore, meet with a great deal of resistance from your conscious, logical mind, which will be constantly trying to prove it wrong. For instance, if you consider that everything is right here and now, including the whole of the future, then the moment of your death must be right here and now. Why are you not dead? If you are working to become proficient in magic, why are you not an expert already? Pay attention to your intuition in this matter, for it will reveal far more than your logical mind ever will. Understanding will come to you as you Work your way through this system.

When you start to experience the Otherworld for yourself, you will notice that time does not pass at the same rate there as it seems to in this world. Practical Work sessions which you felt had only taken a few minutes have in fact taken considerably longer, or, as sometimes happens, what seemed like an exceptionally lengthy Practical Work session has only taken up a few moments of this world time. For now, adopt this new idea of time only when going about your Practical Work. As you progress, you can gradually attempt to bring the concept to bear on your daily routine, until it eventually becomes an integral part of your psychological make-up. The truth behind this new understanding of time will become self-evident, so do not worry too much if, for the present, it seems hard or awkward to come to terms with.

Everything Is Equal

Under this system of magical and spiritual belief and practice, it is accepted that everything and everyone is of equal importance and stature. Everything has its proper function and purpose within the grand scheme of creation. Certain things and certain people will take on a greater or lesser importance under some circumstances, but it must be understood that this is only temporary; eventually, the importance will wane, and the thing or person will slip once again into the background. This has been happening throughout your life as people from the past who played significant roles in your development are no longer important. Objects and possessions which seemed of immense value to you yesterday are discarded junk today.

While on its face, this concept may seem obvious, how far can you take it? Can you honestly say that you believe the alcoholic vagrant sleeping in a doorway is as important as a brilliant brain surgeon who is daily saving lives? Is a shrivelled-up and dried-out

dead leaf as important as the new baby being caressed by its ador-
ing parents? A great deal depends upon your ability to look past the
immediate and see the grander scheme of things. It is not easy, but
it can be done.

Throughout this book, I use the terms *gods* and *goddesses* to
describe certain characters. These terms probably convey the wrong
idea to many people today. The deities in the Irish system are of
exactly the same importance and significance as the human characters, and are of the same importance and stature as the animals
and other life forms of the Green World. These gods and goddesses
were not worshipped by the ancient Celts in the religious sense; they
were looked upon with respect and awe, but they were not considered to be superior or in constant need of placating, as other commentators would have us believe. When reading the Irish legends,
you will note that deities are as mortal as human characters, make
as many mistakes, and are just as deceitful and cruel. They are not
portrayed as all-knowing, all-forgiving, omnipotent beings who play
with the destinies of men and women, as they often are in other
mythologies and cultures. It is true that they are described as being
able to carry out magical acts which humans cannot perform, but
this is no different from the carpenter being able to perform amazing things with pieces of wood which the smith cannot do, or the
smith being able to shape and temper raw ore into weapons, which
the warrior cannot do. It is simply a question of respecting the abilities and skills of others which you cannot copy yourself. This is a far
different thing from worshipping a god or goddess for no reason
other than that they are non-human.

The Irish Celts saw each of their deities as a special kind of friend,
who was just as important as any human friend. These days we would
never consider placating or appeasing a friend with gifts to avoid his
or her fury, or because we believe he or she is superior to us. The
ancient Irish Celts gave gifts to their deities to thank them for deeds
they had carried out on behalf of the individual or clan. This is no
different from what we do today—even if the gift has changed from
a highly-ornate sword to an impersonal, preprinted greeting card.

It is important to get this relationship between deities and humans clear in your mind before you enter the Otherworld and attempt to make contact with a god or goddess. If you attempt contact with your heart in your mouth and quaking in your shoes, you are not going to get very far. The Celtic deities respect dignity and openness in humans, and they have no time for individuals who consider themselves lower than they are. To the Irish Celts, dignity, nobility, and self-confidence were of paramount importance.

Of equal importance is the belief that humans are no more nor less important than the other life forms in the Green World. The life force within a plant is as important as the life force within an animal, which is as important as the life force within a human being, which is as important as the life force within the inhabitants of the Otherworld. To kill or destroy one is the same as killing or destroying any of the others. No matter how much we like to consider ourselves civilised and above the animal level, we are still a form of animal life and are subject to the same Green World laws which affect the animal kingdom. This includes being a part of the food chain, which keeps the whole Green World going. All of us kill to eat, and someday we, too, will be killed for food. We are all the Earth's cattle, and once we die, the great Mother Earth will surely eat our bodies just as we have been eating freely of hers. It does not matter how we die. We may be killed by an animal which, while rare in Western countries nowadays, is still a very real danger in other parts of the world. We may be killed by a virus, which is a vital, living, and integral part of the Green World. We may be involved in a fatal accident, caused by perhaps electricity, gas, chemicals, or even a human-made mechanical device such as a car. All of these have an energy of their own, which is just another form of the life force manifesting in the Green World and playing out its role in the endless cycle of life and death. Most of us will eventually be killed as our own bodies destroy themselves through terminal illness or senile decay. This should highlight in a very personal way the whole concept of true universal equality.

From now on, as part of your magical training, try to adopt this attitude of total equality of everything and everyone. Become aware of just how many judgements you pass on other people as you go about your daily living. Become more aware of the many judgements which are made against you, which probably only registered with you if you felt they were unduly harsh. The next time a beggar accosts you in the street and asks for money, see if you really can accept this individual as being an equal with yourself and those you love and respect most. Situations like this will test you to the limit, but if you cannot cope with them in this world, you will certainly not be able to cope with the much subtler tests of the Otherworld.

Finally, realise that you are just as important as and equal to anyone whom you have looked up to in respect or admiration. Seeing everyone and everything as being truly equal gives you an air of dignity and self-respect. Taken too far, of course, this self-respect and dignity can become snobbishness or even outright arrogance. Keeping things in check, and keeping foremost in your mind the concept of equality, will prevent you from falling into the trap of arrogance or egocentricity. Instead, you will find that you have a much healthier and more sensible attitude toward yourself and the world in which you live.

What Happens after Physical Death

Once your physical body has died, the non-physical parts carry on living, but no longer in this physical world. On this point, all the world's main religions and philosophies agree. The Irish system differs greatly from here on.

As you now know, even the Otherworld, where the afterlife is lived out, has a physical aspect. The physical part of the Otherworld overlaps with this world, and there are many places on the Earth where the coexistence of the two worlds can be felt. To the ancient Irish Celts, one such place was the Isle of Arran in the Scottish Firth of Clyde, which was regarded as the most desirable of all the Otherworld islands. It crops up in various legends under its old Irish name of Eamhain Abhlach (evain avaloch), the Holy Place of the Apple Trees. The word *abhlach* was later corrupted into Avalon, and used by some Celts, and later the Mediaeval romancers, as the name for the Otherworld in the Arthurian legends. The original Avalon, however, was Irish, and can still be visited in its physical manifestation as the Scottish Isle of Arran.

The Irish Celts also regarded several places in Ireland as areas where this world and the Otherworld intermingle. These places are the sites of the many forts such as Tara, Eamhain Macha, Cruachan, Dun Oanghus, and Dun Ailinne, plus the many pre-Celtic megalithic monuments of the Boyne Valley. Other places where the two worlds are believed to meet are Islay, Rathlin, the Isle of Man, Anglesey, Glastonbury, Avebury, Stonehenge, Chartres, and Carnac, to name but a few of the more important ones. There are also many areas which have a very thin veil between the two worlds. Many people still feel the intensity and power of the Otherworld at these sites, but very few understand what they are experiencing. On visiting these special sites and being immediately struck by their beauty, tranquillity, and soft Otherworldly air, many people experience the sensation of time having stopped, and a few even have strong visual images. This shows that to sensitive people (whether or not they realise they are sensitive), the power and the atmosphere of these ancient places is still as alive today as it was thousands of years ago. Those of us who are not psychic or sensitive to these things can be trained to recognise and develop what latent psychic abilities we have. This will be one of the effects of performing the Practical Work given in this book.

The Otherworld, no matter where its physical aspect happens to manifest most strongly, is still an extension of this world. It should not be seen as a place of eternal bliss or eternal damnation, reward or punishment, depending upon how you behaved during incarnation in this world. The Otherworld contains all the same trials, tribulations, pleasures, and periods of boredom as does this world. According to the Irish system it is also possible to die there—a concept which is almost unique to this tradition.

In the Irish legends, the Otherworld is often described as a series of islands or lands, such as Tir Na nOg (cheer nah noak)—the Land of Youth; Tir Tairngire (cheer toyn-ghee-ree)—the Land of Promise; Tir Fo Thonn (cheer foh honn)—the Land under Wave; and Magh Meall (moy mahl)—the Pleasant Plain. Each of these islands or lands has different characteristics and inhabitants. There are several old Irish legends, known as immrama (which literally means "rowings," as in rowing a boat), describing various peoples' journeys to these islands and what they discovered there. The best-known of these are the Voyage of Bran Son of Feabhail, the Voyage of Maol Duin, and the later Voyage of St. Brendan. These fascinating accounts are really no more than allegories describing what happens after physical death, for the purpose of giving the listener some idea of what to expect after his or her own death. They are also used as maps of the Otherworld by Otherworld travellers such as magicians and shamans.[1]

There is a tendency in the Western world to shy away from death and treat it with a certain amount of abhorrence and a great deal of fear. These attitudes are unhealthy and unhelpful when it comes to facing up to either your own death or the death of a loved one. An understanding of the structure of the Otherworld will allow you to journey safely there to get to know and understand it. This will make death less mysterious, and above all, take away the fear and horror of dying and the dead.

---

[1] The modern Celtic writer Caitlin Matthews has published a major work dealing with this aspect of the immrama under the title *The Celtic Book of the Dead,* in which she shows how the Irish legend, the Voyage of Maol Duin, is just such an allegory for the journey of the soul of the deceased after death. She has coupled this ancient knowledge with modern psychological and magical techniques to produce a system which is designed to help the dying, and those left behind, to cope with what lies ahead of them after physical death. This counselling is extremely important and it is to be hoped that many others will follow Caitlin's lead and get involved in this very important aspect of both living and dying.

Because the Otherworld has a physical aspect, it is possible to go there while still in physical incarnation, and to decide upon which particular island or place you would prefer to go after physical death. This implies that the dead and the living can share the same space and intermingle freely, and this is indeed the case. It is believed that the ancient Celts, like all other ancient people, were far more psychic than most of us are today. The realms of the Otherworld, which are hidden to us, were in full view all the time to the ancient Celts, as were its inhabitants, whether deities, the Sidhe, or dead ancestors. Confirmation of this can be inferred from Irish legends, where no mention is ever made of how amazing it is when the deities walk among the ordinary folk and get involved in their day-to day-lives. Should such a thing happen today we would certainly have plenty to say about it, and no doubt be considered hopelessly mad in so doing! When the Sidhe appear, as they often do in the legends, nobody ever declares how odd, wonderful, or amazing this is. It is accepted just as though a group of fellow humans had come on the scene. There is no reason why we should not regain this lost familiarity with the inhabitants of the Otherworld. The practical techniques and suggested Workings in this book should help toward this end those who take the time and effort to carry them out properly.

Although we have concentrated so far on the Otherworld as it affects us after death, this is by no means the most important aspect of death and dying. The Irish Celts not only believed in a life after death in the Otherworld, but also in the possibility that the individual could reincarnate back into this world in another human body. I say the *possibility* of reincarnation, for it was believed that this was no automatic principle: It would come into effect only if the individual concerned wanted it. This is analogous to what happens in this world. We are constantly faced with decisions which will have very dramatic effects on the rest of our lives. In the Otherworld, another decision has to be made: whether to reincarnate or to stay where you are and carry on your existence in the realms of the Otherworld without ever returning to this world.

This may seem odd to readers who do not believe in reincarnation. Those who do may still find it odd, in that the individual has a choice as to whether or not to reincarnate. Keeping in mind that the Otherworld is an extension of this world, and that here we have free will which we exercise all the time, then if life continues after physical death, why should free will stop? The Irish system reflects the natural ways of the Green World where plants are born, grow, die, and eventually reappear as new and complete plants. Some plants repeat this process for several seasons and then, for no apparent reason, do not appear again the following spring. So, too, with humankind. Some will die and keep coming back. Some will die, come back several times, and then never come back again. Some will die and not reincarnate at all. The choice is yours. To me, it makes a lot more sense than other concepts of life after death, where either you remain in a permanent state of bliss or torture as a result of the deeds or misdeeds of one meagre incarnation, or you keep coming back, time and time again, in some futile attempt to sort out mistakes made in an earlier incarnation. Neither of these allows for the exercise of free will. Neither fits the picture of the Otherworld and its inhabitants which I, and many others, have come to know intimately through personal experience. The idea of eternal bliss or damnation, or of an eternal cycle of reincarnation caused by actions carried out during physical incarnation, never crop up in the Irish legends, and play no part in the techniques described throughout this book.

Because, like the three levels, the Celtic view of the world and everything in it always goes in threes, it is not hard to deduce that there must be a third alternative to the choice of either staying in the Otherworld or reincarnating back into this world. This third option is another concept unique to the Irish Celts. The soul of the deceased person can decide to stop living altogether and simply cease to be. Why any soul should choose this option, and whether many do, I do not know, but it is a viable third alternative after physical death; and it is once again an echo of what happens in this world, where there are the same three choices: carry on living without changes, make major alterations in order to change your life, or simply stop living altogether. The general rule of thumb is that if something applies here, then it will apply in the Otherworld—and vice versa—although somewhat differently.

This should not be interpreted as condoning the practice of suicide, whether in this world or in the Otherworld. To attempt to escape the trials and suffering of this world by forcing a complete move to the Otherworld, or vice versa, is to reject a vital and important part of the learning experiences to be had from both worlds. No situation is insurmountable, and all situations, no matter how depressing, painful, or agonising can be turned to your advantage. To try to get away from problems by killing yourself may seem to relieve *you* of an unbearable burden, but that burden will be shifted onto someone else, perhaps in the form of grief at your suicide, and nothing will have been solved.

Finally, it should be stressed that the Irish Celts did not approve of the idea of delving into past lives, and I would warn students of Celtic magic against such unwise prying. This is not just because of traumatic experiences to which you may unwittingly subject yourself by bringing into full consciousness the moment of a very violent death—although this is a very real danger—but it is mainly because of the Celtic view of time, as discussed earlier. If you can accept that time simply is, and that past, present, and future are all here and now at this moment, then the idea of trying to recall something which happened a long time ago really does not make sense. It can also be deduced from this theory that if you are able to remember so-called past lives, then you must be able to "recall" future lives. They are as much a part of the present as your past lives are. Knowing exactly what is going to happen to you in some future life could be far more traumatic than merely reliving a painful memory from a past life. On a more practical note, it is worth considering that your choice to reincarnate into this life indicates that you probably enjoy life in this world and want to get the most from it. Why then waste time during this incarnation trying to look back to ones which have come and gone? As far as the Irish system is concerned, the message is very simple: Let sleeping lives lie.

Involvement in the Physical World

The Irish system is not suited to individuals who constantly strive for Otherworld experiences, or who wish to escape into a state of permanent meditation on the wonders of the universe. The idea of the universe does not even occur in Irish Celtic legend, and even today the Gaelic language has no single word for this concept. Considering that we spend the better part of our conscious life in this physical world, it is only right that we should be as involved and absorbed in this world as we can be.

It is often said that magic is an option not to be chosen by those who cannot control their own lives, or who constantly turn away from the realities of this world. A total grasp of the stresses and strains, pains and pleasures, which govern your day-to-day being is vital to understanding the similarities of the Otherworld. You must be as absorbed as you can be in what is going on around and within you at all levels. It is very easy and very pleasant to experience life and the world when things are going well and you are enjoying yourself, but can you say the same for the bad times? If you review your life, you will find many instances where you have shied away from experiences like watching others suffer, periods of intense physical or mental pain, being told that a loved one is dying or dead, or having to put down a faithful old pet. These experiences have as much to teach us as any of the easier-to-accept lessons of life. There is always a balance, good times and bad times, active times and passive times, progress and stagnation. You must learn to accept one equally with the other.

The Irish system echoes perfectly the laws governing the Green World, and a deep understanding of the Green World is encouraged. This means looking at the wild and desolate places along with the green and luxuriant places; getting to know the Green World during all climatic conditions—rain, sleet, snow—and not just when it is sunny or mild weather; studying the behaviour of birds and animals, and especially the "Nature red in tooth and claw" aspect which most people turn away from. These are all necessary aspects to your full training under the Irish system, and are just as important as more formal magical exercises.

Those of you who live in cities are going to have to go to the countryside and the seaside as often as possible. Treat such journeys as magical ones, and take careful note of everything that happens, even of a totally mundane nature. The forces of Nature to be found in wild areas are very different from those to be found in well-manicured public parks and estates. It is good practice to visit both types of Green World environment regularly, and see how the feel of each place changes with the seasons, the time of day, the weather, and your own moods.

Those of you who live in rural areas should not feel complacent, for there is just as much for you to learn. Many country people take for granted the Green World around them, and pay no more attention to it than the city dweller does while surrounded by buildings. Whether you have to travel far to get into the wild places of the Green World, or whether you simply have to step outside your own front door, do it, and take careful note of all that you find.

Humour and Fun

Despite the seriousness of my comments to this point, one of the most important traits to be developed and encouraged by anyone taking up this system is a sense of humour and fun. The Celts were well known for their love of feasting, drinking, and sport, and there is no reason why we should not also cultivate such earthy pleasures. I said before that a total involvement in this world is necessary to get the most from this system, and this naturally means also becoming familiar with the pleasures to be had. A lot of people brought up with religious backgrounds have unconscious guilt feelings built into them when it comes to pursuing pleasure purely for pleasure's sake. This is not a healthy attitude, and if you recognise this within yourself, work at it until it has been broken down and done away with completely. Of course you must study, practice, and do the Practical Work if all of this is ever to become a living and integral part of your life; but there is ample opportunity for enjoyment, fun, and diversion, and we should take every opportunity to pursue physical pleasures.

Later in this book, we will look at the main festivals celebrated under the Irish Celtic system. You will see that each festival has distinct halves to its celebration—the serious, magical side, and the fun-and-games aspect. This may come as a surprise to people who have only experienced religious festivals under the auspices of one of the more orthodox religions, which have done away with, or considerably watered-down, the fun aspect of their ceremonies. (This has got a very great deal to do with why so many of the orthodox religions are rapidly losing their popularity.) If you feel you cannot equate serious study and physical pleasure as being equally necessary, then you will never be fully at ease with the Irish system. I hope there will be very few readers who feel this way.

Now that we have looked at how the ancient Celts, and the Irish Celts in particular, saw the world, it is time to have a closer look at the structure of Celtic Ireland, and the way in which the all-important Irish mythology developed and blossomed.

Section Three

The Irish Tradition

Chapter Five

The Five Invasions
of Ireland

According to the massive book known as *Lebor Gabala Erenn* (yower gah-bah-lah ayr-een), the *Book of the Invasions of Ireland*—a strange compendium of myth, legend, and fact—there were five successive groups of invaders who arrived in Ireland before the present-day Gaels. The first three groups are known by the names of their respective leaders, and the last two by the names of the races involved. These five invaders were: Cessair, Partholon, Neimheadh, the Fir Bolg, and the Tuatha De Danann. The *Book of Invasions* talks about seven invaders:

> Let us cease from the stories of the Gaedil that we may tell of the seven peoples who took Ireland before them. Cessair, daughter of Bith son of Noah, took it forty days before the Flood. Partholon son of Sera three hundred years after the Flood. Neimheadh son of Agnomain of the Greeks of Scythia at the end of thirty years after Partholon. The Fir Bolg thereafter. The Fir Domhnann thereafter. The Gaileoin thereafter. The Tuatha De Danann thereafter.[1]

---

[1] All of the quotations and poems used in this chapter are taken from R.A.S. MacAlister's translation of *Lebor Gabala Erenn*, published by the Irish Texts Society. See the Bibliography.

This apparent split into seven is a bit misleading. The tribes of Fir Bolg, Fir Domhnann, and Gaileoin all arrived at the same time, and were all descended from a common people. Throughout the text of the *Book of Invasions,* comparisons of dates are given with their Biblical equivalents. This was because the Christian scribes, who set these things down in writing, believed that the Bible provided the only true chronology by which everything else could be dated. This implies that these scribes accepted the events they were recording as being as factual as the Biblical events by which they were dating them. This is an important point: The compilers of these events believed them to be fact. Only by adopting this attitude while studying the texts can we begin to understand what these lengthy allegories really mean on all three levels.

Cessair

The first of the invaders, Cessair, was a woman who arrived with her mainly female companions before the Biblical Flood. She was said to be a granddaughter of Noah, and he, with his inside information, warned her of what God intended for the wicked peoples of this world. She fled to Ireland because,

> She thought it probable that a place where men had never come till then, where no evil or sin had been committed, and which was free from the world's reptiles and monsters, that such a place would be exempt from the Flood. And her wizards, indeed, told her that Ireland was in that case, and that on that account she should come to Ireland.

She arrived forty days before the deluge, but two of her three ships were wrecked on the way. She eventually came ashore at Corca Dhuibhne, which is the Dingle Peninsula in Co. Kerry. The survivors were fifty women and three men. These men were Cessair's father Bith, son of Noah; Ladra, the pilot of the ship; and Fionntan. They felt it would be best to split into small groups in order to survive in this new country, and the men took a roughly equal number of women each and set off on their own. Among the women who went with Fionntan was Cessair herself. The other two men soon died, Bith by drowning, quite a normal sort of death, but the text tells us a bizarre story of Ladra's death:

> Ladra the pilot, from whom is Ard Ladrann named—he is the first dead man of Ireland before the Flood. He died of excess of women, or it is the shaft of the oar that penetrated his buttock: whatever way it was, however, that Ladra is the first dead man of Ireland.

Fionntan, the sole male survivor, was horrified at the prospect of having to see to the fifty women on his own, so he fled. Cessair died of a broken heart at the loss of her husband and her father. Soon after, all the other women died, too, leaving Fionntan all alone in this new country.

Another account of this first invasion states that Noah had refused entry into the Ark to these three men, because he believed them to be robbers (we are not told why). Cessair offered to bring them to safety if they accepted her leadership, which they gladly did. The story, thereafter, is much the same, except that Cessair is given a more important role in this version, in that she is credited with bringing the first sheep to Ireland. This gives her a link with the land and the creatures of the Green World. Sheep were important animals to the Celts and the significance of this apparently mundane act would not have been lost on the listener of the day.

Fionntan lived to be five and a half thousand years old. During these long years he took on various forms, including that of a salmon, an eagle, and a stag—a creature of the Water, a creature of the Air, and a creature of the Earth. This has been interpreted by some as being an allusion to the belief that human souls could reincarnate in animal form, but I prefer to believe this changing is an allegory for Fionntan having full knowledge and experience of all aspects of the Green World and all of its creatures. During his various shape-shiftings, he witnessed all the great events that took place in Ireland, and he passed on this knowledge to the historians before he died. This is how we come to know the story of Cessair and her companions. One version of Fionntan's historical poem reads:

Ireland—whatever is asked of me

I know pleasantly,

Every taking that took her

from the beginning of the tuneful world.

Cessair came from the East,

the woman was daughter of Bith;

with her fifty maidens,

with her three men.

Flood overtook Bith

in his Mountain, it is no secret:

Ladra in Ard Ladrann,

Cessair in her Nook.

But as for me, He buried me,

The Son of God above the Company;

He snatched the Flood from me

above heavy Tul Tuinde.

I had a year under the Flood

in strong Tul Tuinde;

I found nothing for my sustenance,

an unbroken sleep were best.

I was in Ireland here,

my journey was everlasting,

till Partholon reached her,

from the East, from the land of Greeks.

I was here in Ireland,

and Ireland was desert,

till the son of Agnomain reached,

Neimheadh, brilliant his fashion.

The Fir Bolg and Fir Gaileoin

came; it was long ago;

the Fir Domhnann came,

they landed on a headland in the west.

Thereafter the Tuath De came

from Spain, from the south,

so that there was sustenance for me

at their hands, though they were strong in battle.

A long life

to my lot, I shall not conceal it;

till Faith overtook me

from the King of Heaven of clouds.

I am Fionntan the white

Son of Bochna, I shall not conceal it;

after the Flood here

I am a great noble sage.

This poem was clearly composed under Christian influence, and was probably inserted in the text for no other reason than to explain how we know what happened to Cessair and her companions when they were all supposed to have perished. Ireland then lay waste for several hundred years—one version says three hundred and eleven but another says one thousand and two years—after Cessair and her companions died, and until Partholon eventually arrived with his followers.

Partholon

Partholon is a corruption of the original form of the name, Bartholomaeus, which was said to mean, "son of him who stayed the waters." He is associated with the post-deluge invasion of Ireland, whereas Cessair was the pre-deluge invader. According to the *Book of Invasions*, Partholon was a Greek who fled Greece after slaying his father and mother in an unsuccessful attempt to take the kingship from his brother. After seven years of wandering, he arrived in Ireland with his wife and three sons with their wives. Of these it is said that Beoil made the first guest house in Ireland, Brea instituted cooking and duelling, Malaliach was the first brewer who made ale from fern. Partholon also brought with him four oxen, which were the first cattle in Ireland.

At the time they arrived, there was only one clear plain in all of Ireland. They set about making more room for themselves, and cleared another four plains. Upon their arrival, seven new lochs spontaneously appeared, and nine new rivers burst forth. It was as if the very land were welcoming Partholon and his companions. This clearing of plains and bursting forth of waters links Partholon and his family to the sovereignty of Ireland, with all its magical implications. One version of Partholon's sojourn claims that the Fomhoire (fohvoy ra), the rather nasty characters who crop up in the later Mythological Cycle, were already there:

> In the third year thereafter was the first battle of Ireland, and in the princedom of Partholon, in Slemne of Mag Itha, against Cichol Clapperleg of the Fomhoire, namely, men with single arms and single legs: to wit, demons with the forms of men. They fought against him and the battle broke before Partholon. A week were they fighting it, and not a man was slain there, for it was a magic battle.

After thirty years in Ireland, Partholon died. His survivors and
descendants continued to inhabit the country for a further five hundred and twenty years, by which time they numbered over nine thousand. They were all overtaken by a plague, as punishment for
Partholon's murder of his parents, and they all died "between two
Mondays in May." All, that is, except a character called Tuan mac
Cairill, son of Partholon's brother Starn. He is very similar in nature
to Cessair's Fionntan, in that he, too, lived for a very long time, took
on various forms, and subsequently recounted to the latter-day historians and recorders all that had befallen Partholon and his followers. One brief poem relating Tuan's various transformations and
eventual rebirth reads:

Tuan son of Cairill was heard;

Jesus gave to him in his sin,

that he spent a hundred long years

in the form of a man under good appearance.

Three hundred years had he, in the form

of a stag deer on the deserts;

he spent a hundred good years

in the form of a wild boar.

Three hundred years had he on flesh

when he was in the form of a lonely bird;

then he spent a hundred tuneful years

in the form of a salmon under a flood.

A fisher took him in his net,

carried him to the king's fortress;

when she saw the pure salmon,

the queen desired him.

So that it was assigned to her, a good course,

and she ate it all by herself;

the very noble queen became pregnant,

and thence was Tuan conceived.

This poem has also been interpreted as being a hinting at the ancient Celtic belief in the possibility of human reincarnation into animal, fish, or bird form. I prefer to believe that it is a description of a shaman's experiences as he passes through the Otherworld and learns of the many powers of this world and the Green World. This is more in keeping with the rest of the text, and with the Celtic emphasis on experiencing and learning as much as you can of this world before going on to examine metaphysical things.

Neimheadh

The name of the third invader, Neimheadh, comes from an old Celtic word, *nemed,* meaning "a holy or sacred place," thus giving him druidic connections long before the druids were commonly believed to have arrived in Ireland. According to the *Book of Invasions*:

Ireland was waste thereafter, for a space of thirty years after Partholon, till Neimheadh son of Agnomain of the Greeks of

Scythia came hither, with his four chieftains. Forty-four ships had
he on the Caspian Sea for a year and a half, but his ship alone
reached Ireland. These are the four chieftains, Starn, Iarbonel
the Soothsayer, Annind, and Fergus Red-Side: they were the four
sons of Neimheadh.

The reason that the only ship out of the original forty-four to
reach Ireland was Neimheadh's is told in another version of his journey to Ireland which says:

He came out of Scythia westward, voyaging on the Caspian Sea,
till he came in his wandering to the great ocean of the north.
There appeared to them a tower of gold on the sea, and they all
went to capture it and all were drowned except for Neimheadh.

With Neimheadh were his wife Macha, his four sons, their wives
and twenty other people. After a year and a half of wandering, they
landed in Ireland, which, by this time, was being used as a base by
the strange race known as the Fomhoire. After three great battles,
Neimheadh defeated the Fomhoire, and built himself a strong fort
in south Armagh. It is important that, while they were in Ireland,
four new lakes burst forth, twelve more plains were cleared, and two
royal forts were constructed. Neimheadh was carrying on the link
with the sovereignty of the land which Partholon had enjoyed.

Neimheadh eventually died from the plague, along with two
thousand of his people's descendants, and the Fomhoire seized their
chance and returned to Ireland, where they imposed heavy taxes on
his survivors. After awhile, the survivors of the original people
decided they had had enough of the Fomhoire's oppression, and they
staged a revolt. They put up a good fight, but were eventually over-
powered by the evil Fomhoire, and only one ship managed to escape
from Ireland with a crew of thirty warriors on board, the same number which had originally arrived with Neimheadh.

Later legends say that these thirty warriors eventually landed in
Greece, where they were made slaves by the indigenous population,

and put to work shaping the landscape to provide the Greeks with better ground to cultivate—yet another connection with sovereignty in a distorted sort of way. This connection with Greece is interesting, because it is believed that the original people who became the Celts of Europe may have come from the Greek islands. Perhaps this very ancient legend contains more than a grain of truth. According to tradition, later groups of settlers in Ireland were descended from these thirty fleeing warriors. One grandson of Neimheadh's, Semeon, went to Greece, where his progeny later became the race known as the Fir Bolg. Another grandson, Beothach, fathered the race that would become the Tuatha De Danann, and one of his sons, Fearghus Leathdhearg (named earlier as Fearghus Red-Side, one of the chieftains with him on the Caspian Sea), went to Britain and fathered the race that would later be known as the Britonic people.

Several points within Neimheadh's story imply that he was originally of the race later to be known as the Tuatha De Danann. The text may either have been confused in some way, or perhaps it reflects the Celtic understanding of time. Aspects of the story which back up this theory are that his name is a well-known Celtic one associated with druids and the Tuatha De Danann; his wife, Macha, is a goddess of the Tuatha De Danann; his fight was against the Fomhoire, who were the traditional enemies of the Tuatha De Danann; and there are constant references to threes and multiples of three—his was the third invasion, they were thirty years at sea before finding Ireland, they had three great battles with the Fomhoire, thirty warriors escaped Ireland, three of his descendants fathered the three main races. Whether this was deliberate or indicates a corruption in the original story of the Five Invasions, we do not know.

From this we can see that the first three invaders of Ireland all bear striking similarities to each other. They may well have come originally from one source, which was later changed and adapted to suit the tastes of the day. Of the many legends which deal with these three invaders, many claim that each one cleared more and more of the plains of Ireland, and caused more and more rivers to burst forth and lakes to fill up, which accounted for the way the landscape of Ireland appeared to the Celt listening to these histories and legends.

Irish mythology is, in a way, unique among world mythologies in that it does not have a Creation Myth—a story explaining how things came into being—as all other world mythologies and religions do. From what we can gather, the Irish Celts believed that the world, or more specifically Ireland, had always existed, and that it had been changed and shaped throughout its existence by the successive waves of invaders. This means that for the Celts, Creation is an ongoing process, and that they consider everyone alive today to still be participating in the act of Creation. This emphasises the importance personal involvement in this world and the Otherworld has within the Irish Celtic magical tradition, as well as the often-stated fact that it is not an easy option. By adopting this system, you will be consciously and actively taking part in the ongoing creation of this world, and you will be responsible for your actions within it. The fact that the Celts believed Ireland, the physical world, had always existed, shows their belief in the whole of time—past, present, and future—being encapsulated in the present.

The Fir Bolg

The last two invasions were not by individuals, but by whole races of people. The first of these were the Fir Bolg, who were believed to be descendants of Neimheadh, and who were, in a sense, returning to their rightful lands.

The word *fir* means "men," as in a race or people, and the word *bolg* can mean "bag." The name Fir Bolg may mean "Men of the Bag," and there are various legends explaining how they got this curious name. One legend says that, while they were in Greece, they were under bondage to the Greeks, and were forced to carry good soil to the high places and infertile regions to make Greece more suitable for agricultural development. They moved this good earth around in large leather bags, and hence earned the name Men of the Bags. Another legend claims that the sharp cacti and bushes, which they had to brush through while carrying these bags, cut their legs, so they took to wearing trousers instead of their traditional kilt-like garments to protect themselves. They made these trousers from the old and torn leather earth bags, and hence the name referred to their leggings. Yet another tradition claims that, while they were in Greece, they carried around with them little bags containing soil from Ireland, which had the effect of warding off the numerous poisonous snakes and reptiles they encountered in Greece. Again they earned the nickname Men of the Bags because of this.

These three explanations are all highly unlikely, and imply that the mediaeval scribes who were writing down this already very ancient legend were unsure of the meaning of this racial name, and therefore invented these stories based upon what the words meant to them at that time. Another meaning of the word *bolg* is "spear," and it could be that Fir Bolg actually means "Men of the Spear" or spear-throwing warriors. This seems much more likely, especially as in one later legend, specific mention is made to their very effective spears. Whatever the name originally signified we no longer know, and, for our purposes, does not matter. When they arrived in Ireland, which was destitute of people, five brothers divided the land among themselves, and this explains the five fifths of Ireland which we shall discuss in Chapter Seven.

It is also said that, during their captivity in Greece, they became very numerous and actually split into three main sections—the Fir Bolg proper, the Gaileoin, and the Fir Domhnann. According to tradition, the Gaileoin got their name, which means "Javelins of Wounding," from the two words *gai*, "javelin," and *lioin*, "to wound," because they dug the hard clay of Greece with their short stabbing javelins—a favourite weapon of the Celts. The Fir Domhnann were supposed to have been given their name after the "deepness," *domhaine* in Irish, of the clay which they heaped onto the bare Greek rocks. In reality, however, we can compare these mythical peoples with known Celtic tribes. The Fir Bolg were the Belgae people who occupied and gave their name to modern-day Belgium and parts of southern Britain. The Gaileoin were the Laighin, the main tribe of present-day Leinster. The Fir Domhnann were the Dumnonii tribe who occupied vast parts of Britain and western Europe. Even at this early stage, we are able to identify elements within the mythology which are confirmed by later historical and archaeological research.

The Fir Bolg were only in possession of Ireland for thirty-seven years before the Tuatha De Danann invaded and drove them out to Islay, Rathlin, the Isle of Man, and the Isle of Arran—all places considered to be physical manifestations of the Otherworld. Much later, the Scottish Picts drove them out of Scotland, and they ended up back in Ireland. According to the *Book of Invasions*, no new plains were cleared and no new rivers or lakes burst forth while the Fir Bolg were in Ireland. This indicates their very negative nature.

The Tuatha De Danann

The last group of invaders, the Tuatha De Danann (too-ha dje dahnahn), are the most interesting from a mythological point of view. The members of this strange race make up virtually the complete Irish Celtic pantheon. As with the other races we have encountered, the meaning of their name is open to various interpretations. It is most commonly given as "People of the goddess Danu." This, on the surface, appears to be a satisfactory translation, but if we examine in detail the individual words which make up this racial name, we see that this is not an acceptable translation at all.

A lot of nouns in Gaelic have several different meanings, and the word *tuatha* is no exception. One meaning is indeed "people," but this word was only used to refer to rustic people, or people who lived in the wilder parts of the land. It is the root from which the present-day Gaelic and Irish words for "farmer" and "countryside" come. The point, which is lost in translation from Irish to English, is that it is the ordinary or common people who are being referred to, not the gentry or nobility. Tuatha also means "North," and in Cath Maige Tuired, the Battle of Moytura—the main legend dealing with the arrival of the Tuatha De Danann—it is specifically stated that they came to Ireland from the North. They also went on to develop the agricultural potential of Ireland. This information is already contained within the little word tuatha, and would have been obvious to any Celt listening to this tale long ago.

The *De* part of the name means "goddess," and the *De Danann* part means "of the goddess Danu." It was this same goddess who gave her name to the river Danube and to the country of Denmark. There is, however, a major problem in translating Tuatha De Danann as "the People of the goddess Danu," as this implies that Danu was considered to be superior to other deities or that she was seen as the mother goddess of the whole race. When you examine Irish Celtic mythology in detail, you discover that Danu was in fact a relatively obscure goddess and certainly not a mother goddess figure at all. We also know that the Celts held all of their gods and goddesses to be of equal importance, so it is extremely unlikely they would single out a relatively obscure goddess, give her a status which she did not deserve, and which went against one of their main religious tenets, and then call themselves the people of this goddess.

We can resolve this apparent inconsistency by considering the reasons why Danu was chosen as the tribal goddess in the first place. This had nothing to do with status, but with function. All of the Celtic deities have specific functions and associations which are often unique to that deity. Danu's main associations are with artistic ability and craftsmanship. Because the deity's name was often interchangeable with his or her function, it may well be that Tuatha De Danann actually means "the People of the goddess of Craftsmanship," or, to put it simply, "the Artistic People." Judging by the beautiful and incredibly delicate Celtic jewelry, and the intricately decorated weapons and utensils which have been found, this is a far better interpretation of the name.

The Tuatha De Danann arrived in Ireland, fought with the entrenched Fir Bolg, defeated them, and took over the sovereignty of

Ireland. They, too, set about clearing plains and causing new rivers and lakes to burst forth. It is the ongoing adventures of the Tuatha De Danann which make up the whole of what we now call the Mythological Cycle.

These are the Five Invasions of Ireland according to ancient tradition. Things did not stop with the Tuatha De Danann, however. Later stories tell us how the Sons of Mil arrived in Ireland from Spain, and, after many adventures and battles, defeated the Tuatha De Danann and took possession of Ireland. These Sons of Mil are said to be the forebears of the Gaelic people—Irish and Scottish—and their descendants are technically still in stewardship of Ireland. Mil's full name was Miles Hispaniae, which simply means "Soldier of Spain." This association with Spain is due to a fanciful derivation of the Latin word for Ireland, Hibernia, being derived from Iberia or Hiberia. Mil's arrival in Ireland, or, strictly speaking, his sons' arrival—for he died before reaching Ireland—is also related in the *Book of Invasions.*

The legends surrounding the invasions and shaping of Ireland, as described in the *Book of Invasions,* carry on until a comparatively late date, contemporaneous with the writing of the book. According to later sections of the book, the people of Scythia were descended from Noah's son, Japheth. One of their members was a certain Fenius the Ancient, who was among the people who went to build the Tower of Babel. Fenius was a great linguist, and when the languages were separated by God, he alone retained knowledge of them all. His grandson was called Gaedheal Glas, who fashioned the Gaelic language out of the seventy-two languages then in existence.

Gaedheal and his descendants lived in Egypt, and Gaedheal himself was friendly with Moses. According to one story, Moses saved Gaedheal's life, after he had been bitten by a serpent, by touching the affected part with his rod. The skin turned green at this place, and hence his name, Gaedheal Glas, which means Gaedheal the Green. Moses also proclaimed that Gaedheal would forever be safe from serpents, and that whatever land he finally settled would have no serpents to molest him or his descendants. This account rather conflicts with the later story of Patrick banishing the serpents from Ireland.

After many years and many adventures, the descendants of Gaedheal left Egypt and travelled around the Mediterranean and Caspian Seas for a long time before arriving in Spain, which they subjugated by force. This apparently fanciful account of the movements of these people is uncannily close to archaeological evidence found regarding the movements of people at this same time and from these same regions. Perhaps the *Book of Invasions* is far more accurate than we have given it credit for being. For example, another passage states that in 1620 B.C. (as we would date it):

> Tigernmas died with three quarters of the men of Ireland and there followed seven years without a king.

We are not told why Tigernmas and all these people died, but we know from the archaeological evidence that, in the year 1628 B.C., the volcano Santorini erupted and caused a drastic change in the world's weather patterns, resulting in several years of perpetual winter conditions in Ireland. More little snippets from the ancient Irish legends are being proven accurate, as our ability to delve into the past improves.

The king, at the time of Gaedheal, was called Breoghan, and he built a great tower to protect the newly acquired territory. One clear evening his son Ith saw Ireland from that tower. Mil was Breoghan's grandson. He left Spain curious to learn about his ancestors' homes of Scythia and Egypt. His first wife died in Scythia, but when in Egypt, he remarried the pharaoh's daughter, who was called Scota. It was she who gave her name to the tribe who later became the Scots. His first wife bore him twenty-six sons, and Scota bore a further six, called Eibhear, Amhairghin Glungheal, Ir, Colptha, Erannan, and Eireamhoin. All of them would play important parts in the taking and naming of Ireland from the Tuatha De Danann.

Mil set sail for Ireland, but stopped on the way in Spain to sort out some trouble that was brewing, and there, he was killed. Meanwhile, his uncle Ith had already set sail for Ireland, and landed just as the kings of the Tuatha De Danann were holding a counsel to determine how best to divide the land among themselves. Ith came up with a suggestion which on the surface seemed very fair, but, on his way back to his boats, the Tuatha De Danann became suspicious of his motives and killed him. His followers returned to Spain and teamed up with the Sons of Mil to return to Ireland and take it by force.

As they approached Ireland, Erannan climbed the mast to have a better look at the place, fell, and was killed. Another of Mil's sons, Ir, rowed ahead, but his oar broke, he fell backwards into the sea, and was drowned. Finally they landed at Inbhear Sceine (Kenmare Bay in Co. Kerry), and Amhairghin the poet was the first to set foot on Irish soil. As he did so, he uttered the following poem, which is clearly of a magical nature:

> *I am Wind on Sea,*
>
> *I am Ocean-Wave,*
>
> *I am Roar of Sea,*
>
> *I am Bull of Seven Fights,*
>
> *I am Vulture on Cliff,*
>
> *I am Dewdrop,*
>
> *I am Fairest of Flowers,*
>
> *I am Boar for Boldness,*
>
> *I am Salmon in Pool,*
>
> *I am Lake on Plain,*
>
> *I am a Mountain in a Man,*
>
> *I am a Word of Skill,*

I am a Point of a Weapon that poureth forth combat,

I am God who fashioneth Fire for a Head.

Who smootheth the ruggedness of a mountain?

Who is he who announceth the ages of the Moon?

And who, the place where falleth the sunset?

Who calleth the cattle from the House of Tethys?

On whom do the Cattle of Tethys smile?

Who is the troop,

who the god who fashioneth edgse in a

fortress of gangrene?

Enchantments about a spear?

Enchantments of wind?

Once all the men were ashore, Amhairghin uttered another, shorter poem, which was clearly a magical invocation to the fruitfulness of the sea around Ireland:

A fishful sea!

A fruitful land!

An outburst of fish!

Fish under wave,

In streams as of birds,

A rough sea!

A white hail

With hundreds of salmon,

Of broad whales!

A harbour song—

An outburst of fish,

A fishful sea![2]

The Sons of Mil then encountered the three Tuatha De Danann goddesses, Banba, Fodla, and Eriu, each of whom asked that Ireland be named after her in turn. This was granted, and Ireland, Eire in Irish, still bears the name of one of these ancient goddesses. The Sons of Mil also encountered the goddesses' respective husbands, Mac Cuill, Son of the Hazel; Mac Ceacht, Son of the Plough; and Mac Greine, Son of the Sun—all clearly linked to the fertility of the land. These connections, along with the naming of the island, gave the Sons of Mil a very important magical link with the sovereignty of Ireland and the fecundity of the land. These three gods, Mac Cuill, Mac Ceacht, and Mac Greine, asked that they be allowed to keep the kingship of Ireland for three days more, and that, during this time, the Sons of Mil should return to their ships, and wait off the Irish coast a distance of nine waves. (Note the references to threes and multiples of three; this is always indicative of something magical being described.) They agreed to this, but while they were sitting out in their ships, the Tuatha De Danann druids tricked them by causing a great storm to spring up, which swept them further out to sea. They were in danger of being swamped until Amhairghin, the only one who realised it was a magical storm, sang the following magic verse, which calmed the seas and allowed them to return:

---

[2] The similarity between these utterances and those of Fionntan and Tuan, who likewise both proclaimed to have been in many different shapes, cannot be ignored. Much has been made of these shape-shifting poems, including similar ones from the Welsh tradition, and for a good overview of what they may mean and what they have to tell us today I would recommend John Matthews' book *Taliesin: Shamanism and the Bardic Mysteries in Britain and Ireland.*

I seek the land of Ireland,

Coursed be the fruitful sea,

Fruitful the ranked highland,

Ranked the showery wood,

Showery the river of cataracts,

Of cataracts the lake of pools,

Of pools the hill of a well,

Of a well of a people of assemblies,

Of assemblies of the king of Teamhair;

Teamhair, hill of peoples,

Peoples of the Sons of Mil,

Of Mil of ships, of barks;

The high ship Eriu,

Eriu lofty, very green,

An incantation very cunning,

The great cunning of the wives of Breas,

Of Breas, of the wives of Buaigne,

The mighty lady Eriu,

Erimon harried her,

Ir, Eber sought for her—

I seek the land of Ireland.

This magical evocation to the sovereignty of Ireland, symbolised in the poem by Teamhair (an old name for Tara), and Eriu, had the desired effect, and the Sons of Mil were able to regain the land. In a fit of anger at the treachery of the Tuatha De Danann, Donn threatened to kill everyone in Ireland once they arrived there, and at this, the wind blew up again, and he and his brother Aireach were drowned. The surviving Sons of Mil landed in Ireland at the Boyne estuary, and after a great battle against the Tuatha De Danann at Tailtiu (Teltown in Co. Meath, named after the god Lugh's foster-mother), they were victorious. From them, it is claimed, are descended the present-day inhabitants of Ireland and Scotland, known collectively as the Gaels.

From this amazing diversity of ideas and pseudo-history mingling with known factual history, we can begin to see why Irish mythology is so vast and complex. This brief look at the Irish "coming into being" legends should also serve to point out that, to them, Creation was and is an ongoing event. We are all taking part in changing the structure of things, which ultimately shapes this world and the Otherworld. This is perhaps the first truly holistic philosophy to appear anywhere in the world. It is only now, several thousand years after the Irish Celts worked this out, that modern science is beginning to understand the incredible consequences of it all, and that true ecology involves a sound understanding of the effects of everything we do on all three levels. I wonder how long it will be before science latches onto the power and importance of magic?

PRACTICAL WORK

First Things First

To get the most from the Practical Work, the first thing you must do is read, look, and listen. You must read as many of the legends, folklore, and stories of Ireland as possible. You must look at examples of Celtic art, both ancient and contemporary, as well as Celtic artifacts on display in museums. You must listen to Celtic music, as well as some of the many audio cassettes now available which tell the legends, often with musical backing. Suggested sources for these are given in the back of this book. All of this will help you to build up a picture-and-sound library in your head which will provide the material you will need for your Otherworld journeys, to make them as realistic and authentic as possible. Fortunately, all this learning will be going on subconsciously, leaving your conscious mind free to enjoy the legend, artwork, or music you are taking in at any particular time.

As with all things under the Irish Celtic magical tradition, pay attention to what your intuition tells you as you read, look, and listen. Which particular legends or characters from the legends appeal to you? Which picture, painting, or drawing feels right to you? Is there one piece of music, style of music, or even band or group, which appeals to you more than any other? Make a mental note of these leanings, and follow them up by reading more legends about that particular deity or hero, chasing down more artwork by that particular artist or in that style, listening to more music by your favourite band or from your favourite country. All this will leave deep impressions in your subconscious mind which will be invaluable later. Do not try to determine why you feel the way you do about these things. In so doing, you would be bringing into play your logical mind—the part which tries to make decisions based on analysis and reason—and this is totally opposite to the source of your leanings, your intuition. We in the West have been indoctrinated into using our logical faculties to the almost total exclusion of our intuitive ones. Now is the time to reverse that process. This change in the way you think and behave will be made so much easier through the use of this technique of pursuing pleasurable activities, such as reading and listening to music, than by trying to achieve the same results through deep meditation or other more arduous methods.

From now on, read a book, study some artwork, listen to some music, and realise that you are taking the first steps along the long road of the Irish Celtic magical tradition. Do not stop these activities while you perform the Practical Work, but carry on and enjoy them just for the fun of it. Think about the legends from time to time, and start to build up a mental picture of the deities and characters they describe. Try to recall stories, or parts of stories, from memory, and ponder how the deities and characters relate and react to each other. Do not, at this stage, try to analyse the intricate symbolism the stories contain; that will come later. Simply give them due care and attention as you Work your way through them. This will help later when you make conscious contact with the deities and characters themselves.

Chapter Six

The Four Cycles
of Irish Mythology

The account of the Five Invasions of Ireland is outside the main body of legends referred to as the Four Cycles of Irish Mythology. The four cycles are usually called the Mythological Cycle, the Ulster Cycle, the Fenian Cycle, and the Historical Cycle, sometimes also known as the Cycle of the Kings. So seriously were these tales taken, that they were covered by legislation under the Brehon Laws. In the category known as the Prim Scela—main tales—are Battles, Voyages, Tragedies, Adventures, Cattle Raids, Military Expeditions, Courtships, Elopements, Concealments, Destructions, Sieges, Feasts, and Slaughters. The other category, the Fo Scela—lesser tales—deals with Pursuits, Visions, Banishments, and Lake Eruptions. From this we can see that just about every conceivable event was covered in one way or another by the tales, and subsequently by the law. Today we have examples, although some only fragmentary, from nearly all of these classes of tales.

The Mythological Cycle

The most interesting collection of Prim and Fo Scela, from a magical point of view, is the Mythological Cycle, which deals almost exclusively with the adventures of the Tuatha De Danann. All the legends surrounding these beings involve a great deal of magic, shape-shifting, and deep and passionate emotions of love, jealousy, hatred, and comradeship—not all emotions you would normally associate with deities—plus many tales of great battles and deeds of heroism. The Mythological Cycle deals with the gods and goddesses, particularly the better known deities such as Lugh, Nuadhu, Aonghus mac Og, Manannan, Breas, Goibhniu, Dian Ceacht, Oghma, Cian, Miach, Airmed, Brighid, Mor Rioghain, Macha, Badhbh, Balar, Eriu, and Elatha.

This cycle also discusses the Fomhoire: the enemies and negative aspect of the Tuatha De Danann. Broadly speaking, it can be said that the Tuatha De Danann were the gods of Light, and the Fomhoire were the gods of Darkness. The meaning of the name Fomhoire is open to debate. Some claim it is made up of the two words, *fo* and *muir,* which mean "under" and "sea," respectively. They were considered to be sea pirates, who came from a strange, far-off land. Some Victorian writers said that the Fomhoire were based on the invading Viking sea rovers, but we now know that tales of the Fomhoire were being circulated in the first century B.C., long before the Viking era. The name may actually mean "underworld phantoms," from fo, "under," and another meaning of mor, which is "phantom" or "ghost." In view of the tales told about them, this is much more apt.

The Ulster Cycle

Some of the characters and deities from the Mythological Cycle spill over into the later Ulster Cycle. This serves to warn us not to look upon these artificial divisions in this ongoing body of knowledge as hard, fast, and definite. It also shows the endurance of these deities in the minds and beliefs of the later Celtic warrior caste. The Ulster Cycle deals mainly with the exploits of King Conchobhar mac Neasa and his Knights of the Red Branch, who were based at Eamhain Macha, the ancient capital of Ulster. The stories in this cycle tend to centre on battles, violent disputes between individuals, human conceit and deceit, and magical events. They are much more human than the tales of the Tuatha De Danann, and there is much we can still learn from them on a psychological level. Among the many characters featured prominently in the Ulster Cycle are King Conchobhar mac Neasa himself; the greatest of all Irish heroes, Cu Chulainn; Fear Diadh; Bricriu; Ailill of Aran; Queen Meadhbh of Connacht; Fearghus; Conaire; Connla; Fand; Midhir; Eimhear; the great druid Cathbhadh; and a whole host of other warriors, great ladies, and Otherworld men and women.

The stories surrounding the hero Cu Chulainn literally run into the hundreds. Today they are still passed on orally in Ireland, and to a lesser extent, in Scotland. The ancient fortress of Eamhain Macha is the subject of extensive archaeological investigation by the Northern Ireland authorities, and has revealed a colossal amount of information to back up the many detailed descriptions given in the Ulster Cycle. Also from this cycle of Irish mythology come the tales of Deirdre of the Sorrows, perhaps one of the finest and most moving tragedies ever written; the Sorrow of the Children of Lir, a magical tale of heartbreaking intensity and passion; the Tragedy of the Sons of Uisneach, which reveals human frailty and deceit in a tale of jealousy and hatred; plus many other not-so-well-known tales which are still told today, albeit in a corrupted form.

The Fenian Cycle

The later Fenian Cycle overlaps the other two, but deals almost exclusively with the other great Irish and Scottish hero, Fionn mac Cumhaill and his roving warriors, known as the Fianna. These tales, although violent even by today's standards, are more romantic and can be compared to tales surrounding King Arthur and his Knights of the Round Table. Among the characters of this cycle are, of course, Fionn himself, Oisin, Oscar, Diarmaid, Grainne, Caoilte, and many more warriors, heroes, and champions. The Fenian tales are very popular in Scotland, and many variations of well-known Irish themes are found throughout the Western Isles of Scotland. Many place names in the highlands and islands still reflect their ancient Fenian connections.

The Historical Cycle

The final cycle, the Historical Cycle or the Cycle of the Kings, is a curious mixture of mythology and fact. Most of the characters, places, and events mentioned in this body of tales can be verified to have existed or occurred; however, among these known people and places are events of a quite magical and Otherworld nature. Even though they are dealing with factual persons and events, these tales are considered mythological because they describe events not recorded in known history. We will not become too involved with this cycle, although, as with the others, there is an inevitable amount of overlap.

PRACTICAL WORK

Exercise One: Visualisation

By now you should have a fairly good picture of how Ireland, according to the mythology, came to be shaped the way it is, and what types of people lived and died there in ancient times. Now you must try to feel what this was like for Ireland itself. This idea of discerning how a country feels may seem totally illogical, but you must keep in mind that everything, including the very countries and nations of this world, has a mental and spiritual aspect to its being. Countries, like people, can and do feel emotions. Perhaps if more people realised this, it would not be so necessary for organisations such as Greenpeace and Friends of the Earth to constantly remind us of the very great damage we are doing to the planet.

Start this emotional learning experience by visualising Ireland as a flat plain with no rivers, lakes, or mountains on its surface. Despite this, it is teaming with wildlife and many different types of trees and plants. There is a feel of tranquillity and stability about the place and you instinctively know that everything is in perfect harmony.

Once you have a good mental picture of this virgin Ireland, visualise the arrival of Cessair with her original ships and crew. See her vessels in the form that feels most suitable to you. Visualise her and her companions as clearly as possible. Hear them speak in whatever voice or language feels appropriate. Most important, while you are visualising all of this, see and feel how the land of Ireland itself reacts to this incoming of people where there were no people before. See and feel new rivers, lakes, and mountains erupt forth from the smooth plains. Feel how the island joyously becomes aware of its growing potential. Realise that the coming of Cessair has awakened the energies of Ireland and helped it start to progress and mature from the influences and energies the people bring with them, just as human beings, as infants, learn from the influences and energies of others around them, and start to become individuals in their own right.

Eventually Cessair and her companions die, but the changes made to the land remain. A period of inactivity now follows, and the consciousness of Ireland, which had been so stimulated, starts to slip back into a sleeplike state. See now the arrival of Partholon and his followers. Again, see and feel how the land reacts to these newcomers. More rivers, lakes, and mountains appear, and the consciousness of Ireland advances a bit more. Like Cessair's people, though, Partholon's also eventually die, and Ireland falls back into its state of inactivity. This is interrupted by the arrival of Neimheadh, and the whole process starts again, with the outer face of Ireland changing once more, and with its mental and spiritual self progressing and learning from these new shapers of its appearance.

Feel these changes taking place, not only on the surface of the island, but also deep below in the regions inhabited by the beings who Work with the four Elemental building blocks of the physical world— Earth, Water, Fire, and Air. Carry on this visual and emotional exercise by studying the various invaders and their effects on Ireland, right up until the arrival of the Tuatha De Danann. Remember to include the arrival of the Fir Bolg, even though they did not change the land, and, to a certain extent, had a negative influence on it.

Once you reach the stage of the arrival of the Tuatha De Danann, stop your mental advance through the centuries and see how Ireland looks and feels at the time of her most influential invaders. Realise that the Tuatha De Danann were the first invaders who recognised, understood, and Worked with the creative forces of the physical level, and who were aware of, and Worked with the creative forces of the mental and spiritual levels as well. It is this state of total awareness and harmony which these exercises are designed to help you achieve. If you go through this visualisation process again and again, starting with Cessair and working up to the arrival of the Tuatha De Danann, you should eventually realise that what you see happening to the island of Ireland, how it is shaped and changed, and how it reacts to all of this and learns from it, is really a metaphor for what is happening to you as you learn and apply the other levels of existence. Every one of us is more closely linked to the land than we realise. The way we behave toward the land and the Green World reflects not only our present state of awareness, but also what progress we are ever likely to make in achieving harmony with these two aspects. The importance of this will become clearer as you continue through the next few exercises and come to terms with the basic structure of this ancient system.

This exercise is the foundation upon which the rest must be laid. Repeat it as often as you wish, until you feel deep within yourself a true understanding of how the physical land of Ireland responded to its several invaders and shapers. Once you feel you have achieved this, you should repeat the process, but this time change the emphasis from a study of Ireland to an examination of the influences and changes in your own life, from as early an age as you can remember, which have shaped you into the individual you are today. Think over all the people you have known, family and friends. Think on the various places you have lived. Think on the many cultural influences to which you have been subjected from a very early age. Look objectively and subjectively at how you reacted to these things at the time, and try to understand how they have shaped you into the being you are today. Some of this will be painful and some of it will be pleasurable, just as it was for Ireland, but all of it is necessary.

On occasion, come back to this basic exercise and do it again, both from Ireland's point of view, and from your own. You will find that your perceptions and understanding of this invading and influencing process will change as you progress in your Workings. You will also find that your reactions to events in your earlier life will change as your understanding of why they happened and what effect they had on you becomes clearer.

In a sense, you are reshaping the past, which serves to highlight the subtle nature of the Celtic belief that past, present, and future are all here at this moment.

As with all of these exercises, make careful notes of your conclusions and experiences in your Magical Diary at the end of each session. Looking back at these notes at later stages will let you see how you have changed as you progress.

Chapter Seven

The Structure
of Celtic Ireland

Despite the fact that the Irish Celts were all descended from the same racial roots, they became split into many different tribes and extended families, who were constantly at war with each other. Sadly, this racial characteristic is still manifest in Ireland today. It is this tribal warfare which provides the bulk of the Irish legends, particularly the Ulster Cycle. From these often gory stories, we can glean an amazing amount of information about martial training and techniques and about Celtic society in general. It is also possible to weed out details regarding philosophical, magical, and spiritual views, despite the fact that the legends do not specifically deal with these subjects.

Many of the legends, especially from the Ulster Cycle, describe how warriors of one province were the traditional enemies of warriors of another; and how for example, cattle raiding, between tribes in different provinces became so common it was almost a social event. Within each of the provinces were various Celtic tribes, as

IRELAND

The Five Provinces of Celtic Ireland

recorded by the Greek and Roman merchants and explorers who visited Ireland during the latter days of the Bronze Age. These tribes were named as follows:

Ulster—Vennicnii, Robogni, Darini, Voluntii
Leinster—Ebdanii, Cavci, Manapii, Coriondi
East Munster—Vsdiae, Brigantes
West Munster—Iverni, Vellibori, Gangani
Connacht—Ernae, Nagnatai, Avteini

These names were given by the Greek and Roman visitors, and were not the names by which these tribes called themselves. The Cavci, Manapii, Coriondi, and Brigantes are tribes found outside of Ireland, throughout the massive Celtic realms. The main Irish tribes and their locations can be deduced from the many references to them in the existing stories and legends, and we can list their native names and locations as follows:

Araidh—Northern Tipperary-Limerick Border
Calraighe—Co. Sligo
Ciannachta—Co. Meath
Ciarraighe Luachra—Co. Kerry
Conailli—Co. Armagh, Down, and Louth
Conmhaicne—West Connacht
Connachta—Connacht
Corca Baiscinn—West Clare
Corca Dalann—Co. Laois
Corca Duibhne—West Munster
Corca Loighdhe—West Munster
Creagraighe—Ossory
Dal Corbmaic—Leinster
Dal Fiatach—Co. Down
Dal Gcais—Co. Clare
Dal Messin Corb—Leinster
Dal Naraidhe—South Antrim and North Down

Dal Riada—Antrim and West Scotland
Deise—Tara and later Munster
Eoghanacht—Munster
Fir Chuil—around the Shannon
Fir Morca—Munster
Fir Rois—Monaghan, Armagh, and Louth
Fotharta—Leinster (St. Brighid was of this clan)
Gaileanga—South Meath
Gamhanra—Co. Mayo
Laighin—Leinster
Laighis—Aran Islands
Luaighne—Tara
Masraighe—Co. Leitrim
Muscraighe—Munster
Osraighe—South Co. Laois and Co. Kilkenny
Rudraighe—Ulster
Ui Bhriuin—Connacht
Ui Chinsealaigh—Leinster
Ui Dheagha—Co. Kilkenny
Ui Dhunlainge—Leinster
Ui Eachach—Ulster
Ui Failghe—Mid Leinster
Ui Fiachrach—Connacht
Ui Fidhgheinte—East Limerick
Ui Gharrchon—Leinster
Ui Mhail—South Wicklow
Ui Mhaine—Connacht
Ui Neill—Leinster and later Tara
Ulaidh—Ulster[1]

---

[1] *ui* means either "grandson" or "descendant of."
(r)aighe means "of a region."
dal means a "division," "sept" or "tribe."
corca means "race" or "offspring of."

Modern Ireland still comprises the four provinces mentioned in the legends—Connacht, Ulster, Leinster, and Munster—and their origins go back long before recorded history. Curiously, the Irish word for province is *coiced,* which actually means "fifth," not "quarter," as we would expect. Even today, reference is made to the five fifths of Ireland, and there are two differing traditions to explain how this splitting into fifths came about. In the *Book of Invasions*, there is a story which relates how Ireland was originally divided into five by five brothers who were members of the Fir Bolg. These divisions were the present-day four provinces, but with Munster split into East Munster and West Munster. Throughout mediaeval Irish literature, reference is made to the two Munsters. It was believed that the five provinces all met at the Stone of Divisions, a massive rock situated on the Hill of Uisnech which was considered to be the midpoint of Ireland.

The other tradition says that, as well as the four main provinces, there was a fifth province, called Meath, which literally means "middle." In a ninth-century poem by Mael Mura, based on much older oral tradition, we are told that the vassal tribes of Ireland, under the four provincial kings of Connacht, Ulster, Leinster, and Munster, had a revolt. Fiachu, High King of Tara—the spiritual centre of Ireland—was killed. After a period of anarchy, the legitimate dynasty was restored in the form of Fiachu's son, Tuathal Teachtmhar, who defeated the four provincial kings, and took from each one a portion of their province to create the fifth province in the middle.

This dividing of Ireland into fifths was again mentioned during mediaeval times, in a curious text called "The Settling of the Manor of Tara," which is set during the reign of Diarmaid mac Cearrbheoil from A.D. 545-565. This story is similar to the one above, in that we are told the four provincial kings complained to the High King in Tara that his domain was eating up too much of their tribal lands. Diarmaid was loathe to make a decision as to what best to do. He could hardly ask one of the provincial kings to make a fair decision, so, eventually, all agreed to summon the wise Fionntan mac Bochna. Fionntan could be trusted to give an impartial decision, and to define once and for all Tara's limits.

When Fionntan arrived, the dispute and its implications were explained to him, and he thought on the matter for some time. Then, he began to relate a strange story involving a curious character called Trefuilngid Tre-eochair, which may mean "Triple Suffering on the Triple Cornered Stone," who had suddenly appeared to the men of Ireland on the day that Christ was crucified. Trefuilngid was of enormous stature, and claimed to control the rising and setting of the sun. In his left hand, he had great stone tablets, and in his right, he held a branch bearing three fruits—nuts, apples, and acorns—all important magical symbols from the Otherworld. He spoke to the men of Ireland and said,

> I will establish for you the progression of the stories and chronicles of the hearth of Tara itself with the four quarters around about it for I am truly the learned witness who will explain everything unknown. Bring to me seven from every quarter of Ireland who are the wisest, most prudent and most cunning and also the seannachies of the king himself who are of the hearth of Tara for it is right that the four quarters should be present at the partition of Tara and its chronicles that each may take its due share of the chronicles of Tara.[2]

He then gave Fionntan some berries from his magical branch, and Fionntan planted them at various locations throughout Ireland. From these magical berries grew the Five Great Trees of Ireland.[3] Trefuilngid then set up a pillar stone on the summit of Uisnech. The pillar stone had five ridges on its top, one pointing to each of the five provinces. Fionntan named these five provinces Connacht, Ulster, Leinster, and the two Munsters.

---

[2] "The Settling of the Manor of Tara," translated by R.I. Best and published in *Eriu*, Vol 4, 1910.

[3] These will be looked at in more detail in my forthcoming examination of the Tree Alphabet and its uses under the Irish Celtic magical tradition.

Trefuilngid seemed to have passed on his divine knowledge to Fionntan, for Fionntan went on to describe the attributes of each of the five directions—knowledge in the West, battle in the North, prosperity in the East, music in the South, and kingship in the centre. This suggests that we have now reverted to the division of four provinces surrounding the centre. Fionntan is giving the attributes of the five directions—not the five provinces—a subtle but important point. The attribution of kingship to the centre should not be read as solely the centre of Ireland, but also of each province, which had its own king and symbolic spiritual centre. On an even more personal level, the centre is wherever each individual happens to be. Each one of us is our own High King, and, therefore, each one of us has our own spiritual centre.

These provincial attributes were further expanded by Fionntan, and from a practical magical point of view, we can enhance our knowledge of these attributes (or directions) by consciously Working with the symbols and personages associated with each province. Fionntan's complete list follows.

West: Connacht, Knowledge

Foundation, teaching, alliance, judgement, chronicle, counsels, stories, histories, science, comeliness, eloquence, beauty, modesty, bounty, abundance, wealth.

Connacht is associated with the famous Queen Meadhbh and her exploits. She is best known for starting the great Cattle Raid of Cooley, which tends to put her in rather a bad light. She is a goddess of sovereignty, and one well worth getting to know for that reason alone. Some of the early legends make her seem barbaric, selfish, and even cruel, but the traits portrayed in such legends are what you must expect if you wish to encounter the sovereignty of the land. Among many occult groups today, especially ones designating themselves as New Age, there is a tendency to look upon this aspect of divinity as a gentle, ever-caressing, ever-loving mother figure. This is most definitely not the case. Like all sensible mothers, Meadhbh realised the best way to teach her children was to balance security and protection with freedom and a risk of danger, and let them learn from their mistakes. This can be painful, as most of us know, but we learn from these knocks and tumbles, and learning is the main attribute given to Connacht.

Like all the provincial rulers, Meadhbh is closely connected with the other provincial monarchs, and with the High King at Tara. She has particularly strong connections with Ulster, which are made clear in several tales which mention her association with King Conchobhar mac Neasa of Ulster. In the main legend dealing with Meadhbh, the Cattle Raid of Cooley, we are told that she had many Ulstermen fighting on her side against their own Ulster brethren. This was not so much to do with certain Ulster warriors wishing to fight with Meadhbh, but more because they did not wish to fight with Conchobhar. Among the non-Connacht warriors fighting with Meadhbh were not only Ulstermen, but also Leinstermen of the Gaileoin tribe.

There is another Meadhbh mentioned in some legends, Meadhbh Leathdhearg—Meadhbh Half-Red—who is associated with Tara. Not far from the main Tara site, we can still see the remains of her fortress. The legends dealing with Meadhbh Leathdhearg are so similar to those dealing with Meadhbh of Connacht, that it is probably safe to say they are one and the same person. Although the Meadhbh Leathdhearg aspect is associated with Tara, Meadhbh of Connacht's own fort was said to have been at Cruachan, which is probably the modern-day Rathcroghan in Co. Roscommon.

It is repeated many times in the legends, that Meadhbh had several husbands, and never had one man without another standing in his shadow. Her favourite ruse for getting her way was to offer sexual favours, either her own or those of her daughter, Fionnabhair. By modern standards, she seems the epitome of promiscuity. She also seems the epitome of hypocrisy, by the fact that any man who wished to be her husband—and many clearly did—had to be without stinginess, without fear, and without jealousy—all traits she herself showed on several occasions. This apparent contradiction was necessary, because any man who became her husband not only married the woman Meadhbh of Connacht, but also symbolically wed the sovereignty of the land itself. Any fault in her husband's character would become manifest in her, and more importantly, in the land of Ireland as a whole. It is for this reason that she places such stringent conditions on any who wish to be her husband and mate, and also why she has taken so many partners. Think carefully on this point before you decide to try your hand at wedding with the land. Are you prepared and able to undergo such severe and cruel testing?

There are many legends connecting Meadhbh with lakes and rivers, and these are links with her fertility aspect. She is said to have been killed by her own nephew, Furbaidhe, whose father was Conchobhar mac Neasa of Ulster, and whose mother was either Meadhbh's sister Clothra, or her other sister, Eithne. Accounts differ as to what actually happened, but most agree that Meadhbh killed her sister, and when Furbaidhe was old enough, he took his revenge for his mother's murder by killing Meadhbh. Death legends aside, she is very much alive today, and should always be thought of as a vital, living being, who is as conscious and sentient today as she was to the Bronze Age Celt.

Anyone wishing to advance his or her learning and knowledge of the attributes given to Connacht, must make some sort of contact with Meadhbh, and voluntarily undergo the many tests of character which she will impose. It is clear from the legends dealing with her, that if she is treated with the respect she deserves, and if you can approach her without stinginess, fear, or jealousy, you may well succeed in your efforts. Perhaps it would be a good idea to start your learning on a lower level, by approaching other characters from the legends before you attempt to handle Meadhbh herself. At this early stage in your progress, it is unlikely that you will genuinely feel ready, capable, and willing to go so deeply into these more mystical aspects of the Irish system. It should be sufficient for you to know that these deeper aspects exist, and that you may be called upon to face them one day.

North: Ulster, Battle

Contentions, hardihood, rough places, strife, haughtiness, unprofit-ableness, pride, captures, assaults, hardness, wars, conflicts.

Of all the attributes given to the provinces, the ones given to Ulster are clearly still manifest today. This should serve as a warning to be cautious if you wish to cultivate Ulster contacts; however, because this system is Celtic, and because the Celts were warriors, it is something which you must accept and face.

The most famous king of Ulster was Conchobhar mac Neasa. He was very much a warlord, and his fort was known as Eamhain Macha, which is a modern-day Navan Fort, outside Armagh in Ulster. This was not a fortified encampment, as the name suggests, but more of a military training academy and assembly point for the warriors of Ulster. The facilities and training available there were not only taken by seasoned fighters, but by young boys, who were taught the skill of arms from a very early age. Conchobhar had a special troop of young warriors known as the Boy Troop, in whom he took a great personal interest. Despite their tender years, they are recorded as having fought valiantly in the great Cattle Raid of Cooley, when the adult warriors were under the curse of Macha, depriving them of their strength when they needed it most. The adult warriors could not go to the assistance of Cu Chulainn, who was single-handedly hold-ing off Meadhbh's armies from invading Ulster. The Boy Troop, unaf-fected by Macha's curse, went to his assistance, but were cruelly slaughtered by Meadhbh's seasoned warriors.

Just as Conchobhar was Ulster's most famous king, Cu Chulainn was Ulster's most famous warrior. According to some accounts, Conchobhar was Cu Chulainn's father. This came about one night when he slept with his own sister, Deichtine, while drunk, and Cu Chulainn was incestuously conceived by her. There is more to this than meets the eye, however, which we will look at when we examine Cu Chulainn in more detail.

A great many warriors were trained by, and fought for, Conchobhar. They were known collectively as the Knights of the Red Branch, a name they got from the fact that the halls of Eamhain Macha were decorated with branches of carved red yew. The red branch aspect is remembered today in the flag of Ulster, which bears an upheld red hand. Although most translations of this name use the word "knights," they were not mediaeval knights in armour, riding saddled horses, for they predate this method of dressing and fighting by several centuries. Conchobhar is almost unique among these great heroes in that he was given his mother's name, Neas, as opposed to his father's name, as was usually the case. This links him strongly to the figure of sovereignty, who is always female, and indicates that he is a true king, who has been wedded to the land. His father may have been the druid Cathbhadh, the main druid at Eamhain Macha, who advises Conchobhar wisely and consistently.

It was through his mother's wiles that Conchobhar attained the throne in the first place. The reigning king of Ulster was originally Fearghus mac Roich, who lusted after Neas and made it known he wished to wed her. She agreed to this on condition that her son Conchobhar be allowed to take the throne for one year. Fearghus hastily and very stupidly agreed to this unusual condition, wedded Neas, and stepped down from his throne for the allotted period. When the year was up, however, the men of Ulster said that they had prospered so well under Conchobhar's wise rule, they did not want Fearghus back. They also felt they could no longer trust a king who was willing to abdicate his throne, and hence his responsibility for all of his people, for lust. On hearing this, Fearghus left Ulster in a rage, and joined the forces of Ulster's great enemy, Queen Meadhbh of Connacht, which explains his appearance in the Cattle Raid of Cooley, fighting against his own Ulstermen.

An earlier story says that Conchobhar's first wife was Queen Meadhbh herself, who was resident at that time in Tara, but who moved to Eamhain Macha to be with her new husband. She eventually left him to return to Tara, and Conchobhar went on to marry her sisters, Clothra and Eithne. This implies a uniting with the triple-aspected goddess of sovereignty, in the form of Meadhbh and her two sisters, and also makes the connection which all the provincial rulers have with each other and with Tara.

It is recorded that throughout Conchobhar's reign, Ulster prospered, and there was peace in the province (despite its magical attributes as named by Fionntan). Conchobhar studied the lengthy and complicated laws, made good decisions and judgements, and took a great interest in the craft of the warrior, as well as training in arms himself. One of the greatest of all legends to come out of the Ulster Cycle, the legend of Deirdre, portrays him as becoming very jealous, deceitful, treacherous, and cruel toward the end of his life. Whether or not this was a later addition to the original tale made by someone unsympathetic to Ulster, we do not know, but it certainly is not in keeping with the many other legends dealing with him and his reign.

His death is said to have come about when a warrior from Connacht, Ceat Mac Maghach, struck him in the head with a brain ball which he threw from his sling. This brain ball was the brain of the Leinster king, Meas Geaghra, who was killed by the Ulster hero Conall Cearnach. The brain had been removed from his skull and mixed with lime to shrink it and make it solid. It had been kept as a battle trophy by the Ulstermen, but Ceat had stolen it in the hope of killing Conchobhar with it during battle. The blow itself did not kill him, although the brain ball lodged in his skull, and his physicians said it would be too dangerous to remove it. As long as Conchobhar did not exert himself, he would continue to live, which he did, for another seven years. According to the clearly Christian version of the story, he got into such a rage on hearing the news of

Christ's crucifixion, that his blood boiled, and he ran amuck with his sword, slashing at the trees which had been used to hold the crucified Christ. All this exertion was too much for him, and the ball burst forth from his head, his blood spewed out, and he died.

This legend seems totally fantastic, and is clearly a later addition to the original Ulster Cycle, but it is known that the ancient Celts practiced an elementary form of brain surgery. By cutting away part of the skull to relieve pressure on the brain, physicians attempted to cure diseases such as meningitis, and to treat battle wounds without killing the patient. Several skulls with holes cut in them have been found in Ireland, which date from the later mediaeval period. There have been several found in Austria, which date from the third and fourth centuries B.C., implying that this surgical skill had been used for several centuries. The fact that scar tissue and new bone had grown around the edges of these incisions shows that the patients lived on for several years after their operations. This also shows that the Celts must have known about antiseptics, and, probably, powerful anesthetics. The graves of surgeons have been found, and, buried along with them were their surgical instruments, including minute saws for cutting away the skull. Some of these instruments are remarkably similar to ones still in use today. In light of these finds, perhaps we should look at this legend of Conchobhar and his brain ball with less skepticism than before. We should also reconsider the legend of Nuadhu, in the Mythological Cycle, being fitted with an artificial hand after losing his own in battle, as not being as fantastic and impossible as it may at first appear.

Although the body of legends of the Ulster Cycle concentrate on warfare and combat, they still have a great deal to tell us by way of magical instruction and guidance. These legends and symbolic instructions were composed by and for a society which was based on the craft of the warrior. To many nowadays, this is no doubt a rather barbaric and outmoded concept, but be that as it may, we must accept it. If you can lay aside your misgivings about warfare and warriors while Working with these legends and characters in an

Otherworld situation, you will find that they do have a great deal to tell modern humankind, and that they are well worth the effort that goes into unravelling them.

East: Leinster, Prosperity

Supplies, beehives, contests, feats of arms, householders, nobles, won-ders, good custom, good manners, splendour, abundance, dignity, strength, wealth, house-holding, many arts, accoutrements, many trea-sures, satin, serge, silks, cloths, hospitality.

The greatest provincial king associated with Leinster is the famous Cormac mac Airt, grandson of Conn Ceadchathach. His mother, Achtan, was the daughter of a druid, and his father, Art the Bear, was a great warrior. Art was killed in battle the night that Cormac was conceived. His story parallels the legend of King Arthur, from Welsh tradition, in this and many other ways, the most obvious being their very similar names. It may well be that the Irish Celts used the legends of Cormac in the same way that the Welsh Celts used the legends of Arthur: to convey deep truths and hidden instructions in highly allegorical legends and stories.

Upon his birth, his druid grandfather made a magical invoca-tion over the infant, decreeing that he would always be safe from wounding, drowning, fire, sorcery, and wolves. As an infant, he was snatched away by a she-wolf, who suckled him and raised him as her own pup. Later, he was protected by a herd of wild horses, before he was eventually brought back into his human family. These two ani-mals, the wolf and the horse, are clearly totem beasts associated with Cormac and his followers. Such legends give useful hints as to what type of imagery to use to contact Cormac during Otherworld journeys.

The king during Cormac's boyhood was Lughaidh, and one day Cormac was in Lughaidh's court while he was giving judgements in legal disputes. A woman had been brought before Lughaidh, who had been found guilty of allowing her sheep to stray into a neighbour's field of woad, which they duly ate. Lughaidh had to decide upon a fit punishment for the woman. His decision was that the sheep should be forfeit as payment for the lost woad. Cormac rather impetuously stepped forward and challenged the king's judgement, by saying a more fitting compensation would be to give the neighbour the first shearing of wool from the sheeps' back, as both the wool and the woad would eventually grow back again. So good was this judgement that half of Tara, which had fallen down in response to Lughaidh's bad judgement, lifted up and restored itself better than it had been before.

To challenge any king's judgement on any matter would have been a very dangerous and risky business, the most likely outcome being death to the challenger. This shows that Cormac realised, even at this early age, that truth and correct judgement are of paramount importance, and must be upheld at all times. It would be best to keep this in mind when attempting any sort of contact or dialogue with Cormac.

From this incident relating to Tara, it is clear that, as well as being a provincial king, Cormac was also looked upon as being the symbolic High King whose seat was Tara. This seems to be the case with all four provincial rulers. Cormac's association with kingship and the fertility of the land is further emphasised by claims that, during his reign, the trees were always in fruit, the cows always in milk, and the rivers always full of salmon. There was no strife, and no battles were fought during his reign. He is also credited with installing the first mill in Ireland, which not only helped cope with the plentiful yield of the fields, but was done as an act of compassion when he saw how hard one of his servant girls—who may also have been his mistress—had to work. He is clearly meant to be seen as a very influential character, as far as links with the land are concerned.

Like the other provincial kings, he, too, has connections with other provinces. One legend claims that his father's first wife was none other than Queen Meadhbh of Connacht, which links him to that province. Another source states that the famous Ulster hero, Cormac Conn Loingeas, was named after Cormac mac Airt. Cormac also had another name, Cormac Ulfhota, which literally means "Cormac of the Long Beard." It may be that Ulfhota is a corruption of Uladhta, which would mean "Cormac of Ulster." His daughter Ailbhe was married to the great Fionn mac Cumhaill, and his other daughter is reputed to have been the errant Grainne, who forced the great hero of the Fianna, Diarmaid, to elope with her. His son Cairbre Lifeachair was responsible for the defeat of the Fianna in their last battle. All these connections have great significance, and it is through such symbolic connections cropping up during Otherworld Workings that a great deal of information is given to you.

Cormac is connected with Manannan, the great god of the sea of the Tuatha De Danann, who gave him a magical goblet which would break into three pieces if a lie was spoken in its presence, but restore itself if the truth should be told. This, once again, emphasises his kingly attribute of truth at all times, and echoes his earlier judgement after which Tara, which had been broken in response to Lughaidh's bad judgement, restored itself. Cormac is connected with the attainment of ancient knowledge in several legends which feature the ancient symbols of knowledge—salmon and rivers. Like all of the other provincial and High Kings, there are several varying accounts of how he died, one being that he choked on a salmon bone. This may be an allusion to some divine knowledge, which the salmon was believed to impart, being passed on, the nature of which necessitated his removal from the purely physical level. When his druids went to lay his body in Newgrange on the Boyne, the traditional burial place of important kings according to legend (although not according to the archaeological evidence), the barge on which his body was being carried broke free, and did not stop until it arrived at Ros na Riogh, further down river on the opposite side. The druids wisely decided that this must be his intended burial place and laid him to rest there.

There are many legends involving Cormac and the heroes of Leinster, and all are well worth reading and meditating upon, if you wish to make Otherworld contact with the powers and energies behind the provincial attributes given by Fionntan.

South: Munster, Music

Waterfalls, fairs, nobles, reavers, knowledge, subtlety, musicianship, melody, minstrelsy, wisdom, honour, music, learning, teaching, warriorship, fidchell-playing, vehemence, fierceness, poetical art, advocacy, modesty, fertility.

The most famous king of Munster, and the most useful from a magical point of view, is Cu Roi, a name which may mean "Roaring Warrior." His father was said to have been Daire, but Daire is often confused with the great god of the Tuatha De Danann known as the Daghdha. It may be that they were one and the same person. If this is the case, then Cu Roi is from a very prestigious line. His own son was Lughaidh mac Con Roi, who according to some versions, slew the Ulster hero, Cu Chulainn. A place associated with him in the legends is Cathair Chon Roi, which simply means Cu Roi's Fort, and this has been identified as Caherconree in the Slemish Mountains.

He also had a fort called Teamhair Luachra, which seems to have been purely symbolic, as no remains of such a fort have been found in Munster, and there are no place names that look as though they could be derived from this ancient name. As is the case with all places named in legend, however, Teamhair Luachra's true location is in the Otherworld, and should not be too rigidly connected with any identifiable physical-level location. Teamhair is actually the old form of Tara, and it could be that we are meant to understand that Cu Roi held court at Tara in Meath, just as the other High Kings reputedly did. A curious passage from one of the ancient legends says of him:

> Cu Roi never reddened his sword in Ireland from when he took arms until he died, and the food of Ireland did not pass his lips since when he had reached the age of seven for as long as he lived, because Ireland could not contain his pride or his fame or his supremacy or his valour or his strength or his courage. In whatever part of the world Cu Roi should happen to be, he

chanted over his fortress every night, so that it revolved as quickly as a millstone, and the entrance was never to be found after sunset.[4]

This clearly gives him magical associations, and also gives us several very useful symbols for use when attempting Otherworld contact with him. He is closely associated with cauldrons, as are Daire and the Daghdha, and his soul is supposed to live in an ancient salmon, clearly linking him with ancient knowledge and with Cormac of Leinster. He has shape-shifting abilities, and is a great tester of courage, as indicated in the legend of the Feast of Bricriu. In this legend, three of Ulster's greatest heroes, Cu Chulainn, Conall Cearnach, and Laoghaire Buadhach, are tricked into a situation by the tester Bricriu, where they end up arguing over who is the bravest. As they cannot settle the matter themselves, and as they can hardly ask their own king to decide (and thereby imply the other two are not so much in his favour), they travel to Cathair Chon Roi to ask Cu Roi to decide. When they get there, they face all sorts of magical challenges, and it is only Cu Chulainn who appears to be the bravest. However, the matter does not finish there. They journey back to Ulster, and once there, a hideous great warrior comes to the court and demands that the bravest warrior present cuts off his head on the condition that, as soon as the blow is struck, he can do the same to the Ulsterman. Again, it is only Cu Chulainn who passes this magical beheading game. Cu Roi then reveals himself to have been the warrior and the adversaries they faced at Cathair Chon Roi, and declares Cu Chulainn the Ulster champion. This peculiar beheading game occurs in other mythologies and in the Welsh and mediaeval-English legends of King Arthur. On the surface, it appears to symbolise the passing of the seasons, and this is the most frequent interpretation, but there are far deeper implications which only serious Otherworld Work will reveal.

---

[4] Translated by Whitley Stokes and published in *Eriu,* Volume 2.

Like all of the other important provincial kings, Cu Roi has a link with Queen Meadhbh of Connacht, in that he is recorded as fighting on her side during the great Cattle Raid of Cooley. This, coupled with his connections to the other provinces and Tara, shows that all four provincial rulers and the High King are closely linked, and should not be seen as independent beings, but as being separate aspects of one composite being. From a magical point of view, we could say that the provincial king or queen represents our physical selves and mundane personalities, and the High King represents our higher selves or mental and spiritual parts. You should start to understand the implications of this as you Work through the exercises in this book, and as you make your own conscious Otherworld contacts.

Cu Roi's death is given in two or three different ways depending upon which legend you happen to read. All of them agree that it was Cu Chulainn who actually did the deed. This explains why Cu Roi's son eventually killed Cu Chulainn. Cu Chulainn was egged on in this deed by a woman called Blathnaid, and she, in turn, was killed by Cu Roi's famous poet, Feircheirdne, when he grasped her and flung himself over a cliff in revenge for what she did to his king and patron. The above information should be enough to enable you to contact Cu Roi and learn more about the attributes given to Munster and the South. As these are some of the nicer and more acceptable ones, you will probably find it easier to progress through this province than any of the others.

Centre: Meath, Kingship

Stewards, dignity, primacy, stability, establishments, supports, destructions, warriorship, charioteership, soldiery, principality, high-kingship, ollaveship, mead, bounty, ale, renown, fame, prosperity.

Any of the provincial rulers can be considered to be the High King. This is borne out by the legends where each of the provincial rulers is described as being in Tara. The kings and queens of the provinces, however, are all testers, and their particular realms are symbolic of areas of your personality which they will test. These areas can be determined by Fionntan's list of provincial attributes. The testing with the High King and Tara is of a much more Otherworld nature, and tests your relationship to the land. Many legends deal with a High King and events at Tara, and I urge you to read as many of these as you can. The way to get to know Tara, and your own relationship with the High King and the land, is through Otherworld journeys—a practical, as opposed to a theoretical, approach. It is still possible to visit the present-day sites of Tara and most of the other royal forts. This helps to give you a very real and personal link with the land and the sovereignty of Ireland, as well as providing the always-important physical aspect needed for all magical Workings.

It is not possible, nor advisable, for me to tell you the best way to attempt Otherworld contact with Tara or the High King, as everyone is different, and everyone has different things to learn from this experience. All I can do is urge you to spend some time examining each province, and how each one's different attributes manifest within yourself. If, during such a Working, you find that things start to shift from the province in which the Working started and move off to Tara, or the provincial ruler is suddenly replaced by the High King, then go with what is happening, and prepare yourself to face up to some higher challenge. You can also start your Working by visualising yourself at Tara, and let things take off from there. Try whichever seems right to you. If it does not work, try something else. Never be afraid to experiment. There is a great deal of Work we can all do in the five provinces, and there is no set order in which this should be done.

All of this splitting into areas with specific, individual characteristics is purely symbolic, and is not meant to be understood as a description of the way ancient Ireland actually was. What we are looking at in the attributes of the five provinces, is a map of the spiritual level, which is widely reflected in Irish mythology. An understanding of this will help to explain passages which could be baffling, or which could lead to errors in interpretation in both physical and spiritual magical Working.

Despite the constant references to the High King, it must be understood that this in no way implies this status is only attainable by men. The status of High King is genderless, and women are equally capable of making this grade. I use the masculine term, High King, simply for convenience, and because this is the term you will find when reading through the original legends. The modern concept of sexism was unknown to the ancient Celts, who enjoyed a society which was truly balanced as far as men and women are concerned, and in which all were accepted as being of equal value to the tribe. This is the way things are in the Otherworld, and is the way we should be striving to make things in this world.

PRACTICAL WORK

Exercise Two:
A Celtic Identity

In order to fully understand and Work the ancient Irish magical system, it is vital to be able to approach the subject from the same point of view as an ancient Irish Celt. The more you understand about the world in which they lived, and the more you can put yourself in their shoes, the easier it will be to Work with the same deities, heroes, heroines, and Otherworld characters as they did. Having an understanding of how they saw their history, how they saw their place in society, and how that society was structured, all give you as full an understanding as possible of the Irish Celt, and the way he or she viewed this world and the Otherworld.

This exercise is to visualise yourself as a warrior in the army of each of the five provinces in turn. Remember that, in ancient Ireland, warriors were of both sexes, so the following exercise applies equally to women and men. Start with whichever province appeals to you most, and spend several weeks visualising yourself being trained in the attributes associated with that particular province. The ancient Celtic warriors were not only trained in fighting, but were also expected to be learned and skilled in all of the attributes which make up a complete being. The easiest way to achieve this daunting task is to study the attributes of each province, and to identify which ones are strong and which ones are weak within yourself. Then, concentrate on the weak ones, and try to build them up to the same level as the strong ones, before going on to the next province and repeating the exercise there.

The only way you will be able to tell how you are progressing, and if you are succeeding in this exercise, is to put into practice in your day-to-day life the attributes being studied and Worked. This is making magic real and useful on a personal level, and is bringing it into effect in the physical world, instead of leaving it floating about in some vague, higher realm. A suggested visualisation to help you achieve this is to identify yourself with one of the tribes native to each particular province. Some of you may be able to identify your own family name from these ancient tribal names, and, if this is the case, then that is the tribe with which to start your Otherworld investigations.

See your role within the tribe as a trainee warrior who is attending classes given by the druid of the tribe who will instruct you in the various mental, spiritual, and physical aspects. These classes take place outdoors, in a leafy grove, and are in the form of lectures on each topic. Now you will start to realise the importance of reading as many of the old legends, myths, and stories as possible. You must carry on reading and rereading the legends, but this time, with a view to identifying the instructions which lie beneath the surface story. By visualising your druid instructor there with you as you read, you will see what each story and legend is really saying, despite what the related events seem to describe. You will also be starting to bring closer together your magical Work with your day-to-day life, and this in itself, will be very beneficial. Likewise, when performing the purely magical side to this exercise, you will have the advantage of having more and more legends in mind, which your Otherworld instructor can use as examples to explain the provincial attributes to you.

Because there are quite a few attributes listed for each of the five provinces, and because it is going to require a great deal of reading on your part to make this exercise successful, it will take you several weeks, probably months, to complete. This exercise can be ongoing, and should not stop you from carrying on with the next one. Work first on your weakest character attributes; then, once you feel you have made some progress with them, go on with your studies and further exercises. When you have time, come back to this exercise, and complete your Work with your druid teacher on the rest of the provincial attributes.

Section Four

A Who's Who of the Otherworld

Chapter Eight

Otherworld Gods and Goddesses

There are many Otherworld guides and contacts you may encounter as you Work your way through the Irish Celtic magical tradition. Most of them are named in one or more of the Four Cycles of Irish Mythology. The cycle which will concern us most is the Mythological Cycle, which basically deals with the Tuatha De Danann and their adversaries, the Fomhoire and the Fir Bolg. These are the legends which tell us most about the different gods and goddesses, who they were, what they did, and how they related to each other. By studying the legends surrounding these non-human characters, we become familiar with the deities and their actions, and discern the seeds of the Irish magical system.

Also of some interest to us will be characters from the Ulster Cycle, which deals with the great human heroes and their interactions with each other and with the inhabitants of the Otherworld. These legends are far more down-to-earth than the magical legends of the Mythological Cycle. We will also consider the Fenian Cycle, but to a lesser extent, as the goings-on of Fionn MacCumhaill and his band of roving warriors contain less of a magical element than do the legends of the Ulster Cycle. There is something of value in all of these old tales, even if it is something as simple as an interesting piece of folklore or an old custom or belief which helps to complete our image of how this system developed and changed over the centuries.

From a practical point of view, each god and goddess has a different personality, psyche, purpose, and function, just as all of us in this world are different and unique. Knowing who does what will help tremendously in your Magical Workings. The gods and goddesses are archetypes, non-human beings who are symbols of macrocosmic and microcosmic principles which apply to and affect us all. Their functions rarely alter, and the experiences you will have with them while in the Otherworld will give you an understanding of cosmic principles and laws which explain the workings of the universe, this world, the Otherworld, and everything which they contain.

It is not possible to go into detail in a book this size, but the most important deities and their functions are listed below. For more information, read the books listed in the Bibliography. Make conscious contact with as many of these characters as you can, and try to develop deep, personal relationships with them. There is no substitute for personal experience.

Deities are listed in alphabetical order, with the normal Irish spelling of the name, pronunciation, any common variations in the spelling, and, where known, what the name means. By its very nature, the following list is cold and impersonal, and reads more like an Otherworld telephone directory than a list of friends and companions willing to share life's journey with you. Please do not make the mistake of considering these deities as being no more than certain aspects of your own psyche, or some sort of insentient, abstract forms of energy. They are much more than this, just as you are much more than a mobile conglomeration of meat, fluid, and bone. The following notes are guidelines to help you quickly identify which god or goddess may be the best one to help or advise you in any given situation. You must remember that there is an inevitable overlap of function between the deities, and the only way to really understand who does what, and under what circumstances, is to meet and get to know as many of them as you can. Over the years, they will become true friends. Their very vitality and intelligent contact with you will remove any doubts as to their existence, as well as the need for you to know just what they are and how they are made up. Read the following brief descriptions, and do not make any judgements at this stage. Rather, look upon this as the membership roll of a new club or society which you are about to join.

Aonghus (ah-nish)
Also given as Oengus and Angus, "True Vigour"

One of the best known of the Tuatha De Danann, who appears in many legends, Aonghus' *sidhe,* or dwelling, is the great tumulus on the Boyne known as Newgrange. In the older Irish, it was called Brugh na Boinne, and for this reason, he is sometimes referred to as Aonghus an Brogha, which means "Angus of the Brugh." He is more often known as Angus Mac Og, which means either "Angus the Young Boy" or "Angus Son of Youth."

He was conceived at the Festival of Samhain. His father is the Daghdha, and his mother is Boinn, the goddess who gave her name to the river Boyne, upon whose banks lies Newgrange. His foster-father is the great king of the fairy folk, Midhir. According to legend, the Daghdha lay with Boinn, and then magically halted her awareness of the passing of time, so that nine months later when Aonghus was born, to Boinn it seemed as if only one day had passed. This is why he was called Angus the Young—his mother believed he had been conceived and born within one day. His associations with time crop up in many of the legends involving him. Boinn is also a goddess of cattle, and there are several later legends, extending right up until late mediaeval folklore, which associate Aonghus with cattle. He is one of the few deities of the Mythological Cycle to feature prominently in the Ulster Cycle and in the Fenian Cycle, where he assisted the runaways Diarmaid and Grainne from being discovered by the pursuing Fianna.

Some legends claim he obtained possession of Newgrange from his natural father, the Daghdha, by trickery. The story says that he asked the Daghdha for possession of it for one day and night, to which the Daghdha agreed. The next day Aonghus refused to give it back, saying, "it is in days and nights that the world is spent," and that therefore he could keep it for eternity. This is a hint as to his sometimes-wily nature, and another reference to his associations with time. Those of you who may be experiencing difficulty in understanding time as discussed in Chapter Four should seek help from Aonghus.

He is a god of love, and his beautiful appearance is enhanced by four white doves, representing his kisses, which permanently circle his head. He is a helpful Otherworld contact who seems well-disposed toward human beings, but who should be treated with caution, as he is a great trickster and player of practical jokes, although these are never intended to be malicious or harmful. He features in the Battle of Moytura, and in many of the tales from the Mythological Cycle. He is specifically associated with love and lovers, and there are many legends concerning his involvement with love and lovers, the main one being Aisling Aengusa, the Dream or Vision of Aonghus, in which he falls in love with a girl seen only in a dream, but whom he later meets in the flesh at the Festival of Samhain, and with whom he eventually lives. This legend shows that he has had first-hand experience of love, and the pains and pleasures it brings; thus he is very much a deity who will be helpful to lovers, especially ones in trouble.

Badhbh (bove)
"Raven"

One aspect of the triple-aspected goddess of war was that, together with her sisters, Macha and Mor-Rioghain, she would fly over warriors in battle and give out terrible screams, both to frighten them and incite them to even braver and mightier deeds. In this role, she is known as Badhbh Catha, the "battle raven." It is claimed that she appeared, shrieking hideously, above the heads of the warriors during the Battle of Clontarf in 1014, when Brian Boramha defeated the Vikings. She is associated with sexual desire and fulfillment, as are all the deities of war and battles, and often appears in the guise of a beautiful young woman. She can also take the form of a crow or a hideous old hag. When she appears in the Ulster Cycle and incites Cu Chulainn to his last battle knowing he will die, she then takes the form of the raven, and waits to pick his corpse clean. She is clearly a deity who appealed to the warrior nature of the Irish Celts, but I would suggest she is not a contact to be cultivated nowadays.

Balar (bahl-or)
Also given as Balor and Bolur, "the Flashing One"

We do not know much about Balar's lineage other than that he was one of the kings of the Fomhoire, and grandson to an obscure character called Net. His father was Buarainech and his own daughter, Eithne, gave birth to Lugh, the great hero of the Tuatha De Danann. He is sometimes called Balar Birug-derc, which means Balar of the Piercing Eye, for he had a poisonous eye which was covered by a great eyelid, requiring four men to lift it by the use of large ring set into it. Whomsoever this eye gazed upon fell dead. He obtained this power when he was a child, and spied on his father's druids as they were preparing a noxious potion. The fumes from the potion drifted upward and settled in his eye, causing it to be permanently destructive.

He is associated with the North (the source of all Otherworld power, beneficial or malevolent), and, in particular with the Irish Tory Island and the Scottish Hebridean Isles. Conversely, he is sometimes symbolically associated with the South, as the scorching or searing aspect of the sun which withers and kills the harvest. He was finally killed by his own grandson, Lugh, who represents the opposite, beneficial aspect of the sun. The manner of his death was prophesied at the time of Lugh's birth, and is the source of another legend concerning Balar, in which he tries in vain to keep his daughter from seeing any man, to prevent her bearing the fated grandchild. This scheme failed, and Lugh was the result of Eithne's association with Cian of the Tuatha De Danann. As with all members of the Fomhoire, his acquaintance is not to be encouraged or cultivated.

Boinn (boyin)
"Illuminated Cow"

Boinn is a very ancient goddess who gave her name to the River Boyne, was the mother of Aonghus and wife to the Daghdha. She appears in one form or another in various pantheons stretching from India to Ireland. She is always associated with fertility and divine inspiration. One legend featuring Boinn states that there was a magical well owned by Nechtan at which only he or his cup bearers could look; the eyes of anyone else who gazed upon it would burst. Boinn, however, approached this well to look at it, and three gushes shot forth injuring a hand, a foot, and an eye. She ran from the well, but the water followed her all the way to the sea, and hence the River Boyne came into being. Note that this act of creation took place while Boinn had only one foot, one hand, and one eye due to the injuries inflicted upon her by the enraged waters. This motif crops up time and time again in the legends, where someone who is about to perform some very powerful magical act is very often described as standing on one foot, lifting one arm, and closing one eye. It is not clear exactly what this signifies, but it is an area in which a good deal of magical research could be carried out.

Her main symbol is a cow, an ancient and very widespread symbol in itself. She is magically associated with the Moon and its phases, as, according to one source, she had a herd of cattle of all different colours, which represented the different phases of the Moon: *bo finn* (white), *bo ruad* (red), *bo donn* (brown), and *bo orann* (dark). The word *bo* means "cow." These are all symbols which can be successfully invoked during Otherworld journeys to make conscious contact with Boinn. As with all of these very ancient deities, contact may prove to be a bit disturbing for those approaching with incorrect attitudes or an incomplete understanding of what Otherworld Working involves.

Breas (brass)
Also given as Bres, "Beautiful"

Although Breas is of the strange race known as the Fomhoire, he became one of the kings of the Tuatha De Danann after Nuadhu had to abdicate as a result of losing his hand in battle. His mother was Eriu of the Tuatha De Danann, a goddess of the land, and his father was Elatha, a king of the Fomhoire. He was, in a sense, the other half of Lugh, who had a mother of the Fomhoire and a father of the Tuatha De Danann, and who eventually gained the kingship from Breas. Despite his name, he was a bad ruler who made many mistakes and did not learn from any of them; worse than this, he also proved to be utterly selfish and miserly—the exact opposite of what a Celtic king should be. Because of his niggardly ways, he holds the dubious distinction of being the first king in Ireland ever to have had a satire uttered against him. This came about when the poet Coirpre visited, and was not given the hospitality and respect his status deserved. As he left Breas's fort the next morning, Coirpre said,

Without food quickly on a dish,

Without cow's milk on which a calf grows,

Without a man's habitation after darkness remains,

Without paying a company of storytellers —

let that be Breas's condition.

Breas's prosperity no longer exists.[1]

Direct contact with him is not to be encouraged; however, he still serves a useful function, in that reading and thinking about what he did wrong and how you would have handled similar situations can be instructive, while it points out some of the darker areas

---

[1] Translated by E. A. Gray and published by the Irish Texts Society.

of your own personality—something we all have to face up to at some point in our progress. He is an example of what not to be: the complementary other half of Lugh, who is the example what *to* be. The main legend dealing with him is the Battle of Moytura.

Brighid (bree-yit)
Also given as Brigit, "the Exalted One"

Some legends say the Daghdha had three daughters who were all called Brighid, and these are the goddesses of poetry, smithcraft, and healing. A goddess of the Tuatha De Danann, her festival is the Spring festival of Imbolg. She is an important deity throughout all of the Celtic countries, and the large Celtic tribe known as the Brigantes took their name from her. She is associated with guardianship of the land and the well-being of domestic animals. In the *Book of Invasions*, it is said that she brought to Ireland two oxen, called Fea and Feimhean, a great pig called Triath, and a huge boar called Torc Triath. These animals would cry out if Ireland were under attack or any sort of threat. This gives her a connection with the land and the fertility of the domestic beasts, and a role in protecting the land.

According to the Battle of Moytura, she was mother of Ruadhan by Breas, and was the first person in Ireland to keen the death of her son. (Keening is a form of weeping and wailing as a sign of mourning.) The same legend also credits her with the invention of a whistle which the Celts used for signalling to each other at night. According to other sources, she was mother by Tuireann of the Three Gods of Danu, who, in some versions, are named Brian, Iuchar, and Iucharba, but in other versions, are Goibhniu the smith, Luchta the wright, and Credne Cerd the metalworker. The latter association would seem more appropriate, as she is often described as matron of smiths and metal-workers. She is sometimes confused with the goddess Danu, as both have similar functions. It may have been the case that the word Brighid was not a personal name, but actually a title given to all goddesses. She is often confused with the later Christian St. Brigid, as both share common symbolism and attributions surrounding their births and close associations with fire. The Christian St. Brigid probably is this ancient pre-Christian goddess, as adapted by the incoming Christian church to be acceptable to followers of Christ and His saints. Because of this, both Brighid, the pre-Christian goddess, and Brigid, the Christian saint, are contacts to be encouraged and nurtured. Both have a great deal to offer by way of instruction and guidance, especially on spiritual matters (see Chapter Twelve for more details of Brighid and her festival).

Credne Cerd (kreethne kart)
"Worker of Tin"

The best metalworker of the Tuatha De Danann, he was the son of Brighid, and brother to Goibhniu the smith and Luchta the wright. These together comprised the triple-aspected god known as the Three Gods of Danu, according to some accounts. He and his brothers played a significant role in the Battle of Moytura, by making new weapons and repairing broken ones for the Tuatha De Danann to use against the Fomhoire. Earlier in that same legend, he helped give the injured king of the Tuatha De Danann, Nuadhu, an artificial metal arm, after his real one had been cut off in battle. He is sometimes described as a goldsmith, and is a contact worth developing by those interested in such crafts.

Cridhinbheal (kree-hin-vahl)
Also given as Cridenbel, "Heart in Mouth"

A satirist of the Tuatha De Danann mentioned in the Battle of Moytura, his name probably refers to the practice of poets and satirists speaking with emotions from the heart, as opposed to logic from the mind. Originally, poets and satirists were treated with the utmost respect, and their requests were never refused. Toward the end of the Celtic heyday, they began to abuse their power, and became so hated that eventually the institution of the satirist was banned altogether. It would appear that Cridhinbheal represents this later decadent stage. He was killed by the Daghdha after he consistently abused his position of authority by demanding that the Daghdha give him the best bits of his every meal. The Daghdha was slowly wasting away because of this until, on advice from his son Aonghus, he gave Cridhinbheal food which contained three pieces of gold, which killed him. He is rather a deceitful character, and probably only features in the legends for political reasons, in an attempt to point out to the people just how corrupt the institution of the satirist had become. His is not a contact to be encouraged.

Daghdha (day-a)
Also given as Dagda, Dagdae, "the Good God"

Although the Irish Celts did not recognise any "first parent" type of deities, the Daghdha can be considered the father of the gods and goddesses of the Irish pantheon. The "good" part of his name refers not to a moral standpoint, but more to his skill and expertise in all things. He has many other names describing his many talents and functions: Eochaidh Ollathair, "Horse Father of Many"; Ruadh Ro-Fheasa, the "All-Knowing Noble"; Aedh, "Fire"; Fios, "Knowledge"; and in one legend, he gives his full title which runs to twenty-six names. He was father of Aonghus, Brighid, Cearmaid, and many others, and was brother to Nuadhu and Oghma, and, according to some sources, Dian Ceacht.

He features prominently in the Battle of Moytura, where he is clearly associated with very basic, earthy functions such as eating, drinking, sexual intercourse, passing bodily waste, and generally enjoying oneself. His description in this legend is totally unlike that of the other deities, in that he is portrayed as an ugly, unkempt buffoon whose,

> ...belly was the size of a house cauldron...his appearance was unsightly; he had a cape to the hollow of his elbows and a grey-brown tunic around him to the swelling of his rump. He trailed

behind him a wheeled fork which was the work of eight men to move...his long penis was uncovered. He had on two shoes of horsehide with the hair outside.[2]

This is a theme which recurs in many world mythologies, where the greatest of the gods, or the wisest of humans, appears physically to be the exact opposite. There is a valuable lesson here for the student of magic and the Otherworld—never accept things as they appear to be, always look for what may be hidden below the surface. This also emphasises the Celtic belief that everyone, no matter how ugly or absurd he or she may appear, is equal to everyone else.

The Daghdha is associated with the magical cauldron which was brought from the Otherworld city of Murias and which nourished all who sat at it other than cowards and liars. His other symbols include a club which had a smooth end and a rough end. The rough end killed anyone it touched and the smooth end brought them back to life again. He had a harp on which he not only played the three strains of music—Suantraighe the sleeping strain, Geantraighe the laughing strain, and Goltraighe the weeping strain—but with which he called forth each of the seasons of the year in turn (the Celts only recognised three seasons, Winter, Spring, and Summer). He is the master of druidry and closely associated with the oak tree, the fertility of the land, and agriculture, roles usually adopted by goddesses. His function is to fertilise these earth goddesses, which is why the legends recount his sexual prowess over and over again. His festival is the Feast of Samhain. The Daghdha is a very important deity, well worth getting to know.

---

[2] From "Cath Maige Tuired," translated by E. A. Gray and published by the Irish Texts Society.

Danu (don-oo)
Usually given as Danann or Anu, "Wealth"

Danu is a goddess associated with the land and found throughout nearly every Celtic pantheon in one form or another. Traces of her influence can still be seen in names such as Denmark and the Danube. Very little is mentioned of her specifically in the legends, although she seems to have been associated with Mor-Rioghain and Brighid. She is a deity it would be best not to attempt contact with during Otherworld journeys or rituals, for hers is a very ancient and primeval form of consciousness, which most modern-day magicians find disturbing and hard to handle. The fact that we do not know any legends dealing specifically with her also means it is impossible to build up the necessary imagery in your mind before attempting contact.

Dian Ceacht (gee-un kehkt)
"He Who Travels Swiftly"

A god of the Tuatha De Danann, associated with healing, who is mentioned in many legends and is a central character in the Mythological Cycle, Dian Ceacht helped fit Nuadhu with his artificial arm, replacing an arm lost in battle. He may also be associated with reincarnation, or return from the Otherworld to this world, by a passage in the Battle of Moytura which can be interpreted this way. Contact with this deity is encouraged for those interested in healing work. It should be understood that his healing is purely physical, and he is unlikely to be able to assist in healings requiring work on the mental or spiritual levels which, ultimately, all healings do. Further advice and assistance will need to be sought from other deities with broader knowledge of truly holistic healing.

In light of the emphasis I have placed on the fact that all things exist on the three levels, why is one of the deities incapable of operating on all three? The answer to this is that Dian Ceacht, like many of the rest of the Tuatha De Danann, is what could be termed a first-generation Tuatha De Danann. In other words, he was one of the original group to arrive in Ireland, when it was still being formed and shaped. On arrival in the physical world, this first generation of gods and goddesses were not yet complete on all three levels, although their subsequent actions resulted in the triple unity which we know today.[3]

Eadaoin (aid-een)
Also given as Etain

A goddess of the Tuatha De Danann associated with poetry and inspiration, Eadaoin is quite clearly meant to be understood as one of the fairy folk, the Sidhe. Although not a central character in herself, she does crop up in several legends connected with various other deities such as Midhir, Aonghus, Ailill, and Eochaidh. According to some sources, she is the wife of Oghma and daughter of Dian Ceacht. There are several characters named Eadaoin in the Mythological Cycle, all described as being of the Sidhe. It is sometimes difficult to tell one from the other. One of the main legends dealing with her describes how she was changed into different forms and reborn several times to different mothers. She is clearly connected with the mysteries of death and rebirth.

Eadaoin is a contact to be cultivated by those interested in the Sidhe and the fairies, but be careful, as contact with these beings can be quite unnerving. They are not well-disposed to humans, due mainly to our flagrant abuse of the earth and its resources, and they can cast a glamour over visitors to their realms which, at times, can be hard to shake off. Read up well on the Sidhe, and on fairy stories generally, before you attempt any conscious contact with them. They are not to be trifled with.

---

[3] See my book *The Irish Celtic Magical Tradition* for a fuller explanation of this.

Eochaidh (yo-khi)
Also given as Eochu, "Horse"

Many characters in the Irish legends and historical annals have this name, which seems to refer to the times when the Celts revered the horse, and used horses in their magical and religious rituals. It is difficult to make conscious contact with Otherworld beings of this name because there are so many Eochaidhs with so many different functions and symbols. Should someone bearing this name appear spontaneously during an Otherworld journey, it may well indicate an important contact, probably closely associated with horses and the earth energies.

Fir Bolg (fir bull-ug)
"Men of the Spears," "Men of the Bags"

One of the early races inhabiting Ireland, the Fir Bolg were driven out by the Tuatha De Danann at the Battle of Moytura. They fled to the Scottish islands and Scottish West Coast, but according to one tradition, returned to Ireland after being driven out of Scotland by the Picts. They are generally considered to be a warlike race and one not renowned for their liking of humankind. Best to leave them alone.

Fliodhais (flee-ish)
Also given as Flidais, "Liquid or Milk"

A goddess of the Tuatha De Danann associated with deer, cattle, and sexual fulfillment, Fliodhais is a rather obscure deity, apparently associated with the earth energies and how they manifest through quadrupeds and human sexual desire. She is, in a sense, the female equivalent of the well-known Continental Celtic god Cernunnos. She appears in the Mythological Cycle, the Ulster Cycle, the Fenian Cycle, and even in later mediaeval folklore.

Fomhoire (foh-voy-ra)
Also given as Fomor, Fomoire, "Underworld Phantoms"

These are the nastier characters found within the Mythological Cycle, who can be considered to be our own darker, primeval side, and who are complemented by the Tuatha De Danann, representing our brighter, benevolent side. They are a powerful race, representing very early and basic earth forces and energies which modern humanity can no longer handle. Contact with these pre-human forces should be avoided, just as deliberately dredging up your own dark psyche is not to be encouraged. They are always portrayed as oppressors, as in the Battle of Moytura. They are also mentioned in the *Book of Invasions* as being in Ireland when Partholon arrived. Ireland was only a temporary base for them at that time, and they should not be considered as the indigenous race of Ireland. As with the Fir Bolg, it is best to leave the Fomhoire alone.

Goibhniu (gwiv-new)
Also given as Goban, Gobniu, "Smith"

The great smith of the Tuatha De Danann is one of the central characters in the Mythological Cycle. Like smiths from nearly all world mythologies, he is closely associated with magical powers, due to the seemingly magical ability of smiths to take lumps of solid earth and turn them into useful metal tools and weapons. He is one of the triple-aspected gods found throughout the Irish Celtic pantheon, his brothers being Luchta the wright and Credne the bronzeworker. He has a magical ale feast, and those who partake in it are rid of disease and decay forever. He is also associated with spears as magical weapons, with cows, and with the earth's fecundity generally. He is one of the original leaders of the Tuatha De Danann and a powerful contact. His name appears throughout the Celtic lands, and Govan, the great shipbuilding area of Glasgow, takes its name from him and his function. His is a contact to be encouraged by those interested in smithcraft, metallurgy, and shaping the earth forces and powers.

Lir (leer)
The Sea

A rather obscure character, his children are better known than he. It is never specifically mentioned in the legends if he is one of the Tuatha De Danann, and he does not feature in the Mythological Cycle very much. The only legend naming him specifically is the tragedy the Fate of the Children of Lir, in which he plays a minor role; but his name occurs in several legends through his son, Manannan mac Lir. He seems to be a later deity, as far as written references to him are concerned, and there are no real symbols associated with him other than, perhaps, the sea. Contact with him may be quite disturbing because so little is known about him, and also because the sea signifies great motions and upheavals, hidden depths, and unknown areas. Contact with him is likely to bring such things to the fore in your own consciousness. Be careful!

Lugh (loo)
Also given as Lug, "Light," "An Oath"

Lugh's full name is Lugh Lamfhada, "Lug of the Long Arm." He is one of the main deities of the Celtic pantheon, whose name is found all over the Celtic realms. His mother was of the Fomhoire, being Balar's daughter, Eithne, and his father was Cian of the Tuatha De Danann. This combining of opposing races into one person symbolises Lugh as being equally and consciously aware of both worlds, and both the dark and light sides of his nature. The all-important third aspect to his being is identified in the legend of the Battle of Moytura where, on arriving at Tara, the spiritual centre of Ireland, and after a lengthy discourse with the doorkeeper, he declares that he is Samildanach, master of all crafts at once. He is the image of perfection for which we should all be striving.

Lugh is the central character in many legends, especially the Battle of Moytura, which is an allegory of the progress of the human race, and of the individual, which is what Lugh represents in that legend. He is also an important character in the legend known as the Fate of the Sons of Tuireann, one of the Three Sorrows of Story-Telling, in which three warriors kill his father Cian. Lugh imposes a dreadful *eric*, or fine, upon them as compensation. In that legend, he displays distinct signs of jealousy, hatred, a lust for revenge, and cruelty, which are not normally associated with deities, and which are rarely associated with Lugh. He features in a better light in the Ulster Cycle, in that he is described as being the spiritual-level father of the great hero Cu Chulainn. His foster-father was Manannan, and he was raised and instructed in his many crafts in the Otherworld realm of Eamhain Abhlach, which is the Scottish Isle of Arran in the Firth of Clyde. In some legends, he plays the role of a saviour figure.

His is a contact to be cultivated by those who have both a deep desire to learn as much as they can about physical crafts and skills, and who have a deep spiritual calling. He is associated with the spear as a Magical Weapon, especially the spear brought from the Otherworld city of Gorias. His festival is the festival of Lughnassadh to which he gave his name (see Chapter Fourteen for more details of both Lugh and Lughnassadh).

Macha (makh-uh)
"A Pasture"

One aspect of the triple-aspected goddess of war, her sisters being Badhbh and Mor-Rioghain, she features heavily in the Ulster Cycle, and the Ulster capital of Eamhain Macha was named after her. Eamhain Macha means the "Twins of Macha," and one legend states that she was forced to race King Conchobhar's horses while she was pregnant. She won the race, but gave birth to twins as soon as she crossed the finish line. In her shame and anger, she cursed the men of Ulster that, whenever they needed their strength most, such as on the eve of battle, they would be as weak as a woman in childbirth for nine days and nights. An alternate version of the naming of Eamhain Macha is based on a fanciful derivation of the meaning of

Eamhain as "neck brooch." This version claims that she drew out on the ground, with the pin of her brooch, the limits of the fort that would eventually be built there.

She has a further connection with Ulster through the hero Cu Chulainn. On the day Cu Chulainn was born, a nearby mare gave birth to twins foals. One of these was called the Grey of Macha, and eventually became one of Cu Chulainn's chariot horses. It is clear from these fragments of legends, that Macha is associated with twins, horses, and the earth energies. Originally, though, she was probably of the Tuatha De Danann in the Mythological Cycle, despite these strong Ulster Cycle connections.

Like her sisters, she is associated with war and with sexual gratification and the fecundity of the land. According to the *Book of Invasions*, she was wife of Neimheadh, the third invader of Ireland, and she has therefore been closely associated with the sovereignty of the land from a very early date. She is closely connected with battle trophies of the goriest nature, especially severed heads, which were known as Macha's Acorn Crop. As with her sisters, she is not a contact to be encouraged.

Manannan (man-an-awn)
"He of Mana (the Isle of Man)," or perhaps, "Crickster"

A strange deity who crops up in the Mythological, Ulster, and Fenian Cycles, like his father, Lir, Manannan is never specifically mentioned as being one of the Tuatha De Danann, but he is closely associated with them. One legend recounts how it was Manannan who divided up the sidhe—the underground retreats—to the deities of the Tuatha De Danann, when their rule in this world was over and they were forced to live hidden away underground. He was so diligent in this task that he forgot to allocate a sidhe for himself, and consequently, his permanent home became the many islands of the Otherworld, particularly Arran. The fact that the Tuatha De Danann asked him to do the dividing may imply he was not one of their number and could therefore be considered an independent arbitrator.

Although he is very much connected with the Otherworld as it manifests physically in the many islands around Scotland and Ireland, he is also connected with the Isle of Man, which is said to derive its name from him. One description of him states that he has three legs, which make it easier for him to roll across the sea. This three-legged symbol is still used today by the Manx people as a symbol for their island. To him the sea is dry land, and he rides across it in his magnificent chariot; the fish are his cattle, and the great white breakers are his horses.

He is a contact to be cultivated by those wishing to make serious journeys to the various parts of the Otherworld. He is also closely connected with magic and magical accoutrements, and possesses a crane-skin bag which contains many marvellous and magical objects. His connections with the sea are emphasised through this bag, as it is always full at high tide, but empty at low tide. He has a herd of pigs which, if slaughtered and eaten one day, will be alive and well the next. He usually appears carrying a silver apple branch, a powerful symbol which can still be used to invoke Otherworld journeys. The legend, the Voyage of Bran, gives a very lengthy description of Manannan and his perceptions of the Otherworld.

Midhir (mee-djeer)
Also given as Midir, Midyir, "Judge"

One of the Tuatha De Danann, he is foster father to Aonghus, and very closely associated with the Sidhe—the fairy peoples and fairy realms. He is Lord of Illusion and the Otherworld, and lover to Eadaoin. According to some legends, he is brother of the Daghdha and father of Macha. He is a contact to be cultivated by those wishing to explore the realms of fairy, and to become familiar with the fairy folk; but be careful. He can be deceptive and not always what he may seem at first. This is the way with the fairy realms; hence the many stories of people becoming lost there. Even today, we describe somebody who is not fully in this world as being "away with the fairies."

Mor-Rioghain (more-ree-en)
Also given as Morrigan, Morrigu, "Phantom Queen" or perhaps "Great Queen"

A goddess of the Tuatha De Danann, she, along with her two sisters Badhbh and Macha, forms the triple goddess of war. She appears in both the Mythological Cycle and the Ulster Cycle, particularly in the the Cattle Raid of Cooley, which is very heavily battle-oriented. Memories of her survive in modern Celtic folklore as the Washer of the Ford, who is seen as a weeping woman washing blood-stained shrouds at a ford in a river. This is obviously a bad omen, especially if you happen to be a warrior on your way to battle! She appears in this guise in the Battle of Moytura, where the Daghdha encounters her washing blood-stained clothing in a stream. At the end of that legend, she gives a dire prophecy as to the fate of humankind and the world. Because she is associated with war, grief, mutilation, shapeshifting, and sexual gratification for its own sake, she is not a contact to be encouraged.

Nuadhu (noo-uh)
Also given as Nuadu, Nuada, "Catcher"

One of the main gods of the Tuatha De Danann, his full name is Nuadhu Airgetlamh, "Nuadhu of the Silver Arm." He lost his own arm during the first Battle of Moytura, and had an artificial arm of silver fitted by Dian Ceacht. He is an important deity, connected with magic and knowledge, especially in the form of the salmon of the Boyne, which was said to know all things. He represents the experiences of gaining that which we desire most, losing it through no fault of our own, and having to struggle to regain it. In a sense, he can be seen as the epitome of the motto, "Don't give up." He is associated with battles, kingship, and swords, especially the magical sword brought from the Otherworld city of Findias. A useful contact to establish.

Oghma (oam-uh)
Also given as Ogma

This great champion of the Tuatha De Danann is credited with the invention of the Ogham script, and is associated with eloquence and poetic inspiration as well as the physical skills and abilities of a champion. His full name is given as Oghma Grian Aineach, "Oghma Sun-Faced," or Oghma Grian Eces, "Oghma Sun-Poet," and he is a god to be found throughout the Celtic realms. He is a contact useful to those interested in both poetry and physical development by way of martial or military training. He is also a tester on the spiritual level, and anyone advancing along the slow road to spiritual fulfillment will inevitably encounter him.

He appears in the Battle of Moytura as the champion of the Tuatha De Danann, who is forced to carry out degrading manual work. This may refer to the hardships to be endured by those pursuing the spiritual and mystical paths. In that same legend, it is stated that his sword could speak, and it was this sword which related what had happened throughout the battle itself. This emphasises his associations with both eloquence and the role of champion, and gives a hint at possible symbolism which could be used to contact him during Otherworld journeys.

Samildanach (sow-eel-dahna)
"Master of All Crafts at Once"

Strictly speaking, Samildanach is not a character or deity at all, but one aspect of the god Lugh. Samildanach is mentioned in the Battle of Moytura as coming to the royal residence of Tara and demanding entrance. The doorkeepers tell him he can only enter if he has some skill which the king may be able to use. He then goes through a long list of the many skills he has, but each time the doorkeeper says they do not need him, as there is someone in Tara already who can perform that particular task. Eventually Samildanach tells the doorkeeper to ask the king if there is one person in Tara who has the ability to

do all of these things at once, and if there is, he will not enter. Of
course, there isn't such an individual within Tara, so he is admitted,
and given the honour and respect which his status demands.

Most commentators on this part of the legend assume that
Samildanach is in fact Lugh himself, but this is not the case, and it
is vital to appreciate this point in order to make any sense of the legend as a whole.[4] It is sufficient to consider Samildanach as representing the spiritual part of us which has the potential to achieve
everything and anything. Any aspiring magician must seek to
become aware of his or her own Samildanach aspect. An understanding of both Lugh and Breas will help in this process, as they are
the other two aspects of his being.

---

[4] For more information on this point, see my book *The Irish Celtic Magical Tradition*.

PRACTICAL WORK

Exercise Three:
An Otherworld Landscape

The next exercise in our series of Practical Work involves the construction of an Otherworld landscape, in which you will eventually meet and converse with the many Otherworld contacts who Work through the Irish Celtic magical tradition. You will have started this exercise with the visualisation in Exercise Two, concerning the leafy grove where your druidic instruction took place. The landscape which you need to develop now should be on a much grander scale, although it can still include the grove which you have already created. The purpose of this personal Otherworld landscape is to give you territory with which you are familiar, where you can visualise legends unfolding and where you can create scenes in which you consciously meet, and have conversation with, the various deities and Otherworld guides.

Ideally, this Otherworld landscape should contain a river with a ford, a large open plain, mountains, woodlands (which can include your own grove), a seashore, and a large, Celtic-style fort. This fort should be constructed of wood and surrounded by a palisade, and should be typical of the period (definitely not a later, stone-built mediaeval castle). Examples of reconstructed Celtic forts can be found in several of the books listed in the Bibliography if you are not sure what yours should look like. Many of the legends, especially from the Ulster Cycle, also give quite detailed descriptions of forts.

Spend some time on this exercise, and construct in your visual imagination, as clearly as possible, this Otherworld version of the physical Green World. You will be spending a good deal of time here as you progress through the rest of the exercises in this book, and later as you progress under your own steam. When you get the chance, even in daydream if not actually in meditation, close your eyes and see your Otherworld landscape unfolding before you. Go for walks in the woods. Stroll along the banks of the river. Cross the ford and see what is on the other side. Climb the mountains. Watch the wildlife on the plain. Have a good look around the outside of the fort and see what it is like inside. Explore its many rooms and outbuildings until you are completely familiar with it. Remember to open up all of your Otherworld senses, not just sight, and do all the things you would do in this world. Smell the air, and the scents of the trees and flowers around you. Touch the earth, the trees, rocks, and anything interesting lying around. Feel the wind on your face, and notice any changes in temperature. Listen to the birds singing, hear the river bubbling over the wet rocks. Feel totally at one with the Otherworld life forces as you walk about this green and fertile place.

Do not, for the moment, visualise anyone else being with you. That will come later. For the time being, just enjoy the solitude and feeling of belonging that comes with the construction of your own Otherworld place of Work and study. Remember how things felt in Exercise One, which involved relating to the very soil of Ireland during the Five Invasions, and see how that fits into things now. Build up this whole scene and relationship slowly and carefully, and return to it whenever you can. In the later exercises, this will be the place where you will meet your Otherworld contacts, see the legends played out before you, and get to know the forces which Work through the Green World of this place and of the physical world.

Chapter Nine

Otherworld Guides Other than Deities

The deities listed in Chapter Eight will give you guidance, instruction, and information on matters relating to cosmic principles and laws which apply to everybody. The function of the other guides drawn from the Ulster and Fenian Cycles is to show you laws and principles which apply to you alone. These guides will make you realise areas of your personality or character which are weak and need to be strengthened. They will reveal other areas which are negative, outdated, or obstructive, and which should be changed or done away with altogether. This instruction is, again, given through Otherworld journeys involving a good deal of symbolism, which you will need to Work on and interpret for yourself.

Most of the legends from the Ulster and Fenian Cycles are allegories providing clues to each character's function and purpose. The situations these characters experience are meant to point out specific life patterns which may crop up in your life. In some cases, the legend you are Working on may contain the complete answer to a problem or situation in which you find yourself. If the complete answer is not there, enough information will be given for you to make conscious contact with the relevant hero or heroine who will be able to help you find the answer and solve the problem. Like it or not, we all have problems to deal with, and it is the function of these Otherworld guides to help us realise our problems and negative attitudes, and to point out ways to cope with or correct them.

The following is a necessarily brief list of known contacts. During your Otherworld journeys, you will often make spontaneous contact with characters not mentioned here. When this occurs, go with the flow of the Working and see what this unexpected guide has to offer. It is often these new Otherworld contacts who become true personal friends and guides, and who understand you as an individual. Do not seek out spontaneous contacts to begin with (which is a contradiction anyway), but stick with the ones given here until you are familiar with them and their overall functions. I recommend that you read as many legends as you can from all of the Four Cycles, to give your visual imagination a large library of characters upon which to call.

Aithirne (a-heer-nay)
Satirist from the Ulster Cycle

Son of the great poet Feircheirdne, he is known as Aithirne Ailgheasach, "Aithirne the Importunate," Aithirne Ahmnach, "Aithirne the Savage," and Aithirne Dibheach, "Aithirne the Miserly." He represents the latter days of the institution of the poets and satirists, when they started to abuse their considerable power, and became objects of fear and mistrust. There are several legends dealing with him which all point out how mean, stingy, and self-centred he is. He can be seen as the Ulster-Cycle equivalent of Cridhinbheal from the Mythological Cycle.

You may think it odd that I should encourage contact with such an unsavoury Otherworld being, but he serves a very necessary function in pointing out negative qualities in us. To progress under the Irish system, you must face up to characters like him, and as a result, the flaws in your own personality. The hardest thing you will have to do under this system is face up to what you are really like on all three levels. Aithirne will be merciless in helping you recognise these things.

Amhairghin (our-ghin)
Also given as Amergin, "Song Conception"

Two Amhairghins are mentioned in the old legends: Amhairghin
Glungheal, from the Mythological Cycle, and Amhairghin mac Eigit
Salaigh, from the Ulster Cycle. The first Amhairghin arrived in
Ireland with the Sons of Mil, and was the first one to actually set
foot on Irish soil. He negotiated with the indigenous Tuatha De
Danann over sovereignty rights. The second was a druid in the court
of King Conchobhar mac Neasa and instructor to Cu Chulainn. He
married Findchaem, daughter of King Conchobhar mac Neasa's
druid, Cathbhadh.

The earlier Amhairghin recited two magical poems, which were
given in full in Chapter Five as examples of the word imagery used
by Otherworld characters to convey magical meanings or invoke
magical powers. One poem was recited to still a raging storm, created by the druids of the Tuatha De Danann to stop the Sons of Mil
from landing on Irish soil. The other was an invocation to the spirit
of Ireland, after they had landed. The true meanings behind such
powerful symbolism and provocative descriptions will take a lot of
interpretation, but this is what Otherworld journeying is all about.
The benefit of having these better-known invocations in writing
before you is that you can spend time meditating over them before
you decide to attempt any conscious contact with the originator of
these magical lays. Today, this Amhairghin's main function is as a
contact for those who wish guidance or information about new ven-
tures or moves. Being, symbolically, the first Gael to set foot in
Ireland, he has set the symbolic precedent for being the only one able
to advise on such matters.

The other Amhairghin is also an instructor, but on matters more
modern and of immediate relevance. According to the legends, he
was an ugly child, who was apparently mentally backward. He
worked as a simple serving boy until, one day, he uttered a very pro-
found poem, and his true worth and status were recognised. This has
overtones of a ritualistic, initiatory, awakening experience, and

serves as a strong hint as to his function. As well as being a fine poet, he is also a strong, fierce, and valiant warrior, and, therefore, manages to combine the spiritual and mental abilities of the poet with the physical abilities of the warrior. This is the condition for which we should all be striving.

Aoife (eef-ih)

A great warrior queen from the Ulster Cycle, Aoife lived with her sister, Scathach, in the Scottish Isle of Skye, where they ran a military training camp. Skye takes its name from Scathach (sky-ah). It is clear from the legends surrounding the training camp that it was not only a place of physical training, but of mental and spiritual instruction as well, comparable to the *dojos* of Eastern martial arts systems. According to legend, Aoife not only trained Cu Chulainn, but also gave him his ultimate weapon, the powerful magical spear, called the Gae Bulga. She also bore his son, Conlai.

The legend of Aoife shows that there was frequent contact between the Ulster warriors and the people of the Inner and Outer Hebrides of Scotland. It also confirms the historical fact that women were trained as warriors alongside their men, and often surpassed the men in ability. She is a contact to be cautiously encouraged for anyone interested in reviving Western-style martial arts, as opposed to the Eastern disciplines.

Art (ort)
"Bear"

A son of Conn Ceadchathach, "Conn of the Hundred Battles," and father to Cormac, he is seen in legend as showing justice, wise counsel, and fair dealing to all. He is also associated with Otherworld voyages and with bringing back knowledge from those realms. He is therefore a good contact for anyone seeking help in these areas. Both in name and function, he closely resembles the British King Arthur, even to the extent that Art was said to be protected by angels, as was

Arthur, even though neither was Christian. Because of this, he can be seen as a link between the pre-Christian and Christian traditions. (This is an important aspect for anyone studying this magical and spiritual system, which goes beyond such artificial religious boundaries.)

Bran Mac Feabhail (bron mak-fayvil)
"Raven son of Feabhail"

Bran is a character very much associated with Otherworld voyages and the return of knowledge from those realms. He is also associated with the phenomenon of time passing at different rates in this world and the Otherworld. A beautiful and instructive poem exists, which describes in detail his journey to the various Otherworld islands, how he encountered the sea god Manannan on the way, and what happened upon his return to this world. This type of poem or legend is known as an *immram,* which literally means "rowing a boat."

Although the "Voyage of Bran" is written in fantastic poetic terms, there is a lot of wisdom in this ancient verse. The journey, as it is laid out in poetic form, can be used as prescripted imagery to help access the Otherworld for those who are experiencing difficulty in this area.[1] Bran is a very useful guide, as he has been to all of the Otherworld islands many times, and is a trustworthy and knowledgeable companion.

Bricriu (brik-roo)
Sometimes given as Bricne

It is not clear what this name means. It may be related to a specific type of poetry, called in Irish *breac,* "speckled," which intermingles

---

[1] The modern-day singer, songwriter, poet, and bard, Robin Williamson, has produced a spoken version of the "Voyage of Bran," accompanied by the clarsach, on cassette. This is an ideal form in which to fully experience the beauty and Otherworld power of this ancient lay. Details of Robin's cassettes are given in the Discography at the end of this book.

praise with satire. Bricriu is usually given the full name, Bricriu of the Poisonous (or Evil) Tongue. This gives a good indication as to his nature.

Although his being a satirist is never specifically mentioned in the legends, it would appear that he is, for he invariably uses clever words to stir up trouble, even to the extent of inciting mass slaughter. Despite the clearly deliberate nature of his actions, he is never punished or even reprimanded for his evil ways. In fact, in the Ulster Cycle legend, Bricriu's Feast, it is recorded that he is permanently guarded by eight swordsmen, implying that his proper function is to provoke and test the heroes and heroines of Ulster by skillful satire and use of words. Obviously, while carrying out this rightful function, he may require protection from those who cannot take his satires without giving in to blind rage and revenge.

In the Cattle Raid of Cooley, it says that after the great war between Meadhbh's forces and the Ulstermen, Bricriu was asked to judge the outcome of the dreadful fight between two bulls, which had been the original source of contention. To give him such an important task shows that he must have held a position of high authority within the tribal structure, and that he was by no means considered a mere troublemaker. Unfortunately, during the bulls' terrifying combat, Bricriu accidentally got in the way and was trampled to death. This may signify a ritual sacrifice connected with the bull cult and the earth forces bulls represent. We do not have enough information on this cult to come to any firm conclusions on this possibility.

He is best regarded as a necessary tester, who makes you face up to certain aspects of your life or personality which you have been avoiding, but which need to be grasped and dealt with before further progress can be made. So, while he does serve a useful function despite his bad press, he is an Otherworld character to be dealt with cautiously, and not one to be deliberately contacted unless you are fully prepared to face up to what he will most definitely have to say to you.

Caoilte (kweel-tchi)
"Slender and Fierce"

His full name is Caoilte mac Ronain, and he is nephew to the great Fionn mac Cumhaill himself. He continued to appear in both Irish and Scottish folklore right up until this century, and was clearly a very popular figure from the Fenian Cycle. He is always portrayed in the legends as being an incredibly swift runner and, in some legends, is given the name Caoilte Cos Luath or "Caoilte Fleet Footed." He also was associated in some way with the goddesses of sovereignty—in some instances as a friend and helper, in others, an aggressor and foe. It is no longer clear what his true association with the land is; however, he is very closely associated with the animal kingdom, and is a contact for those wishing to learn more of the animal world.

In the legend, Agallamh na Seanorach (ahk-allahv nah shon-orah), or the Colloquy of the Old Men, we are told that Caoilte lived so long, he was still in Ireland when St. Patrick arrived. He spent many days and nights relating all the adventures of the Fianna to the saint. This gives him a place in both pre-Christian and Christian mythology, which indicates he may be a good contact for anyone who feels they are biased as far as religious beliefs are concerned, especially against the pre-Christian or Christian faiths.

He is associated with the Otherworld, and a famous poem describing the Otherworld in the form of the Isle of Arran is attributed to him:

Arran of the many stags,

the sea impinges on her very shoulders!

An island in which whole companies were fed

and with ridges among which blue spears are reddened!

Skittish deer are on her pinnacles,

soft blackberries on her waving heather;

cool water there is in her rivers,

and mast upon her russet oaks!

Greyhounds there were in her, and beagles;

blaeberries and sloes of the dark blackthorn;

dwellings with their backs set close against her woods,

and the deer fed scattered by her oaken thickets!

A crimson crop grew on her rocks,

in all her glades a faultless grass;

over her crags affording friendly refuge,

leaping went on, and fawns were skipping!

Smooth were her level spots,

her wild swine they were fat;

cheerful her fields,

her nuts hung on her forest-hazels' boughs,

and there was sailing

of long galleys past her!

Right pleasant their condition all when the fair weather sets in.

Under her rivers' brinks, trout lie;

the seagulls wheeling round her grand cliff

answer one the other.

At every fitting time delectable is Arran![2]

Cathbhadh (koff-uh)
Also given as Cathbad, "Battle-Slayer"

Druid of King Conchobhar mac Neasa in the Ulster Cycle, Cathbhadh was, according to some sources, Conchobhar's natural father. Although there was no system of hierarchy among the Irish druids, Cathbhadh is probably the most famous and most important of all the druids mentioned throughout the various Irish cycles. He taught the warriors of Eamhain Macha magical skills, which they had to learn and master along with the normal skills and abilities associated with the warrior craft. Unlike the Gaulish druids who held aloof from war, the Irish druids felt no qualms about becoming involved in the thick of battle, and Cathbhadh is also a great warrior. This is highlighted by not only his name, but also by the fact that he was grandfather to both Cu Chulainn and to Naoise, the lover of Deirdre.

He is always portrayed as being a man of vision, and a great predictor of the future. Many of the legends relate how he laid various *geasa* on people, which implies he also could affect the future. He is scrupulously just and fair, and not open to any sort of persuasion or coercion. Those wishing to further their magical skills (particularly of a druidic nature) should attempt to contact Cathbhadh, but be prepared to be subject to a hard, thorough master.

---

[2] From *Silva Gadelica,* translated by S. H. O'Grady.

Cessair (kessir)

According to the *Book of Invasions*, the first settlers in Ireland arrived with this woman, who is described as daughter of Bith, son of Noah. With her came fifty women and three men, one of whom was the celebrated Fionntan. She is clearly a goddess figure, associated with the land and sovereignty, but of a very ancient type. There is little point in attempting conscious contact with her now, for she exists only to show that Ireland has a very ancient lineage. Indeed, it is recorded in the legends that she actually died in Ireland. Her death is described to show that she is now part of the land itself, and no longer a conscious Otherworld contact.

Conaire (kun-er-ay)
"Warrior Lord"

The High King of Tara in the Ulster Cycle, who is much associated with sacred kingship and all which that implies, Conaire's mother, Meas Buachalla (mash boo-ahallah), was from the Otherworld. His apparent father was a king of this world, called Eterscele, although unknown to him, Meas Buachalla had already conceived by an Otherworld man, called Nemglan, who appeared to her in the guise of a bird. He is, therefore, half of this world and half of the Other-world, and closely connected with shamanism and Otherworld knowledge and journeying. The main legend dealing with him is Togail Bruidne Da Derga, Destruction of the Red God's Hostel.

Besides being closely associated with birds, a quality synony-mous with the shaman and Otherworld seers and travellers, he is also associated with blood and sacrificial death, which are both linked to the institution of sacred kingship. It is recounted that he was chosen for the High Kingship following an enactment of the mysterious Tarbh Fheis, the druidic bull-feast ritual, in which he was seen in vision. He later fulfilled the prophecy as to how the next High King would be recognised. There were more geasa laid on him than on any other High King, which indicates his extreme importance and magical significance. From these various associations and legends, it is clear that he was being presented as the image of the perfect High King, whose role was much more magical than political. During his reign, Ireland was at peace, and there was much prosperity. Contact him if you are wishing to improve your aspect of the sacred kingship and shamanism.

Conall Cearnach (kun-ul kar-nok)
"Strong Wolf, Triumphant"

One of the great heroes of the Ulster Cycle, who is a great friend and compatriot of the other magnificent Ulster hero, Cu Chulainn, he appears in legends such as the Cattle Raid of Cooley, the Cattle Raid of Fraoch, and the Story of the Pig of Mac Da Tho. He is a valiant and fierce warrior, never showing fear, who is scrupulously fair in battle and will never take unfair advantage over an opponent. According to all of the legends, he is closely involved in the cult of the head as a battle trophy. He lived to a ripe old age, and is the epitome of the strong, just, and proud warrior. He is a contact to be cultivated by those who are lacking in any of these areas.

Conchobhar mac Neasa
(kunna-voor mak nassa)
"One Who is Desirous of Warriors"

This great king of the Ulster Cycle was seated at the royal capital of Eamhain Macha. It is interesting that mac Neasa which means, "son of Neasa," refers to his mother, and not his father, as is usually the case. According to some legends, his father was Cathbhadh, who later became his druid and counsellor. As the story goes, Cathbhadh passed Neasa's home one day, and she asked him to divine what the present hour was lucky for. He told her that any child conceived at that moment would be known in Ireland forever. Because there was no other male present, Neasa immediately took Cathbhadh into her home, and Conchobhar was conceived. It is also related that he was in his mother's womb for three years and three months before finally being born. The number three is always symbolic in the legends of something or someone very magical and important.

Like the other important monarchs, he is very much associated with the archetype of sacred kingship and the heavy burdens and duties which that imposes. Conchobhar's name probably refers to his military training school, and his band of warriors who were later known as the Knights of the Red Branch. He had a magical shield, called Ochaoin, which would cry out if he was in danger during battle. This can be used as a magical symbol today by those wishing to make contact with him on an Otherworld level.

Although he is a powerful and potent character, I would advise caution when dealing with him. In the legend of Deirdre, he loses his kingly detachment, and gives in to the overpowering and destructive emotions of jealousy and hatred. This should be interpreted as a warning that even the most enlightened can fall victim to very basic human emotions. It should also be kept in mind that few individuals today could meet the high standards of physical fitness and mental and spiritual discipline expected of a Celtic warrior. If you are not capable, he may well reject you.

Cormac mac Airt (kurmok mac art)
"Warrior Son of the Bear"

Son of the great king Art, and grandson of the famous Conn, Cormac is the Leinster equivalent of the Ulster Conchobhar—connected with the institution of sacred kingship. Although he was originally a Leinsterman, later stories set him in Connacht, and whereas Conchobhar was very battle-oriented, and ultimately succumbed to his own human frailties, Cormac was a much more peaceful ruler. It was recorded that during his reign, Ireland had never been more prosperous or bountiful in grain, fruit, and milk yield. He is also well known for his wise and shrewd judgements in awkward and difficult legal cases. Cormac eventually took the royal seat of Tara, the spiritual centre of Ireland. Because the High King represents the spiritual aspect of all of his people in physical incarnation, we can see that Cormac is a very important figure for anyone wishing to develop their own spiritual aspect, especially in the service of others and of the land itself.

He features as a very important character in many legends. His connections with the Otherworld are recounted in several tales. One particular legend states that he was given the silver apple branch, a symbol of the Otherworld, by Manannan mac Lir. When it was shaken, it had the effect of calming, or perhaps putting into a trance, all present. He is also associated with wolves, and this would appear to be his totem animal. From these two pieces of information, it should not be too difficult to construct suitable visual imagery to use in attempts to contact him during Otherworld journeys.

Cu Chulainn (koo hool-inn)
"Hound of Culann"

The greatest and most famous of all the heroes from the Ulster Cycle, his exploits are recounted in literally hundreds of legends and stories stretching from the Iron Age right up to the present-day folklore of Ireland and Scotland. So important a character is he to the Irish, that even today, a magnificent statue of him stands in the General Post Office in Dublin. The *cu* part of his name means "hound" or "wolf," but it can also mean "warrior," and this is probably a more apt description of his function throughout his short life.

According to legend, his mother was Conchobhar's sister, Deichtine, and he was born three times, with three different fathers. This came about when Conchobhar, Deichtine, and the Red Branch Knights were hunting birds near Newgrange. They spent the night in a little bothy near Newgrange, and while there, the woman of the house gave birth to a son. Deichtine nursed the baby while the woman slept, but in the morning when they awoke, they found that the woman, the house, and everything in it had vanished, except the baby boy. Deichtine took him back to Eamhain Macha and reared him as her own.

He soon died, but on that night, the god Lugh came to her in a dream and told her that the child was actually hers, and that his father had been one of the birds they were hunting that night in the magical house at Newgrange. He also told her that she was now pregnant by him—he had impregnated her through a drink she had consumed earlier that evening. As she grew heavy with child, rumours spread in Eamhain Macha that Conchobhar had lain with his own sister while drunk one night. Conchobhar, in an effort to dispel these malicious stories, gave her as a bride to one of his warriors, Sualdam mac Roich. So ashamed was Deichtine to go to her new husband while pregnant, that she was sick, and the child "spilled away in the sickness and she was made virgin and whole again and went to her husband." She conceived by Sualdam, and, in due course, bore a baby boy.

Coincidental with his birth was the foaling of a mare and the appearance of a large flock of birds over Ulster—another magical association of threes. His connection with horses and dogs, which is very strong throughout the many legends about him, shows that these are his totem animals. It is known that at the time of Cu Chulainn, the Irish Celts bred large dogs as a source of meat, but one legend describes how Cu Chulainn was specifically debarred from eating dog flesh. This, again, indicates that the dog is one of his totem animals. The appearance of the birds during his birth is symbolic of his first father, and also of the shamanic Otherworld traveller. This hints at his Otherworld connections and powers.

His original name was Setanta, but this was changed while he was still a child, after he slew Culann the smith's massive guard dog. He promised to take its place until the dog's pups had grown to maturity. Hence his new name, Cu Chulainn, or "Hound of Culann." Whenever a change of name occurs in a legend, we can take it to mean that some sort of magical initiation has taken place. All these factors combine to emphasise just how important a character Cu Chulainn is.

He is the fiercest and bravest of all of King Conchobhar mac Neasa's Red Branch Knights. He has a terrible weapon, the Gae Bulga, which is a barbed spear thrown by the feet. He was given his military training by the great warrior queen, Scathach, on the Scottish Isle of Skye. It is clear from the legends which refer to this period in his life that his training was not just on a physical level, but also combined mental and spiritual disciplines. The legends give a long list of the warrior feats he was taught and mastered in Skye, but we are not told exactly what they were, presumably because the ancient Celt listening to the tale would have known. The passage is as follows:

> Cu Chulainn's training with Scathach in the craft of arms: the apple feat—juggling nine apples with never more than one on his palm; the thunder feat; the feats of the sword edge and the sloped shield; the feats of the javelin and rope; the body feat; the feat of Cat and the heroic salmon leap; the pole throw and the leap over a poisoned stroke; the noble chariot fighter's crouch; the Gae Bulga; the spurt of speed; the feat of the chariot wheel thrown on high and the feat of the shield rim; the breath feat with gold apples blown up into the air; the snapping mouth and the hero's scream; the stroke of precision; the stunning shot and the cry stroke; stepping on a lance in flight and straightening erect on its point; the sickle chariot; the trussing of a warrior on the points of spears.[3]

It is recorded that he had an uncontrollable temper, and when his full battle fury—referred to in the legends as his warp-spasm—comes upon him, his whole body distorts hideously. Even his own men are not safe from him during such times. This serves to show

---

[3] There is much material here for research and study by anyone interested in the martial arts who wishes to attempt to reconstruct the native Celtic martial and military training disciplines. Reprinted from *The Tain* by Thomas Kinsella, Oxford University Press.

that the forces of the physical level can be uncontrollable, and must be handled with great care. This is a point often overlooked by those seeking "higher" powers. Several legends tell of his various exploits in the Otherworld, which he is able to enter and leave at will. He is the image of the perfect warrior, who is not only supremely capable in battle and has an unshakable sense of honour and loyalty, but is also fully in control of his mental, spiritual, and magical powers. A very powerful figure indeed, and one well worth contacting by those interested in the martial arts of the West. Beware, however: he is a sore tester, and will push you to your physical, mental, and spiritual limits. He is not a character to be treated lightly.

Cu Roi (koo-ree)
"Roaring Hound"

The king of Munster in the Ulster Cycle, he is the equivalent in sacred kingship to Conchobhar of Ulster and Cormac of Leinster. He is associated with a Cauldron of Plenty, and also with the Salmon of Knowledge, in which, according to some sources, dwells his own mortal soul. Like all kings, he had many geasa laid on him, and most of his seem to be connected in one way or another with the sun. He is, therefore, an ancient solar deity. He is connected with the ancient and very magical beheading game, which occurs in nearly all Celtic and British mythology, where a mysterious stranger (in this case Cu Roi) challenges the bravest heroes to cut his head off, but afterwards, he has the right to cut off theirs. In the Irish version, several people are challenged but refuse out of fear, until Cu Chulainn steps forward, accepts the challenge, and thereby displays himself to be the true champion. This echoes both of ancient head cults and also a reincarnation or rejuvenation theme, perhaps connected with winter and spring, and the return of life in the earth following a period of apparent death. An important character, he has enough symbolism to make contacting him during Otherworld journeys all the easier.

Dearg (jarr-ig)
Also given as Derg, "Red"

An obscure but important character who appears throughout Irish mythology, Dearg's name literally means "red,"—and is really a synonym for death. He is one of the Celtic gods of death, and is associated specifically with violent death, as opposed to death by natural causes. All the legends in which he appears (sometimes in triple form) are concerned with violent deaths and bloody feuds. He is also associated with wild places, the stag, and several other wild creatures. He can be regarded as the Irish equivalent of the well-known Continental Celtic god Cernunnos. His violent-death aspect can be interpreted as death through the wild hunt, or death in order to survive. He is a character who would be useful to those wishing to live as close to Nature as possible, and those who find it difficult to accept the more violent and death-dealing aspects of Nature, which manifest in the need to kill to survive. Due to his powerful and gory associations, he is probably a character most of us should be happy to leave alone.

Deirdre (dair-dir-eh)
"Sorrow"

Her Ulster Cycle legend is probably the finest piece of tragic prose ever composed, and, even today, it is heartbreaking to read. Although her name does not literally mean "sorrow," Deirdre has become synonymous with sorrow and heartbreak due to her short and unhappy life. She is personified as a great beauty, and is the image of the perfect female. At her birth, the great druid Cathbhadh prophesied that she would be the source of eternal sorrow and the destruction of the Red Branch Knights. The warriors of King Conchobhar, on hearing this, demanded that she be killed before the prophecy could come true. Conchobhar took her into his own special care, and attempted to prove the prophesy wrong by preventing her from seeing any men. This action was doomed to failure, and the story which unfolds is one of treachery, deceit, bloodlust, jealousy, and senseless death and destruction.

Deirdre herself is almost incidental to all of this, and is no more than a pawn of Fate. She is described as having psychic powers, and knowing in advance what is going to happen during the various stages of her life and the lives of those close to her. The implication is that she is a victim of her own psychic powers, and sees them as a curse which she cannot remove. This can still be seen in those people today who have genuine psychic powers, but regard them as a dreadful curse which they cannot control. Although Deirdre's tale is one describing the effects of malevolent and negative emotions, she is still a character worth contacting today. All of us at some time or other are put into situations involving such emotions, and usually we can do nothing about them. To learn to cope with such situations during Otherworld journeys is a good way to cushion the blow when these events occur in our daily lives. This is one of the very practical uses of Otherworld journeying.

Diarmaid Ua Duibhne
(jee-oor-mid oo doov-neh)
"Unenvious"

One of the important figures from the Fenian Cycle, the second part of his name means "descendant of Duibhne," but is often incorrectly translated as "brown." In a sense, Diarmaid is the masculine equivalent of the very feminine Deirdre in that he, too, was the tragic victim of negative human emotions and personal lust. He does not have the same psychic abilities as Deirdre, because such intuitive powers are more natural to the feminine than they are to the masculine. On the other hand, legends portray him as using his logic and intellectual abilities to get himself out of the many predicaments he gets into. This is no more than the balance between the intuitive, instinctive, feminine powers of Deirdre, and the intellectual, logical, masculine powers displayed in the legend of Diarmaid. Neither one is more important than the other.

He has a curious mark on his forehead called the love spot. Should any woman gaze upon it she falls instantly in love with him. This may seem a desirable blemish to possess, but Diarmaid keeps it hidden by wearing a cap over his forehead, because he cannot control the effects it has—it is a curse rather than a blessing. This uncontrollable aspect is equivalent to Deirdre's unwanted psychic powers. Both the legends of Deirdre and Diarmaid have survived to the present day in the folklore of Ireland and Scotland, and this helps to show the very deep level at which they speak to the individual. We unconsciously know they are important allegories, and therefore remember them and pass them on from generation to generation, as a means of instruction and learning.

Diarmaid can be a useful Otherworld contact for those who are torn between personal loyalty and conflicting obligations to others. He can help to advise on those situations in which it seems that, no matter what option we choose, we are going to hurt ourselves or someone else. Diarmaid may not be able to show a clear way out of such unwanted situations, but he will be able to show you how to cope with their results—which is, after all, more important.

Donn (dun)
"Dark"

An ancient figure who occurs throughout Irish mythology and folklore to the present day, Donn is a god of death and Lord of the Otherworld. Just as Dearg is a god of violent death, Donn presides over natural death. He is connected with horses, which can be used as symbols for making conscious contact with him.

Today talk of death is often taboo, and not considered to be particularly pleasant, but the Celts believed that they were born from death, and that Donn was a father figure. Because they had no fear of death, or of what happened afterwards, their whole attitude to death, dying, and the god of death was completely different than ours. There is a well-known magical meditation in which the meditator visualises his or her own death, and studies his or her own reactions to it.

Consciously contacting the character of Donn during Otherworld journeys is a good exercise for those wishing to get the most out of this Irish system of magic and self-development. This is a far more pleasant experience than contacting his violent counterpart, Dearg.

Fear Diadh (far jeea)
Also given as Ferdia, "Man of Smoke"

A hero from the Ulster Cycle, and great friend of Cu Chulainn, his name appears with several different spellings: Fer Dea, "Man of a Goddess," Fer Deoda, "Divine Man," and Fer Dedh, "Man of Fire." He is meant to represent a being who is half man and half god. He was trained in Skye along with Cu Chulainn, and is, therefore, a true warrior on all three levels. During the epic saga the Cattle Raid of Cooley, Fear Diadh and Cu Chulainn are forced into a position where they must fight each other, despite their extreme reluctance to do so. In this part of the legend, Fear Diadh has been compromised to such an extent that, for the sake of his honour, he must fight his greatest friend. Cu Chulainn is mistakenly under the impression that Fear Diadh is doing this for no other reason than that he had been promised Queen Meadhbh's daughter, Fionnabhair, in marriage if he would fight. Cu Chulainn appeals to Fear Diadh not to fight with him for such a trivial reason, and recites the following poem:

> Fear Diadh son of Daman,
>
> noble warrior, do not come.
>
> You will suffer more than me
>
> and bring sorrow to your company.
>
>
> Do not come, and in the wrong place,
>
> or here you'll find your resting place.

How can it be that you alone
could escape my fatal rage?

I'll overwhelm you with my feats
despite your horn-skin and red rage.
Son of Daman you will never have
the girl that you are boasting of.

Meadhbh's daughter Fionnabhair,
for all the fairness of her form
and all the sweetness of her shape,
will never yield to your assault.

Fionnabhair the royal daughter
she is nothing but a snare.
She played false with the others
and ruined them as she ruins you.

Don't break our friendship and our bond,
don't break the oath we made once,
don't break our promise and our pledge.
Noble warrior, don't come.

This is the same girl who was promised

falsely to fifty men.

They got nothing but my spear

as I showed them to their graves.

Ferbaeth, they said, was brave enough

and had a houseful of fine heroes,

but a short moment quenched his fire,

I finished him with one throw.

Srubdaire found a bitter end.

A hundred women held him dear.

There was a time his fame was high,

but neither wealth nor weapons saved him.

If they had offered her to me,

if I were the one that Meadhbh smiled at,

I wouldn't think to do you harm

or touch the least part of your flesh.

Despite this impassioned plea from his old friend, Fear Diadh realises he has gone too far and, for the sake of his honour, cannot back down. In reply he simply states,

Cu Chulainn, you bear your cunning lightly,

but I have mastered the same trade.

Our friendship is finished, through foul-play.

Prepare to face your first defeat.

Forget that we were foster-brothers.

Squinter, you are past help!

The reference to horn-skin in the third verse is a reference to a type of body armour worn by the Celts, which was constructed from animal horns. The word squinter, in the last line of Fear Diadh's reply is an insult derived from a pun in Old Irish, which is lost in translation. An abbreviated form of Cu Chulainn's name is *cu* (warrior), but *cu cu* in Old Irish means "squinting" or "cross-eyed." Eventually, after three days of fighting, Cu Chulainn slays Fear Diadh with his terrible weapon, the Gae Bulga, and he utters a very moving lament over the death of his great friend and companion.[4]

Fear Diadh can teach you much about the craft of the warrior. The legends surrounding him warn us that, to be a true warrior you must at times fight even those whom you love most. In other words, honour and duty must come before personal desires or friendships. Think carefully on this point before choosing the craft of the warrior, as it is not everyone who can face up to this aspect of military discipline.

---

[4] This lament, and the poems extracted above, can be found in Thomas Kinsella's excellent translation of *The Tain*.

Fearghus mac Roich (far-ish mak ro-ik)
"Virility, Son of the Great Stallion"

A character from the Ulster Cycle who features prominently in the Cattle Raid of Cooley, he is clearly associated with sexual prowess both because of his name and because, after leaving Ulster, he fled to Queen Meadhbh, who is well known for her own sexual prowess and appetite. One of his physical symbols is the sword, which likewise has obvious sexual imagery. His sword is called Caladbolg, and appears in the Welsh tradition as Caledvwlch. This, in turn, was Latinised in later legends, where it became Caliburnus, and eventually, Excalibur, the sword of King Arthur. Its roots lie deep within the Irish tradition, as do many of the facets of the Arthuriad. He is closely associated with both the kingship and sovereignty of the land, despite the fact that he allowed himself to be tricked out of the kingship of Ulster by Conchobhar's mother, Neasa, who played on his own lust.

Like Conchobhar, Fearghus' name, mac Roich, comes from his mother and not his father. Several points link him symbolically with the feminine energies of the Green world: the taking of his mother's name, being tricked by a woman, having the same status as another king bearing his mother's name, and his great sexual prowess. All of this hints at his very close link with the sovereignty of the land.

He is rather an obscure character, and one who is difficult to pin down, as he seems to change allegiances throughout the legends dealing with him. This was not because of a fickle nature, but because he had been cheated or deceived by the monarch he was loyal to at that particular time. He features in the legend of Deirdre, where he was used and cheated by the jealous King Conchobhar mac Neasa.

His role is one of learning by example. In all of the legends we read that whenever he gave his word on a matter, he kept it, but this was rarely the case with those who gave their word to him. He is therefore a victim of his own honour and other people's dishonour. He is a useful contact for those who find themselves in the unenviable position of constantly being deceived by others, while at the same time trying to be honest and open with them. He may also be of use to men and women wishing to develop their own sexual prowess, although it should be understood that such physical power brings with it much responsibility on the other levels as well. Anyone contacting Fearghus for this reason is advised to study well all the legends concerning him before going ahead. As is always the case in the Otherworld, things are never quite what they seem.

Feircheirdne (ferr-kaird-neh)
Also given as Ferchertne, "Man of Precise Craft"

Feircheirdne is the archetypical poet, and the personification of the poet's art, skill, and loyalty to his or her patron or matron. He features in the Ulster Cycle, but is also featured in the legends dealing with Leinster and Munster. It is likely that the name, Feircheirdne, was not just a personal name, but a title bestowed upon poets. He is a contact to be encouraged for those wishing to develop their poetic abilities on all levels. He is a fair and just teacher, who is recorded in the legend, Immacallam in Da Thuarad, the Colloquy of the Two Sages, as acknowledging a challenger to his position as chief poet as being equal to, if not better than, himself. How many would be prepared to do that today?

Find (fyoond)
"Wisdom"

Find is a very ancient figure who is almost outside the standard cycles of mythology due to his extreme antiquity. Variants of Find appear in most of the Cycles under different forms of the basic name. He is associated with knowledge, enlightenment, and wisdom, which are obtained specifically by magical means, mainly through communion with the earth forces and goddesses. This can also be achieved through contact with Otherworld beings and deities, and through magical rituals, which help to bring into consciousness that which is deeply buried in the subconscious. In the legends, this is displayed by Find sucking his thumb like a baby whenever he wishes to divine something of importance. His triple aspect is portrayed in the legends, where he can appear as a baby, a young man, or an ancient ancestor, which is meant to symbolise his knowledge of time in what we would call the past, present, and future. He is closely associated with the River Boyne, and his main Otherworld symbol is the salmon.

Fionn mac Cumhaill (fyoon mak koo-il)

Fionn is the great progenitor of the whole Fenian Cycle, and is a figure featured heavily in ancient Irish folklore. Even today, his stories and legends are told in Ireland and Scotland, and especially in the Scottish Western Isles. All of these areas still have many geographical features named after Fionn and various members of the Fianna. Many attempts have been made to translate his name. The usual translations are "White (or "Fair") Son of the Hazel," or sometimes, "Fair Son of Destruction." We really do not know what his name signified, as the word Cumhaill is otherwise unknown in Irish. The name, Fionn, is a later corruption of the earlier version, Find. There is an Old Irish word *cumall,* which means "a female slave," but his mother, Muirne, is described in the legends as a daughter of the druid Tadg, and would therefore not have been a slave. The Cumhaill part of his name refers to his father anyway, so whatever it signified originally has been lost to us today.

His original, personal name was Deimne, but this was changed to Fionn after he accidentally consumed three drops containing the wisdom from the Salmon of Knowledge, taken from the Boyne by the druid Fionn. It had been prophesied that one called Fionn would catch and eat the Salmon of Knowledge, and thereby have infinite wisdom, and the druid Fionn assumed that this referred to himself. When he realised Deimne had accidentally consumed this wisdom by sucking his thumb after burning it on the cooking salmon's hot skin, he renamed Deimne, Fionn, and graciously accepted that it was Deimne for whom the knowledge had been intended. Whenever such a name-changing incident occurs in the legends, we know that some sort of important initiation is actually taking place. This legend also explains why Fionn could only invoke his divine wisdom by sucking his thumb. The same story survives concerning Find, and it is clear that Find and Fionn stem from the same source. He is not only a physical warrior of this world, but also a traveller to the Otherworld, and a source of information and knowledge for those seeking it.

Fionn is always described as a great war leader. His band of warriors are given the collective name of the Fianna, which simply means "warriors." His is mainly a guardian's role, and he is the champion of ordinary people and of the oppressed. His warriors all have very special, and, in some instances, clearly magical skills. In many ways, the legends of Fionn mac Cumhaill and the Fianna mirror very closely the legends of King Arthur and his Knights of the Round Table. As an Otherworld contact, he is extremely useful, whether in his warrior-guardian role or in his shamanic-seer role. Individual members of the Fianna are also worth getting to know, as most of them are described in some detail. Their individual skills and abilities are explained quite well in many of the legends from the Fenian Cycle, especially in the collection of legends known as Duanaire Finn, or Poems of Fionn.

Fionn is closely associated with various animals, especially deer and hunting hounds. Many of the legends and contemporary folklore involve incidents which occurred while he was out hunting. He can be seen as a Lord of the Hunt, a figure who occurs throughout nearly all European mythology in one form or another, and who is sometimes depicted in the form of the well-known Celtic god Cernunnos.

Fionntan (fyoon-tun)
"Old Find"

Another variant of the character Find, he is described in legend as having come to Ireland with Cessair, and having lived there for over five-and-a-half thousand years. During this period, he took on various animal and bird forms, and witnessed all that happened during the development of Ireland. He is the archetypal seer, and source of all ancient lore concerning Ireland. His transformations into various creatures imply a belief in the transmigration of human souls into animal bodies after death. It can also be seen as gaining knowledge of the animal and bird kingdoms, as well as of the human world of existence. Fionntan is an important contact for those researching into far-memory and ancient lore, although it should be understood that conscious contact with such ancient characters can be quite disturbing to the modern mind. You are advised to proceed cautiously if attempting to contact him.

Meadhbh (mai-iv)
Also given as Medb, Maeve, "One Who Intoxicates"

The great and powerful queen of Connacht, who features predominantly in the Ulster Cycle, Meadhbh is one of the many goddesses of sovereignty in Irish mythology who are given human incarnations. The legends concerning her do not beat about the bush when it comes to describing exactly what that means. She is clearly of an independent mind, and by no manner or means secondary to her many husbands. She is a great and fierce warrior in her own right. Her lustful ways and enormous appetite for sexual adventures are often referred to in the Ulster Cycle, particularly in the Cattle Raid of Cooley, which was started because of her jealousy. Her overpowering self-centredness and destructive jealousy make it clear that, despite her great power over the land and her close connections with the sacred kingship, she is not a character to be encouraged or deliberately invoked by the faint-hearted. She is a far cry from the Earth-Goddess or Gentle Mother image which most people seem to have today.

Many legends mention the fact that she had several husbands, all of whom had to be "without stinginess, without fear, and without jealousy,"—all the attributes of a High King. Because she is a goddess who is tied to the land, she is eternal, but her human husbands, the High Kings of the day, only lived the normal lifespans of human beings and then died. Meadhbh simply re-weds and lives on.

This means she is still available today as a partner for anyone who wishes to ritualistically adopt their own High Kingship and wed the land. To go ahead with this mystical union will bring with it the sorest testing of any possible magical initiation. Anyone contemplating such a move is advised to think it over long and hard before voluntarily becoming yet another husband to the voracious Queen Meadhbh. On the other hand, it may be a good thing for those interested in the Earth and earth mysteries to make her acquaintance, without the full commitment of a marriage, as she will certainly be able to instruct and guide those with such a calling. This, too, can be a very painful and testing experience, for the Earth and the earth forces are not always pleasant to deal with, due to the great damage humankind has done. Take time to build trust and confidence with the earth energies before expecting them to accept you.

Mil (meel)
Also given as Mil Easpaine, "Soldier of Spain"

Traditionally the ancestor of the Irish and the Gaels, Mil's wife was Scota, an Egyptian, who gave her name to the present day Scots. Although Mil never actually came to Ireland—having died en route—his sons did, and after many battles, deaths, and upsets, they settled in the country and began to populate it. A rather obscure character in his own right, but perhaps one who could be useful to those interested in genealogy and racial roots.

Neara mac Niadhain (narra mak nee-yen)

This character from the Ulster Cycle is associated with Otherworld travelling, communing with the dead, and bringing knowledge from the Otherworld to this world. He is connected to the festival of Samhain, which is traditionally known as a Feast of the Dead. He is an obscure character in his own right, but the legends that remain concerning him clearly intend him to be a useful contact to those wishing to develop any of these aspects.

Neidhe mac Adhna (nai mak aynuh)

A poet who features in some of the earlier legends and literature, he has a famous contest with the poet Feircheirdne for the seat of the chief poet of all Ireland. Although he is technically beaten by Feircheirdne, he is still proclaimed to be a very important poet in his own right. His function today is that of the tester we all need to establish just how good—or bad—we are at becoming master poets, with all that this implies. He is associated with obtaining knowledge from the sea, and was trained in Scotland, which may refer to an Otherworld training on one of the many Scottish islands believed to be physical-level manifestations of the Otherworld.

Neimheadh (nev-eh)
Also given as Nemed, "A Holy Place"

Neimheadh was the third invader of Ireland, who arrived some thirty years after Partholon died. He is described as having defeated the invading Fomhoire, and is closely linked with sovereignty and kingship through his wife Macha, who is one of the many earth goddess figures. He is also credited with clearing many plains in Ireland, and with the fact that, during his stay, many lakes and rivers burst forth, which is an indication of his ability to work competently with the native earth forces. According to legend, he is ultimately the father of both the Fir Bolg and the Tuatha De Danann races, which makes him of exceptional importance in a genealogical sense. In some ways he is a very similar character to Fionntan, and with similar functions. Like all of these early invaders of Ireland, though, he is a character most of us today will find disturbing to contact.

Oisin (ush-een)
Also given as Ossian, "Little Fawn"

Son of Fionn mac Cumhaill in the Fenian Cycle, he gets his name from the fact that his mother, who had originally been human, was turned into a doe by a malevolent magician. According to other accounts, she was an Otherworld woman who took the form of a deer to lure Fionn away from the Fianna during a hunting expedition. Whatever the correct version (if there is one), Oisin is clearly associated with hunting and shape-shifting. There are several legends extant in the group known as the Lays of Fionn, concerning his journeys to the Otherworld and his great poetic abilities. He is a character to be sought after by those interested in such areas.

He is also given the role of historian in the legend, the Colloquy of the Old Men, where his meeting with St. Patrick is described. These legends usually contain a great deal of dialogue between the two, in which St. Patrick tries to convince Oisin that Fionn and the Fianna were heathens, and therefore must be burning in Hell, while Oisin very articulately points out all of Fionn and the Fianna's many noble points, including their generosity, compassion, mercy, hospitality, and so on. He is another character who can be seen as a bridge between the two traditions, who existed at the time of the overlap of the pre-Christian and the Christian traditions.

Oscar (uskur)
"Fawn" or "Champion"

Son of Oisin and grandson of Fionn mac Cumhaill, he is one of the great heroes in this legendary Cycle. Oscar is a strong and valiant champion, who won many single combats against hideous and frightening opponents. He is associated with the spear and the flail, a weapon he used to fight off the devils as he and the Fianna escaped from the very depths of Hell, according to one later Christianised legend. He is, in some ways, another aspect of his father, Oisin, and the two are more or less interchangeable. Like all members of the Fianna, he is closely connected with the hunt and the animal kingdom in general.

Partholon (par-ho-lon)
Also given as Parthalon or Parthalan

A Greek who left his own land, he eventually became the second invader of ancient Ireland, according to the *Book of Invasions*. He fought a magical battle with the visiting Fomhoire, before obtaining control of the land. His people were the first to introduce cattle to Ireland, as well as a guest house, cooking, and the brewing of ale. All of these things imply domesticity and an ordered society. Partholon's people also set about clearing various plains and generally shaping the land of Ireland. From these associations and the magical battle with the Fomhoire, it is obvious that Partholon and his company were considered to be very early manipulators of the earth energies. The warnings given earlier about attempting conscious contact with these first invaders of Ireland apply also to Partholon.

Suibhne Geilt (swee-neh gaylt)
"Mad Suibhne"

Only one legend deals specifically with Suibhne Geilt, called Buile Suibhne Geilt, the "Frenzy of Mad Sweeney." The name Suibhne was very common in ancient Ireland, but there are reasons for assuming that the legend of Mad Sweeney may be based on an actual person. Although he is described as being mad, this should be understood in the sense of divine madness or inspiration, and not as some debilitating mental illness. He is said, in the legend, to have become a bird by growing feathers and living in the trees. This is symbolic of his taking on the role of the shaman, who lived in the wilds, and who wore a cloak of bird feathers.

He is a very important character for those interested in Celtic shamanism, an aspect of Celtic magic which is only now becoming appreciated and better understood. The legend of Mad Sweeney contains some of the finest nature poetry in all of the many Irish Celtic legends, and contains a great many references to different types of trees. He may well be a good source of information for those interested in Irish Celtic tree lore and magic. He is a character who has been very much neglected by many, but one well-worth getting to know by anyone interested in these fascinating areas of the Irish Celtic tradition.

Tuan mac Cairill (too-an mak karill)

The only survivor of Partholon's people, he is very similar to Fionntan in nature, in that he lived for a very long time, took on many animal and bird forms, and witnessed all the great events which happened throughout Ireland's history during this period. His functions are the same as Fionntan's, and the cautions given concerning conscious contact with Fionntan apply equally to Tuan.

PRACTICAL WORK

Exercise Four:
Making Contact

Start this exercise by carefully examining all of the deities or characters listed in the last two chapters. Using your intuition, choose one who appeals to you, and find out what you can about that deity or character from any of the source material listed in the Bibliography. A good introduction to the Irish legends are Lady Gregory's books, *Gods and Fighting Men*, for the Mythological Cycle, and *Cuchulainn of Muirthemne*, for the Ulster Cycle. Once you have built up a good mental impression of what that deity or character represents, what his or her personality is like, and what legends deal with him or her specifically, then formulate in your mind the conscious desire to make contact with him or her.

When you are ready, close your eyes, let yourself relax for a moment or two, and then start to build up your Otherworld landscape as clearly as you can. When you are fully conscious in the Otherworld, make your way to a part of the landscape which is appropriate to the guide you wish to meet. You can determine this by clues hidden in the legends, such as where the main events involving him or her take place. For example, if the legends dealing with your chosen guide frequently involve rivers, then make your way to your Otherworld river. If he or she is often described as being in or travelling through mountains or woodlands, then make your way to the mountains or woodlands. If, however, you are unable to determine an obvious location from the legends, then simply choose

your own. As always, let your intuition decide. Once you are there, concentrate on what you know of this character from what you have read.

If you have a description of his or her physical appearance, then
keep that in mind. If not, make one up which fits in with his or her attributes. Concentrate also on things like what he or she should be wearing
or carrying. A satirist or bard, for example, would be clad in good-qual-
ity clothes, would most likely be carrying a small harp, and would have
an air of dignity and self-assurance about him or herself. A warrior of
either sex would be clad in scant, leather clothing, carrying arms of some
sort, and would appear cautious and tense, ready to deal with any threat.
A god or goddess (if you are thinking big!) would be clad in very colourful clothing, with a good deal of gold and silver jewellery, and would have
a very Otherworldly air about him or herself.

Once you have spent some time setting the scene, and making
absolutely clear in your mind exactly who you want to have contact
with, visualise that person slowly walking toward you. Do not anticipate
what he or she is going to do or say; simply watch the scene before you,
and keep your mind as blank as possible. This is absolutely vital at this
stage, for it is through your own thoughts that these guides will speak
to you. It is true you will see their lips moving and hear voices, but the
actual ideas and information will be originating in your own mind. It is
very important not to clutter it up with your own ideas and expectations.

There is a certain knack to being able to achieve this, and you must
try it time and time again until it starts to work for you. At first, keeping
your mind totally blank while waiting for new thoughts and ideas to
enter will seem contradictory and impossible, but this is exactly the way
the whole system of Otherworld communication works. Building up a
good, clear mental image of your Otherworld guide, and learning all the
legends connected with him or her (as well as any specific qualities he
or she has) will help to make this form of telepathy all the easier, especially from the point of view of the Otherworld guide. If you are still
unclear about this, go back and reread the comments on visualisation
and the inhabitants of the Otherworld in Chapter Three.

It is a good idea to spend as many sessions as you can with the same
guide, until a good, solid link is forged between you. Do not change from

one guide to another in the early stages of your progress; this will only serve to hinder those in the Otherworld you are trying to get to know. Stick with one Otherworld guide, until you know him or her well, and you know you can contact him or her with relative ease whenever you wish. Once you have achieved this degree of familiarity and successful communication, you can think about branching out and contacting other deities and characters from the legends.

At this stage, the purpose of this particular exercise is to become adept at Otherworld communication. Later, you will rely upon this new-found skill to learn and experience things which will help you as you progress through the Irish Celtic magical tradition. For the time being, do not attempt to ask your new friends for advice or assistance on specific matters. It is too early in your learning process to understand how such advice and assistance is given out. Instead, enjoy Otherworld walks with your guides through your own Otherworld landscape. Chat with these new friends about their lifestyles, how they see this world, how they felt during particular episodes in the legends, and so on, and generally get to know each other well.

Remember that your guides will be just as keen to learn about you as you are about them. They may well ask you some very searching and, at times, embarrassing questions. Always answer as honestly, openly, and fully as you can. If you try to deceive these intelligent beings, for whatever reason, or if you tell only part of the story, you will find that any genuine contact you may have had will soon dwindle and be replaced by nothing more than self-deluding daydreams. This can be quite a severe test in itself, but you must learn to cope with it if you are ever to progress.

Spend what time you can strengthening contact with your guides, for they are immensely enjoyable as well as useful, and always remember to write up a full report in your Magical Diary, recording as best you can, verbatim accounts of what was said and by whom. You will learn a lot from these early conversations in the years to come, even though at the moment they may seem like mere trivia. Don't make value judgements at this stage, and don't be too pushy. All of these things take time and cannot be rushed.

Section Five

The
Four
Festivals

Chapter Ten

An Introduction
to the Festivals

T he ancient Celts held festivals and celebrations throughout the year, which served many different purposes. Some were very personal, and related to only one family or immediate group of relatives, as in the case of a birth or wedding. Some took the form of a tribal celebration, and would have been localised, as in a feast to honour heroes, or to commemorate great battles. Some were more widely celebrated, such as the acceptance of a new king or queen, which would affect many tribes and clans. Still others were of a magical or spiritual nature and were celebrated countrywide, as a recognition of certain changes having occurred in the Green World.

The four main festivals in the Irish system fall into this last category. Samhain (sow-in), Imbolg (eem-bolk), Bealtaine (bal-tayn), and Lughnassadh (loonassa) were the most important feasts in the magical and spiritual calendar of the Celts, common to all Celtic peoples throughout Europe. They are still celebrated today, albeit under a different guise from their pre-Christian origins. Samhain falls on the first of November, Imbolg on the first of February, Bealtaine on the first of May, and Lughnassadh on the first of August. Originally, they were not celebrated on set dates at all, but were held when certain events in the Green World indicated that the seasons were changing. These, of course, could have occurred on widely differing days each year.

It is probable that, at first, there were only three main festivals, Samhain, Bealtaine, and Lughnassadh, with Imbolg coming later. Having three festivals certainly fits in better with the Celtic emphasis on threes. This passage from the *Book of Sligo* (now lost) supports this view:

> By Diarmaid and by the men of Ireland the great congregation of Uisneach is held now at Bealtaine; for at that time Ireland's three high gatherings were these: the congregation of Uisneach at Bealtaine; the convention of Taillte at Lughnassadh; the feast of Tara at Samhain; and whosoever of the men of Ireland should have transgressed these, the same that should have violated this their ordinance was guilty of death.[1]

The three festivals are very much tribal, communal celebrations, which would have been enjoyed by all members of the clan, and used as occasions for cementing relationships with other tribes and clans. Imbolg is much more of a personal, family celebration, which takes place in the home, and does not often involve other people. Somewhere along the line, Imbolg became established as one of the main Celtic communal festivals, perhaps because the Irish tradition is a vital, living tradition, which changes and adapts to suit different people at different times. When or why this happened does not matter, though we shall continue to uphold the tradition as we find it today.

The first festival in the Celtic calendar, Samhain, celebrates the end of summer, once the growing and harvesting seasons have come to an end. It is also considered to be the start of the new year. The Celts reckoned a day as starting with the darkness of the night before,

---

[1] From *Keating's History of Ireland* by P.S. Dinneen, Irish Texts Society.

and in the same way considered the year to start with the dark, or winter period. Imbolg is celebrated when spring begins, as the ewes start to lactate, and the first new shoots push their heads through the snow-covered earth. Bealtaine is the start of summer, when the forces of the Green World are at their strongest, and when new growth and life is seen all around. Lughnassadh is celebrated when the harvest is over, and the fruits and grains are stored and ready for use during the winter months ahead.

As each of these events is dictated by the forces of the Green World, and not by some human-made calendar, they should be celebrated only when Green World conditions indicate that the time is right. This will vary from year to year, depending upon the prevailing climatic conditions. It will also vary from district to district, depending upon local climatic variations and factors such as local topography, soil types, proximity to the sea, and so forth. It is true that, in the later years of Celtic rule in Ireland, Samhain and Bealtaine were celebrated on agreed dates throughout the land. This comparatively late practice, however, was connected more with the politics of the institution of the High King than with prevailing Green World conditions.

For those of you wishing to get the most out of this system of magic and celebration, I would suggest that you ignore the calendar dates for these festivals and instead keep a close eye on the Green World cycles going on around you to determine your own dates. This will give them more meaning, and is a good way to get to know the changes which are occurring in the Green World that we often miss, living in artificially heated and lit houses, which effectively put a great barrier of brick and concrete between us and the life forces we should be so eagerly pursuing. Many arguments have been put forward both for and against using set dates for these festivals, and I can see good reasons for both points of view. The danger comes when one person or group proclaims they are using the "correct" dates, and that everybody else is wrong. The truth is that there simply is no such thing as a "correct" date. Even attempts to work the calendar backwards to determine the dates used in ancient times can lead to confusion. This is easy to see when we examine how the calendar we use today has changed over the centuries.

It is fairly certain that the ancient Celts would have counted time by the movements of the sun and the more frequent phases of the moon. On the European Continent, under the rule of the Romans, a calendar based on named days and months which followed the same pattern every year was introduced by Julius Caesar in 46 B.C. The old system of counting by suns and moons was abandoned. The so-called Julian calendar became the standard henceforth. Unfortunately, Caesar's calculations were not quite accurate enough. As the centuries rolled by, things started to get a bit out of line between what the calendar said the time of year should be, and what the Green World conditions showed it actually was. To put things right, in 1582, Pope Gregory XIII did away with Caesar's calendar and introduced one of his own, which allowed for "leap years" to correct the earlier miscalculations. This "Gregorian" calendar was not immediately adopted everywhere in Europe and the Middle East, however, which lead to the confusing situation of neighbouring countries recognising different dates for the same days.

It was not until 1751, almost two centuries later, that Britain agreed to adopt the Gregorian calculations. By this time, a discrepancy of eleven days had built up between the Julian calendar and the Gregorian calendars. Not only did this require introducing a new calendar to Britain more or less overnight, it also involved the removal of eleven days, to bring Britain into line with everyone who had been operating under the Gregorian calendar. Just to complicate matters, the year 1800 was not a leap year, according to the new calendar, which meant Britain was still one day behind, and needed to make even further adjustments. In some parts of Scotland, the people still talk about and celebrate "The Old New Year," which falls on the twelfth of January, by their calculations. In most parts of Scotland, up until 1600, the new year was reckoned to start on the twenty-fifth of March!

From this tangled web of dates, adjusted dates, and readjusted dates, it is clear that any attempt to work backwards in time to calculate an exact date for any given festival is virtually impossible.

Even if exact dates could be determined, since the celebrations were moved from year to year to match the Green World seasons, no standardized dates could be established from them.

These festivals are usually described as religious occasions, and indeed they are. The way the Celts practised their religion, however, was very different from our modern attitudes to things spiritual. The celebration of the major festivals strongly reflected the combination of the three levels. They were occasions for displaying a common religious or spiritual belief, but also for mental and physical pursuits. The mental level would have manifested during the festivals in activities such as law and decision making, which could only be carried out when the whole clan was present. The physical level would have been experienced through game-playing, competitions, and the ever-popular feasting and drinking. The three levels would also have been consciously brought to bear during the critical magical and ritualistic parts of the celebrations, which were performed by specially skilled clan or tribe members. Their physical actions, mental concentration, and emotional input, as well as their spiritual fervour, would have been for the benefit of the whole tribe or clan, and for the very land itself.

The Celts also invited their deities to partake in the festival, alongside the human participants. Although the Celts held their gods and goddesses in esteem, and regarded them with much respect, they were so familiar with them that there was no sense of separateness or remoteness from them, and no fear or awe felt when in their presence. This attitude helped to make these important occasions more relaxed and enjoyable.

Celtic religious festivals were times of great enjoyment for all involved, and were not the sombre, austere ceremonies we have come to expect of religious festivals today. Celtic festivals were not just parts of an annual calendar of events, to be observed every year out of habit; they were vital and necessary, both for the fertility of the land and for the well-being of the clan. This need to celebrate the festivals is an aspect modern society has forgotten. We tend to view festivals or ceremonies of any sort as either quaint customs, a bit of an intrusion, or something that is done out of habit. The festivals were important on the group level as a communal recognition of the changes taking place in the Green World, but they were also important on the individual level, when all members of the clan would acknowledge that similar changes were taking place within themselves. This linking of the personal to the changes in the Green World is an aspect we have, to a very great extent, lost today. It is time we all reforged our links, got back in tune with the Green World and ourselves, and reaped the benefits this fundamental approach to the world, and our places in it, brings. The following sections will help you to achieve this by giving you an explanation of each festival and Practical Work, in the form of a ritual, for you to carry out and use to realign yourself with the Green World.

PRACTICAL WORK

Exercise Five:
Re-enacting a Legend

The next exercise in our series carries on from the previous ones, where you were encouraged to get to know your own Otherworld guides. Now that you will have spent some time familiarising yourself with them, it is time to get to know their functions and duties, as well as their personalities. The way you achieve this is to take a legend involving one of your Otherworld guides, read it again and again, until you are completely familiar with it, and then visualise the whole legend unfolding before you in your Otherworld landscape. Not only should you visualise the legend taking place before you, but you must also see yourself taking an active part in it.

Don't just stand on the sidelines and watch it as if you were watching a film or play. All of the legends have characters within them, either named or implied, which for the purposes of this exercise, you could become, and thereby take an active role in the events unfolding before you. Do not assume the role of the main character, but rather adopt a minor role. Be content to participate at such a slight level that you are still left with plenty of opportunity to observe what the others are doing. For example, if your chosen legend involves a scene at a feast, you could assume the role of one of the feasters. If a battle is described in the legend, and is relevant to the character you are studying, then take on the role of a camp follower. It would not be wise to adopt the role of a warrior in such circumstances, as you are liable to be called upon to fight. If the character and legend you choose are not very active, or spend a lot of time indoors talking, then take on the role of a servant or attendant. This will give you a legitimate reason for being there, and also allows you enough time and freedom to study and really get to know the deity or character.

It is only by becoming an integral part of the legends that you will start to understand what the legend is saying, and not just what it appears to say on the surface. This is also the way that you will understand and appreciate how the many deities and characters interact with each other, and how they behave in any given situation. These are all things which are vital to know, if you are ever to make full use of your Otherworld contacts. A side-effect of all this will be that you will have to react to situations in your Otherworld legendary role, and this, too, will be both revealing and instructive.

At first, do not be too ambitious in this exercise. Pick a character whom you know well from a legend, or part of a legend, which is not too long or too complicated. Once you become more adept at this, however, you can start to re-enact larger legends, involving more and more characters. By its very nature, this is an exercise which you can try over and over again, without the need to repeat any legend or part of a legend. It is also flexible enough to allow you to study the same deity or character in many different situations, limited only by the number of legends you can find involving that person. It is while undertaking this visualisation of legends that you can ask specific questions concerning yourself or your own progress. The answers you will be given will probably reveal themselves in the form of the legend's suddenly going off in a direction new to you. The events which then unfold before your eyes, and in which you will be participating, will hold within them the answer or answers you need. Because these answers will be presented symbolically in the scenes played out before you, you will need to have a sound grasp as to what the events described in the legends really mean, and what each character within those events represents, before you will be able to make any sense of them. This is why I suggested in Exercise Four that you leave aside asking specific personal questions until a later stage. That stage has now come.

As always with any Otherworld Work, remember to record immediately after completion of the exercise all that happened. In this particular exercise, it is especially important to record any realisations you had concerning your chosen character. Did you discover any aspects of his or her personality which you had not seen before? Did he or she react differently in any given situation than you had expected he or she would? How did he or she get on with the other characters involved in the legend? Did he or she display some previously unknown or unrealised skill or ability? All of these things are important, as they all go to building the complete picture of your Otherworld guides, friends, and helpers, and this is central to any competent magical Working under the Irish system.

The rest of the Practical Work involves performing the rituals of the four main festivals of the Celtic year. As each one of these festivals occurs only once a year, it is important that in-between festival times you carry on with all of the exercises given earlier. Each time you perform them, you learn from them, and they will change and advance with you, as you Work your way through this whole magical system. Similarly, as you learn and advance, you will start to be able to formulate your own magical and Otherworld exercises. You will also find that your Otherworld guides will suggest other things you could be doing.

Do not see the exercises in this book as the be-all and end-all of the Irish Celtic magical tradition. They are methods of opening the doors to this huge and complex system, but once the doors have been opened, you will find many more methods to try and things to do which have not even been mentioned in this book. There is no formal structure of grades or degrees of learning under this system, because, by its very nature, it simply goes on and on. Now that you have set your foot on the long road of progress, keep going forward, don't look back, and enjoy the journey!

Chapter Eleven

The Festival of Samhain

The Festival of Samhain would be the most important festival of the year if any festival could be regarded as being more important than any other. In the case of Samhain, the event being marked is the ending of one year and the beginning of the next. The word *Samhain* means "the ending of summer," and comes from two words, *samh,* "summer," and *fuin,* "end." It also signifies the end of the light half of the year and the commencement of the dark half. Another old name for this festival was Oiche Shamhna (oi-chi how-nah), which means "Eve of Samhain," indicating that the festival is considered to start with the darkness of the preceding day.

The Festival of Samhain is celebrated all over the world on the thirty-first of October, and the first of November. In ancient Celtic days, there was no set calendar, and Samhain would have been celebrated at different times in different places, although most would have tried to fit the festival in at the same time as their immediate neighbours. It was only in later Christian times that set dates were laid down for the celebration of religious festivals. The dates were usually set to continue the pre-Christian festivals around their original times throughout the year.

In the modern calendar of the Christian church, Samhain is known as Hallowmas, or the Feast of All Saints. The Christian feast was originally celebrated on the twenty-first of February, the Roman festival of Feralia. It was changed to its present date in 835 by Pope Gregory, in accordance with the Church's policy of using the times of the existing pre-Christian festivals for the celebration of the new Christian ones. The fact that such an important Christian festival as Hallowmas was moved by almost four months to coincide with Samhain indicates that even in the ninth century, Samhain must have been an important pre-Christian festival.

Just as Samhain recognised the start of the new year, it also heralded the start of winter, the cold and dying season. It was at this time of year that surplus cattle were slaughtered for food throughout the winter. This was reflected in the Green World, where many plants and flowers were dying and decaying to nourish the ground and make it fertile for the next year's growing season. It was customary not to eat wild fruits or plants after Samhain, as it was believed that no matter how ripe or luscious the fruit might look, all the goodness and vitality had been taken from it on Samhain eve. Samhain's connection with cattle is reflected six months later in the festival of Bealtaine, which also has strong cattle connections.

The importance of cattle to the Celts is shown in the many tales known as Tana, or "cattle raids," which have come down to us today. This practical association with slaughter and decay is one reason why Samhain became associated with death. Another reason is that the Celts believed they came from death, that death was literally their father. The dying time of this world was also a time of birth and renewal, and was seen to herald the start of the year to come. The apparent contradiction of death and life being one and the same thing also hints at the duality of the two worlds—this world and the Otherworld—which come closer together during Samhain than at any other time of the year. The two worlds are mirror images of each other. If it is summer in this world, it will be winter in the Otherworld. If it is daytime here, then it will be nighttime there; consequently, a time of death here is a time of birth there.

Samhain is very much an in-between time. It is neither part of the old year nor part of the new year. It is too late for the light half of the year, but too early for the dark. It is considered to be outside the effects of time altogether. To be in-between time is clearly a very special state, and it is recognised as being a time when the normal order of things is upset or reversed, and chaos reigns, albeit temporarily. The dead are no longer barred from walking this earth, and can return to their families and home, and join in the celebrations with their loved ones. Similarly, it is at Samhain when the sidhe mounds open, and the people of this world can easily find their way into the Otherworld, and explore those realms without hindrance.

This state of being in-between was very important to the Celts, and is another manifestation of the all-important concept of the three levels of being. Evidence of the importance of being in-between can be found in many of the Irish legends, where many important births and deaths take place at either dawn or dusk, the times in-between night and day. Important meetings and combats are often recorded as taking place at fords in rivers or on beaches. A ford is neither dry land nor a full-flowing river, and similarly, a beach is neither dry land nor the swelling sea; they are in-between the two states. Most of the legends dealing with death are set at dawn or dusk. In The Adventure of Neara, the hero has to carry a corpse upon his back, and sees many visions associated with death and destruction, as well as the riding-forth of the fairy host. The legend known as the Intoxication of the Ulstermen is set at Samhain, when the Ulster heroes stumble across Ireland in a drunken stupor. The death of the great Ulster hero, Cu Chulainn, occurred at Samhain, and the second battle of Moytura also took place at this time. From the sid at Cruachan emerged the god Ellen Trechenn (a corruption of *in tEllen Trechend*—"triple-headed Ellen"). This god was a destructive one, who used to burn Tara, the seat of the High King, every Samhain, until he was eventually killed by Fionn mac Cumhaill. The fact that this god was triple-headed emphasises the importance of the unity of the three levels at this time of year.

The destruction of Tara by fire is symbolic of the purifying of the entire people of Ireland, because the High King represented not only the sovereignty of the land, but also the people themselves. Many major events in the Fenian Cycle are recorded as having occurred at Samhain. It is said of the Fianna that they hunted and lived outdoors from Bealtaine to Samhain, but during the cold months from Samhain to Bealtaine were billeted in the houses of the common people whom it was their duty to protect. It was also at this time that tributes were paid, both to the gods and goddesses, and to the kings and overlords. A tribute was paid to the king of Ulster by the people of the Western Isles of Scotland, which shows the close ties these two countries had, until the Battle of Magh Rath in 637.

Every third year, a *feis* (faysh)—a feast or assembly—was held at Tara, and this was the most important celebration of all. This feis brought together the High King, the provincial kings, and chieftains with their respective *ollamhs*. It commenced three days before Samhain, and carried on for three days after. It was during the feis at Tara that important decisions were made which were likely to affect all the people. This was reflected in the smaller local Samhain gatherings, when each member of the clan was given the opportunity to comment on the events of the previous year, and to make any suggestions or promises to be kept during the year to come. This was sometimes referred to as the Festival of Tongues. During this period of free speech, any member of the clan, no matter how lowly or humble, could speak his or her mind freely, without fear of retaliation or spite from those who were, perhaps, told things they would rather not have heard.

Samhain and its counterpart, Bealtaine, are the most enduring of the major festivals, and ones in which many of the old customs and practices can still be seen. It is interesting to note that even today, thousands of years after Samhain was first celebrated, the Christian Church, especially in the Western Isles of Scotland, still considers it—under the present day guise of Hallowe'en—to be too pagan to accept and actively discourages its celebration. Despite this, the festival carries on and is enjoyed by thousands of people throughout the world, even though most are unaware of its magical and spiritual associations. It is probable that the bonfire celebrations in England now set to mark Guy Fawkes Night, were originally Samhain celebrations. The relatively minor event of Guy Fawkes' unsuccessful attempt at mass murder was simply added on to the existing festivities, presumably to discourage participants from consciously acting out a pagan ritual.

At one time, part of the Samhain ritual consisted of the symbolic sacrifice of the king, or substitute for the king; perhaps Fawkes' attempt at sacrificing the government of the day was unconsciously recognised by the people as a symbolic act which was very appropriate for that time of year. Poor old Guy has now become the victim himself in an ironic twist of fate, with most celebrations ending in the ritualistic burning of his effigy.

Many books on folklore record a vast array of activities connected with Samhain, or Hallowe'en, nearly all of which are concerned with role reversal and the playing of practical jokes. The recognition of and communication with the dead and the fairy folk are also themes in the folklore. There is, of course, the present-day emphasis in the popular mind on witches, broomsticks, and black cats, but this focus on the witchcraft side of the festival is a recent one. It is nonetheless relevant, as the festival is one which modern-day Wiccans recognise and celebrate.

In Ireland and the West of Scotland the festival is still actively celebrated under the guise of Hallowe'en, especially by children. It is a time of fancy-dress parties, when children and adults become recognisable characters or objects, or dress in totally nonsensical ways, such as wearing clothes inside out or backwards. This is a continuation of the ancient concept that Samhain was a time when the normal rules of life were reversed or jumbled up. Another common event in these areas is for gangs of children to go door to door, "guising" (which comes from the word disguising). Usually they are in some sort of fancy dress, and it is customary for the children to perform some entertainment for the householder—a song, story, joke, or simple trick. In return, the householder traditionally gives the per-formers gifts of apples, nuts, or money. This, again, echoes parts of the original celebration, when the dead members of the clan would be invited back to their old abodes, and would be entertained, fed, and given gifts to take back to the Otherworld. Hazelnuts feature a great deal in Irish legend, as do apples, and both of these have much symbolism associated with them, especially on a magical level. Samhain is the time of year when nuts and fruit become abundant, but the apple is especially connected with the Otherworld in many traditions and mythologies.

Samhain is a very ancient festival which has survived the rav-ages of time and the changes in popular thinking in a very success-ful way. It is a festival which seems to appeal even to people with little or no spiritual inclination, but who can, nonetheless, enjoy its purely fun and festive aspects. The following ritual should help you to celebrate Samhain on a more serious level, and in a manner closer to the way it was probably celebrated by the ancient Irish Celts.

RITUAL WORK

The Samhain Ritual

Every magical ritual, no matter how grand or how simple, should always have a specific purpose behind its performance. The purpose behind the Samhain ritual is to acknowledge the end of one year and the start of the next, and to use this time to examine the things that were unnecessary or wrong in the past year. It is a time to determine the things that can be done away with during the next year, and to decide upon any changes, new ideas, or practises which will be beneficial in the year to come. As well as this personal aspect, one of the main purposes behind any Samhain ritual should be a recognition of the fact that this is a period which is outside the effects of time. It is a period when the two worlds open up to each other, and movement from one to the other becomes much easier. It is a time of remembering and thanking the ancestors and those who have gone before us, and who have helped to shape the way we see and understand this world and the Otherworld. It is a time of celebration.

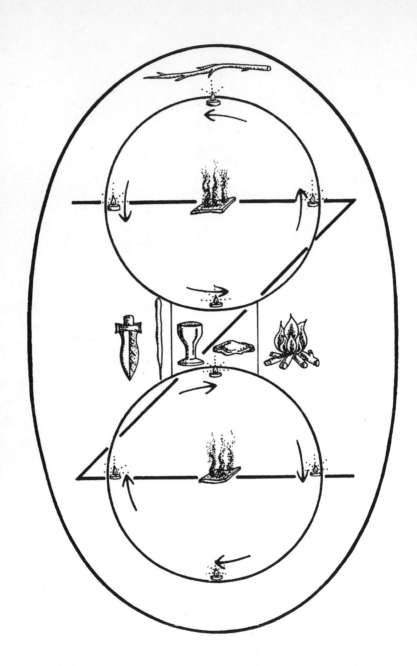

Ritual Working Area for the Festival of Samhain

Preparation

For a few days prior to the ritual itself, spend some time in quiet reflection and light meditation on the events of the year which is about to come to an end. What were the positive points that you would like to see continue? What were the negative points that you would like to do away with? Were there any periods or specific incidents that you did not understand? Were there any opportunities that you missed through inaction or incorrect action? Once you have managed to determine exactly how the year really went, and have decided upon those things you wish to do away with, then start to look ahead to the year to come.

Realise that this is a new beginning, and determine what you need for the year ahead. Decide what you want to achieve (be realistic here!). Are there any new ideas or practices that you wish to introduce, either into your daily life or into your magical Workings? What you are doing is laying out a realistic and achievable plan for the days and months to come. After you have prepared your list of events from last year, and plans for next year, try to narrow these thoughts and deliberations down to a specific number of things to be done away with and things to be achieved. Write them all down on a small card, seal this card in an envelope, and have it ready for the ritual itself.

Equipment Needed for the Ritual

Robes, Knife, Wand, Stone, Cup, Sword, eight "nite-lite" candles, enough paper and kindling to light a bonfire and enough cut wood to keep it burning for some time, two blocks of charcoal, incense, matches, an apple branch, sealed envelope containing your list, food and drink, a compass.

Place and Timing

Ideally, this ritual should be performed when the living things of the Green World surrounding your immediate home environment decree that the growing time has ceased, and that the time of death and decay is about to start. It will take most people quite a few years of careful observation before they will be confident enough to predict just when that time will be. Initially, I recommend that you stick to the now-accepted calendar date for the festival, and start the ritual just before dusk on the Eve of Samhain, preferably outdoors. The reason dusk is recommended as the starting time is that dusk signifies the start of the day of Samhain and therefore of the new year. Performing the ritual at this specific time means that the first act of the new year is a magical one, part of which is intended to shape the course of events for the year unfolding.

If you can find a reasonably flat, secluded area, with a birch tree standing on its own, this would be ideal. This sort of environment may not be easily accessible to everyone, but do make the effort to find such a place, as the very act of looking is a magical ritual itself, if carried out with magical intent. If you are able to perform the ritual outside, then the added atmosphere of the encroaching darkness as the Working is going ahead will certainly lend itself to the efficacy of the magic being Worked. It is possible to adapt the ritual to an indoor situation, which may be easier for some people, but for the purposes of this book, I shall give the ritual based on the assumption that an outdoor Working area is available.

The Ritual Itself

Gather together all that you are going to need, and proceed to your Working area. Remember, if some travelling is involved, to give yourself enough time to get there before darkness sets in (which at Samhain is quite early in the evening). Once you arrive, and before you do anything else, spend a moment or two getting in tune with your surroundings. Feel the atmosphere of the place. Rid yourself of mundane thoughts and concerns, and reflect on what you are about to do. Once you feel calm and ready to start, lay all your equipment at the foot of the birch tree, or if there is no suitable tree, in the centre of what will be your Working area.

Take your Sword and trace on the ground the limits of your full Working area. This will need to be big enough to contain two separate circles within it, representing this world and the Otherworld, plus an area between the two, representing the in-between aspect of existence.

The rough shape of this area should be an ellipse, with its longest axis oriented on a North-South line. As you carefully draw the tip of your Sword along the ground in a clockwise direction, be aware of defining and limiting the area of your existence. Beyond this line there is nothing, and for the duration of the Working, you will be encapsulated within the area you are now describing on the ground.

When you are finished, return the Sword to the centre of your Working area and place it alongside everything else which is there. Put on your robes, and be aware of temporarily covering up your own mundane personality, and assuming your magical personality. It may be a good idea to slip your robe over your ordinary clothes, as nighttime at Samhain can get rather chilly. If you prefer to remove your ordinary clothes before putting on your magical robe, be sure to place them neatly within your Working area, somewhere out of the way.

Take the apple branch and place it at the extreme North of the ellipse, inside the line you have drawn on the ground. As you carry it from the centre of the Working area, where everything is lying awaiting use, start to shut out all worldly thoughts, and feel the magical atmosphere build up around you. Although at this stage you are only preparing everything for use later in the ritual, you should be aware of the significance of what you are doing, and carry out the act with due solemnity and respect.

The next act is to light a fire at the Eastern edge of your Working area, in the space between where the two circles will be. This fire will give warmth and light and will symbolise the Light which is visible at all times from both worlds. Once the fire is burning steadily and safely, return to the centre of your Working area and take up your Knife. Go to the Southern end of your Working area, and in a clockwise direction, draw out on the ground a circle which should take up slightly less than half of your entire Working area, and be big enough for you to move around in. This circle will represent this world.

When this circle is complete, go slowly and consciously back to the central area, but do not leave the Knife in the middle with the rest of your equipment. Instead, carry on through this central region to the Northern end of your elliptical Working area. Once there, describe another circle on the ground, this time in a counterclockwise direction. Again, the circle should be slightly less than half the entire Working area, but big enough for you to move around in. This circle will represent the Otherworld. As you do this, be aware of the fact that you have travelled from this world to the Otherworld, and that you are now making the Otherworld real and solid to your physical eyes.

When this circle is complete, return to the central area, which is now in-between the two circles, put down your Knife, and take up your Wand. Go back to your first circle. Go around it clockwise, tracing the limits of this world with your Wand. Be aware of the fact that as you do so you are making it more and more real, and are making its limitations clearer and clearer. When you have returned to your starting point on the circle, proceed back through the in-between region and into the Otherworld circle. Once there, do as you did in the other circle, but this time in a counterclockwise direction. Be aware of the Otherworld becoming more and more real.

Once you have completed this circuit, return the Wand to the central area, take up your Cup and carry it into the this-world circle. Do as before with your Cup, always being aware of this world becoming more and more solid, and more and more clearly defined and limited, until you have completed your clockwise movements. Go back through the central area and into the Otherworld circle. Trace out its limits counterclockwise, return to the central area when finished, and replace the Cup with your Stone. Take it into the this-world circle and carry it around with the same thoughts and visualisations. Go back through into the Otherworld circle to do likewise, but in a counterclockwise direction, and so on, until both circles have been completed, and your four Magical Weapons are back in the central area between the worlds.

You will now have a Working area which consists of two clearly defined circles within an ellipse. The circle in the South represents this world, and the one in the North represents the Otherworld. A fire burns between them, and your magical equipment and personal belongings sit on the ground between them also. Realise what a very magical and unique position you are in at that moment. You are standing between both worlds, aware of them both, yet affected by neither, and in total control of the situation, with all the potential that lies before you.

After a moment's reflection upon this point, take up four of the little candles and the matches, and go to the Otherworld circle. Place one candle at each of the Cardinal points and light it. Try to be accurate in your siting of the Cardinal points, as this will help the flow of energy to come through all the stronger later. If you do not have a compass, or are not sure of the exact Cardinal points, then at least make a good guess at them. For the purposes of the rest of the ritual, accept that the four quarters which you have decided upon are as accurate as you can make them.

Be aware that this lighting of candles is being reflected on a much higher scale in the Otherworld, and that in a sense, you are activating your symbolic Otherworld and bringing it to life. You may find that, if you are able to perform this Working outdoors, it is a good idea to dig a little hole in the ground to sit the candles in, and thus prevent any gusts of wind from blowing them out. Once you have placed and lit all four candles in the Otherworld, and spent a moment or two visualising the Otherworld coming into life within your circle, take the remaining four candles and do the same in your this-world circle, with the same attendant realisations and visualisations. Spend some time standing in your this-world circle looking across to the Otherworld circle with its little flickering flames. Feel a yearning to be in the Otherworld, and to meet again those who have gone before you.

After the four candles have been lit, and you have spent due time reflecting over what you have done already and what is still to come, return to the in-between part of your Working area, take up a charcoal block and some incense, and return to the centre of your Otherworld circle. Light the charcoal and place it on the ground, or on a little flat stone placed there earlier if the ground is wet, and sprinkle some incense on it. Loose church incense is ideal for this purpose, and has a subtle enough aroma to be atmospheric, but not overpowering. If you cannot obtain loose incense, then any of the proprietary brands of incense sticks or cones will work just as well. If you are using manufactured sticks or cones, avoid any with strong flowery smells, especially Eastern flowers, and try to choose ones with subtle, delicate aromas.

As the smoke starts to rise from the centre of the circle and fill the whole area with its delicate aroma, be aware of the fact that you have now given a spirit to the Otherworld. This is what the incense smoke symbolises. Visualise this spirit shimmering and shining all around you within the confines of your Otherworld circle. Leave the Otherworld circle once the incense is burning steadily, take up the other charcoal block from the central in-between area, and go to the this-world circle. Once again, light the block, place it on the ground, and give it some incense. As the smoke starts to rise, be aware of the spiritual aspect of this world being activated to a higher degree.

As you stand in the centre of this world, turn and look across to the Otherworld circle. Spend several minutes now thinking of the great significance of what you have done so far. Realise that you are now aware of both worlds of existence at the same time. Understand that you are gazing from one to the other. Know that you are in total control of the situation. Consider that you have the potential at this point to do anything you will, within either or both worlds. See in your mind's eye the barriers between the two worlds falling away. As they do, visualise all sorts of people and creatures from each world crossing over into the other. As one world opens up to the other, and as the inhabitants of one joyfully greet the visitors from the other, realise that the passage of time has stopped, and you are now standing within a timeless zone, where the illusion of time will not affect you.

When you have these important thoughts and realisations deeply rooted into your consciousness, step out of your own circle, and go slowly across the central area into the Otherworld circle. As you step into it, take on the mental attitude that you are now a native of the Otherworld, and look back across to this world. Think upon how you now consider this world from an Otherworld point of view. Is it any better or any worse? Do you wish to interfere with the goings-on of this world, or do you prefer to remain an unattached observer? How do you consider the inhabitants of this world to be? Are they thoughtful or careless? Considerate or heartless? Aware of the realities behind the illusion in front of them, or simply blind to what is really going on?

Let these and other similar questions arise in your mind, and try to answer them honestly from your Otherworld perspective. When you have answered as many of these questions as possible, feel a desire to travel to this world to meet and entertain the inhabitants, and to get involved in their affairs, even if only temporarily. When you are ready, take up the apple branch from the Otherworld circle and slowly and deliberately carry it over to this world, both as a symbol of your Otherworld origin, and as a gift to those of this world whom you are about to encounter.

Once back in this world, change your mental attitude from that of the bearer of the apple branch, to that of the recipient of the apple branch. Realise you are back in your own world, and that you have been able to bring through to it a very important gift from the dwellers in the Otherworld. Lay the apple branch on the ground, and if it feels appropriate, close your eyes and commence a spontaneous Otherworld journey. What will happen during this journey, if anything, I cannot say, as it will be intended for you and you alone. Keep a careful mental note of it though, as it may well be of major significance to you in the year to come, even if at the time, it does not make much sense.

Once your journey has come to an end, realise that the old year, too, has come to an end, and that the new year has just started. Because you want to enjoy this new year celebration, and because you want to remain outside the effects of time for as long as possible, you can now leave your this-world circle and step into the in-between area, where your fire is, hopefully, still burning brightly. Take your sealed envelope, and, with intention, place it in the heart of your Samhain fire. As it burns away, realise that whatever was written on the card inside it has now been sealed, and will start to take effect. All the things you decided you wanted to do away with, all the things you decided you would like to initiate or change will now start to come about. This is why you should spend a few days carefully thinking over what you are going to write on your card. Once it is popped into the fire, it is too late to realise you have made a mistake or missed something.

The burning of your card concludes the formal part of the Samhain ritual, but if you feel there is some act or task you still wish to carry out, then by all means go ahead and do it. It is important to move in directions which may appeal to you intuitively or spontaneously while in a ritual situation, always assuming that those feelings or inclinations do not go against the basis of the Work, and do not require you to step outside your defined Working area. It is at this point that you could hold your own Festival of Tongues, and discuss with all the members of the group your plans and aspirations for the year to come.

When the magical part of the ritual has finished, you should relax and enjoy the celebratory aspect of Samhain, which is just as important. Eat and drink, play music, cook food on the fire, dream, or, in short, do whatever you like by way of fun and enjoyment. What better way to start off the new year than with a party? In Scotland, at the changing of the years according to the calendar, the festival of Hogmanay, as it is known, is far more widely celebrated than is the festival of Christmas, despite the fact that most Scots would describe themselves as being Christian. A great deal of emphasis is placed on old doors closing and new doors opening at Hogmanay. It is a time when people who have had a bad year make the conscious decision to put all that has happened behind them and look forward to a new and better year ahead. Although Samhain differs greatly from a traditional Hogmanay celebration, it does have this factor in common.

During your celebrations, it is fine to look ahead with relish to the year that is about to unfold with all of its potential and abundance. The final act you must perform before leaving your Working area (which may not be until the next morning if you have decided to spend the night there) is to redraw with your Sword, in a counterclockwise direction, the ellipse which defined your full Working area. Once you have done this, the complete ritual is finished, and you can pack up and go home. There is no need to redraw, or undo, the two circles representing the two worlds.

Technical Points

Unlike most ritual Workings, the Samhain ritual does not invoke the assistance or protection of any guardians or helpers, and does not conclude with the magic circle(s) being redrawn. This is because Samhain is a time when the barriers between the two worlds have been removed; therefore, there is no need to call through any Otherworld beings for help or protection, as any such beings who are meant to be there will be there already. Because Samhain is believed to be outside the normal effects of time, there is no need to close the circles as, technically, they have never been opened. During the creation of the two circles, there is a constant flow from one to the other, and this flow takes on a double-spiral shape due to the clockwise movement in one circle and the counterclockwise movement in the other. This represents the belief that each world is a mirror image of the other.

If at all possible, this Working is best carried out by a man and a woman. The man shapes the this-world circle and the woman shapes the Otherworld circle, with the appropriate Magical Weapons being passed from one to the other in the central in-between area. If a man and woman carry it out together, it is then possible for the woman to bring the apple branch from the Otherworld to the man in this world. He can then take her hand and go back to the Otherworld, where the Otherworld journey can take place. The ritual is also well suited to a group Working, with each member of the group having responsibility for a particular Magical Weapon. This way everyone can play an active part in the ritual itself. If a group does carry out the Working, the final, celebratory part can become quite a party, and this is, after all, what new year celebrations are all about!

It may be a good idea to take with you a small supply of dried logs for your Samhain fire, as any fallen wood in the area at that time of year may be wet and of no use for starting a fire. As is always the case when building fires outdoors, be thoughtful and be careful. If it is impossible to carry on the ritual outside, then the only adaptations to the above which need to be made are to have a large candle lit to represent the Samhain fire—unless an actual open fire is available in the room where the ritual is being Worked—with a dish handy to catch the burning remains of the sealed envelopes.

Apples can be substituted if it is not possible to obtain a branch from an apple tree. These can be eaten later as part of the Samhain feast, which should consist mainly of appropriate food and drink such as apples, nuts, cider, and homemade wines. Finally, it should be noted that from Samhain until Imbolg, the darkest part of the year, it is traditional for the magician to concentrate his or her magical Workings on personal growth and development. It is a time when most group Workings come to a temporary halt, and the magician has the time and freedom to pursue his or her own contacts, which he or she can then develop in the group Working later in the year. Just as everything else in the Green world turns inward and disappears into its own realm, so, too, should the magician in tune with the forces and currents of the Green world.

This is not to imply that all group Working should be deliberately avoided until Imbolg; far from it. Carry on with group Workings, always assuming that there is a reason for them, but place your emphasis on developing yourself and nurturing your own Otherworld contacts. By doing this, you will start to fine-tune your physical, mental, and spiritual aspects to the rhythms and cycles of the Green world, which will benefit you in the years to come.

Chapter Twelve

The Festival of Imbolg

Just as the ancient festival of Samhain has been adopted and adapted by the Christian Church, so, too, has the festival of Imbolg. The name, sometimes also given as Oimelc, literally means "butter bag," and this is an indication of the festival's pastoral origins, when the festival would have been celebrated as the local sheep started to lactate. This means it would have been celebrated at different times in different places. When the festival was adopted by the Christian Church, the date was fixed on the first of February. Unlike Samhain, which is very much a festival for the whole community and any visiting guests to celebrate jointly, Imbolg is more personal and localised. This aspect was carried forward into the Christian era. The festival tended to be celebrated with the family at home, at least in the Scottish Western Isles, as opposed to through a communal act of worship in the church.

The old name, Imbolg, occurs only in very old literature. The modern Gaelic name for Imbolg is Oiche Fheil Bhrighide (oi-chi ayla vree-jida), which means "Eve of the Festival of Brighid." It is normally called Candlemas in non-Gaelic-speaking areas. This title clearly identifies the festival with St. Brighid, or St. Bride, as she is sometimes called. This is a carry-forward from Celtic times when the festival was associated with the goddess Brighid of the Tuatha De Danann.

Brighid was the daughter of the Daghdha, and wife of Breas, a Fomhorian king and temporary ruler of the Tuatha De Danann. Her son, Ruadhan, was killed during the Battle of Moytura, and Brighid was so overcome with grief that she expressed her sorrow through keening her dead son. This was the first time keening—open weeping and wailing in grief—had been heard in Ireland. Brighid had two sisters, who were also called Brighid, and collectively they were the goddesses of poetry, healing, and smithcraft. This occurrence of a goddess, or sometimes a god, having two brothers or sisters of the same name is common throughout the Irish legends, and indicative of the triple aspect of one god or goddess.

There was an historical Brighid, who is often confused with the mythological Brighid, and who probably owes her existence to her anyway. According to tradition, the historical St. Brighid was born at sunrise, neither within nor without a house. The importance of this state of being in-between has already been noted, and is our first indication of her pre-Christian origin. She was fed from the milk of a white, red-eared cow, which again associates her with the pre-Christian Brighid, whose festival has to do with lactation. The description of the cows being white with red ears is a standard for Otherworld creatures within the Irish legends. She was credited with being able to hang her wet cloak on sun rays to dry, and this brings in the mythological Brighid's mantle, and her association with fire. The fire association is further emphasised by the belief that whatever house Brighid was in shone as if it were ablaze.

She became Abbess of Kildare in 525, and in her sanctuary, which no man was allowed to enter, a sacred flame was kept alight continuously until the Norman invasion of the twelfth century when it was briefly extinguished. It was relit, but eventually dowsed forever during the reign of the English king, Henry VIII. The flame was said to have been tended by nineteen nuns (some versions claim it was nine), for nineteen nights, but on the twentieth kept alight of its own accord. The fiery aspect of the pre-Christian goddess can clearly be seen to have attached itself to the Christian saint.

The importance of this sanctuary at Kildare was so great that the nuns there were considered to be more important than the bishops themselves. This reverence was so embarrassing to the male-dominated Roman Catholic church that a Papal decree had to be issued in 1151 to put an end to it. The skull of St. Brighid was taken by the Normans to Portugal, where until very recently, cattle were driven past it in an act of purification. Clearly, such adoration of what was, after all, a relatively minor saint, stems from a very deep respect, reverence, and remembrance of the ancient pre-Christian goddess, who was called upon by all women during childbirth to make their delivery an easy one.

Although Brighid the saint and Brighid the goddess are both Irish, their appeal stretched across the waters to the Scottish Hebridean Islands, where a great deal of lore, rituals, and sayings evolved around them. In the Isles, Brighid is sometimes referred to as Mary of the Gael, and she almost supersedes the Virgin Mary in importance and reverence. Just as the ancient Celtic women called upon her for assistance during childbirth, so, too, do the women of the Isles. One surviving rune is:

There came to my assistance,

Mary fair and Bride;

As Anna bore Mary,

As Mary bore Christ,

As Eile bore John the Baptist

Without flaw in him

Aid thou me in my unbearing,

Aid me, O Bride!

As Christ was conceived of Mary

Full perfect on every hand,

Assist thou me foster-mother,

The conception to bring from the bone,

And as thou didst aid the Virgin of Joy

Without gold, without corn, without kine,

Aid thou me, great is my sickness,

Aid me, O Bride![1]

This little rune, although plainly Christian in sentiment, displays a great deal of ancient Celtic influence, especially in the reference to foster-mother. Fosterage was a common affair among the ancient Celts, and carried on for a considerable time among the Highlanders and Islanders of West Scotland. The bond between foster-parent and foster-child was regarded as being stronger and more important than the bond between natural parent and natural child. One Highland proverb says, "Fuil gu fichead, comhdhaltas gu ceud" ("blood to the twentieth, fostership to the hundredth").

Other names given to Brighid are Muime Chriosda (mooma kree-osta), "foster-mother of Christ"; and Bana-ghoistidh Mhic De (bana-host-ah veek djay), "godmother of the Son of God." Christ is referred to as Dalta Bride (dahl-tah breeju), "foster-son of Brighid"; and Daltan Bride (dahl-tahn breeju), "little fosterling of Brighid"— a name which is still used as a term of endearment in some of the Gaelic-speaking parts of Scotland. One of her present-day Gaelic names is Ban-chuideachaidh Moire, "the aid-woman of Mary," because of an old legend which says she helped deliver the Christ child. In this legend, it is said that she was actually born the daughter of a poor innkeeper in Bethlehem. During a bad drought her father left in search of water, and gave strict instructions not to give food nor water to anyone, as there was only enough left for herself.

---

[1] From *Carmina Gadelica* by A. Carmichael. See the Bibliography.

Presently, two strangers appeared, an old man and a beautiful young woman heavy with child, who asked for food and drink. Brighid, in her heart, could not refuse this weary couple, and she gave them all she had. The strangers thanked her and went on their way. When she went to close the inn for the night, she found that her food and water had been replenished in full, as if they had never been touched. She went in search of the strange couple, and, seeing a brilliant golden light above a nearby stable, entered just in time to help the young woman with her childbirth. As the young woman slept, Brighid wrapped the silent baby in her mantle, and allowed the exhausted mother to recover. Brighid's father returned, and, seeing the lights, angels, and Heavenly Host above the stable, knew the Messiah had arrived.

In both Ireland and West Scotland, the Eve of Bride is a time for much celebration and ritual. The main form of celebration is for the women to make an oblong basket in the shape of a cradle, called Leaba Bride (lah-ba breeju), "Brighid's Bed," and place within it a sheaf of corn. This sheaf has been kept from the previous year's harvest, specifically for this purpose, and has been fashioned into the shape of a woman. This festival is regarded as signifying the first day of spring, and therefore, the corn woman is bedecked with primroses, daisies, snowdrops, and any other flowers that happen to have pushed their heads through the snow, along with bright ribbons, shells, and stones.

When all is ready, one of the women goes to the door and calls, "Bride's bed is ready." Another woman calls, "Let Bride come in, Bride is welcome. Bride come in, thy bed is made." The corn figure of Brighid is placed in the basket, along with a small white wand of birch, broom, bramble, or white willow. This wand is straight to signify justice, and white to signify peace and purity, and its giving mirrors the coronation ceremony of the Irish Kings when they, too, were given such a wand for the same reasons.

The men of the community are then invited in to pay their respects to Brighid. Note that they are only there at the invitation of the women, another very early Celtic tradition. They, too, give her their gift, which is usually a shell, stone, or flower, and thereafter, rejoicing and celebration take place. Once the main celebrations are over, and any guests have gone, the woman of the house very carefully smooths the ashes of the peat fire, and places the wand among them. The entire household then retires for the night. Next morning, the ashes are carefully examined, and if the marks of the wand are found it is a good sign. If Lorg Bride, the footprint of Bride—a disturbance in the ashes in the shape of a footprint—is found, then the household is especially blessed. If, on the other hand, no trace is found of either, then it is seen as an indication that Brighid is offended. This is very bad luck.

Being the first day of spring, snakes were thought to come out of their winter hiding places, and strange sayings and runes were chanted on this day. Few of them have come down to us intact, and most are only remembered or recorded in fragments, but the main theme is usually,

Early on Bride's morn

The serpent shall come from the hole

I will not molest the serpent

Nor will the serpent molest me.

Some versions change the word serpent to Daughter of Ivor or the Noble Queen, but basically they all make the same announcement. Too little remains of these sayings to form any definite opinion as to their meanings or origins. The reference to the serpent would imply a pre-Christian origin, considering the frequency with which serpents appear in our native pre-Christian tradition. In Ireland, the saying was slightly different, and referred to a hedgehog, presumably because of the lack of serpents in Ireland. It was believed the hedgehog came out of his winter hole on this day to inspect the weather. If he stayed out, it was an indication of a good spring to come, but if he returned to his burrow, it meant that the wintry weather was to continue.

A common practice, and one still carried out in parts of Ireland and the Western Isles, is to make Cros Bride, or Bogha Bride (bo-hah breeju), which means "St. Brighid's Cross." Although a great deal of variation is found, the usual shape is a diamond or lozenge of straw woven around a little wooden cross. Some have as many as thirty lozenges; some are simple crosses within circles; and some are made entirely of rushes bent over on each other. Basically, there are two main types—four-armed crosses and three-armed crosses. The four-armed ones are hung in the house for the benefit of the humans and are a protection against fire and lightning. The three-armed ones are hung in the stable or byre to protect the horses or cattle. It is interesting to note that, despite the very clear pre-Christian associations of these customs, most priests gladly bless the St. Brighid crosses, knowing full well the superstitious use to which they are put. Nine months later, however, these same priests will more often than not actively discourage the celebration of Samhain.

The festival of Imbolg is also the origin of the Christian festival of Candlemas, which is celebrated on the second of February. This is when candles are blessed in the church. There are two slightly differing legends suggesting the beginnings of this custom. The Irish version is that Brighid promised to distract the attention of the crowds when Mary took Christ to the temple. She did this by wearing a headdress covered in lit candles. It worked so well that Mary declared the day should be remembered by the blessing and purification of candles in the church. The Scottish version states that as Mary and Jesus entered the temple, their candles were in danger of going out from the draft. Brighid came from the crowd and took their candles, and walked in front of them into the temple. The candles did not even flicker as she held them, and they seemed to burn with an unnatural brilliance. Again, Mary decreed that the day should be remembered by the blessing of candles. Whichever version you prefer, the ancient Celtic association of Brighid with fire and illumination is still there.

The festival of Imbolg has ancient Celtic origins, honouring the goddess Brighid and the return of spring. It has become Christian, celebrating the saint of the same name and her role in the birth of the Christ. In both its pre-Christian and latter-day forms, it is very much for women, and a mystery to men, who play no part in its preparation or ritualistic side, and who only participate in the cele-bratory part at the specific invitation of the women. It is a very positive festival, marking as it does the return of spring and the lengthening days, with their steady increase in warmth. It does not carry with it the same intensity of purpose as the very magical and mysterious festival of Samhain, the rather gloomy festival of Lughnassadh, or the very down-to-earth festival of Bealtaine. It makes up for this in its own serenity and beauty. Being a man, it is not possible for me to give a full and detailed Imbolg ritual, but I give some notes below which should assist women who may wish to construct their own Imbolg celebrations.

RITUAL WORK

The Imbolg Ritual

The Festival of Imbolg marks the celebration of the coming of spring. It recognises the life force of the Green World making itself evident with the first flowers and plants pushing themselves through the snows and hard ground of winter, and new lambs being born in the fields. It is the time of year when the magician should turn his or her attention away from the very inward and self-oriented Workings of the dark winter months to the more outward and group-oriented Workings appropriate to the light half of the year. The winter should have been spent in preparation for the coming spring, with its new vitality and hope. Now is the time to consciously change your focus and put your abilities and skills to use for the common good. It is also the time when the emphasis on all level, shifts from the very magical days of winter to the more spiritual days of summer, as symbolised by the hours of light increasing each day. In short, the thoughts and actions of the magician should reflect the changes in the Green World, which is becoming lighter and lighter, and giving more and more pleasure and sustenance.

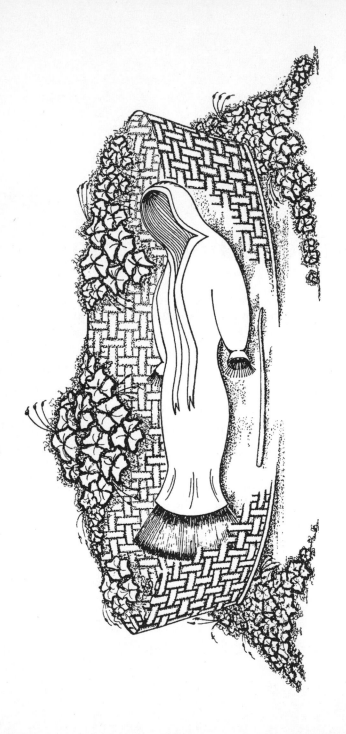

Brighid's Bed for the Festival of Imbolg

Preparation

The ritual involved at Imbolg is based in the home, and most of its preparation will concentrate on getting the house into order to receive the goddess Brighid. Most of this preparation will be a straightforward, old-fashioned, spring cleaning from top to bottom. It may seem a little early for this, considering the nights are still long, and the days are still cold, but if such a spring cleaning is carried out with magical intent, concentrating on the fact that the physical cleaning also represents a spiritual cleaning, then this is in itself a powerful and useful magical act, and should not be seen as a dirty or unwanted chore. Particular attention should be paid to the area around the hearth, as this is where most of the ritual will be centred. This is also a part in which the men can most definitely be involved.

For those of you who live in centrally heated buildings without a proper fireplace, it will be necessary to choose a suitable area of your room to consider as your hearth. Always remember that intention is more important than what you actually have or use. In this cleansed and prepared hearth area, you should construct a small bed or basket in which you will lay the image of Brighid. This should be decorated with fresh flowers and made as attractive as possible, with little shells, brightly coloured stones, feathers, or anything else from the Green World which can be used to make Brighid's Bed a colourful and pleasing thing to behold. You should also be on the lookout for some suitable small gift to give to Brighid during the ritual itself. Ideally, this should be something natural, from the Green World, such as one of the things mentioned above, or something small, simple, and appropriate to the time of year, which you have made yourself. Finally, it will be necessary to find and make a small white wand to be given to Brighid during the ritual. This should be about nine inches long, straight, and made of a white wood such as ash, hazel, rowan, or even a thick bramble stalk, devoid of its thorns.

Equipment Needed for the Ritual

Robes, Knife, Wand, Cup, Stone, several candles, matches, Brighid's Bed, Brighid's Wand, Corn-Doll, personal gift, food, and drink.

Place and Timing

The Working should take place once the ewes start to produce milk, in preparation for the birthing of the spring lambs. As very few of us nowadays keep domestic sheep, it can instead be commenced with nightfall on the Eve of Imbolg. It should be centred on the hearth of the house.

The Ritual Itself

The ritual of Imbolg is one of the type referred to as a Woman's Mystery, and should only be carried out by the women of the family or magical group. The first thing to be done is to clear all the male members of the family out of the house. Next, all the necessary equipment should be placed near the hearth where Brighid's Bed has already been prepared. The participants in the ritual should put on their robes. One woman, who has been decided earlier by the drawing of lots, should wait outside the main room with the corn-doll image of Brighid in her arms (see Chapter Fourteen, which deals with the Lughnassadh Ritual, for details on how to make this corn-doll). The woman appointed to carry out the main part of the ritual, who has also been previously determined by the drawing of lots, then takes her Knife and carries it around the perimeter of the room in a symbolic act of driving away anything which may have taken up residence during the dark and cold winter nights.

As she walks clockwise around the room, with Knife held out threateningly, the rest of the women visualise dark shapes fleeing before the Knife and disappearing out of the room. Next, the Wand is taken up and carried around the room, with the others again visualising all that is not wanted and should not be there, on all levels, quickly departing before these highly charged Magical Weapons. The same process is repeated with the Cup and the Stone, until the room is thoroughly cleansed of all unwanted influences, creatures, thought forms, or anything else which has taken up residence there during the months of winter.

The vacuum created by this exorcism is then filled with light, as each woman takes one of the candles, lights it, and places it on the floor next to Brighid's Bed. Be sure to have plenty of saucers or other heat-resistant mats handy on which to set the lit candles. The woman carrying out the ritual should then satisfy herself that Brighid's Bed is ready to accept the goddess, tidying it up if necessary, or rearranging any misplaced decorations. Once she is satisfied that all is in readiness, she declares that Brighid's Bed is ready and Brighid should be asked to come forth. At this point the rest of the women go to the door of the room and call aloud for Brighid to come forth, declaring that her bed is ready to receive her. A lot of visualisation is necessary, but this is made easier by the fact that the woman chosen earlier will be waiting outside with the corn-doll image of Brighid in her arms. The corn-doll is brought into the room with the utmost care and reverence, and gently laid in the waiting bed. The woman who has been carrying Brighid lights her own candle, and places it beside the others around the bed.

Once she has been laid in her bed, her Wand is placed beside her. Several minutes of quiet meditation should then be spent imagining the room, and then the whole house, filling with light radiating from Brighid's Bed. With this light comes a great feeling of love and protection, like a mother has for her newborn child. A feeling of total comfort and security settles upon the house and all who live within it. What happens next is up to the woman in charge of the ritual, and is the essence of the ritual and this particular Woman's Mystery. For this reason, I, being a man, cannot comment on it, nor will I attempt to do so. If things are going well, the women will instinctively know what to do. Once this very intimate and personal part of the ritual is over, the men of the household should be invited into the room to offer their gifts to Brighid, and to make any requests of her they may have. Each man should go forward individually, light a candle, give Brighid his gift, and make his requests before stepping back and allowing the next man to come forward. Although there is inevitably a feeling of awe and wonder experienced by the men at this stage, it should be kept in mind that this is not only a time for reverence and respect but also a time for enjoyment. To this end, a communal feast can now be celebrated, while Brighid stays in her bed, surrounded by her colourful gifts and shining candles.

Once the festivities are over, all the men and the women leave the room except for the woman carrying out the main part of the ritual. When they have gone, and all is quiet, the woman should light a new fire in the hearth (it is advisable to have cleaned out the hearth and prepared the fire earlier in the day). As she does so, she should be aware of Brighid's presence—stronger than it has been up until now—as if she were actually in the room and standing immediately behind her. If this is you, as the fire catches and the flames start to leap upward, be aware of Brighid's love and protection likewise getting stronger and brighter, and burning and clearing away anything which has managed to linger in any dark recesses of the house. Eveyone in the house should be sharing this visualisation.

When the fire is burning well, go to Brighid's Bed and carefully remove Brighid's Wand, taking it to the fire and laying it across the flames. As it starts to burn, leave the room, closing the door securely behind you. The entire household should then retire for the night. In the morning, the day of Imbolg, the woman of the house can take the corn-doll from Brighid's Bed and hang it somewhere in the house, to act as the physical embodiment of the spirit of Brighid and the protection she offers for the household during the year to come. By tradition, the previous year's corn-doll is taken outside and fed to the cattle; but as most of us do not keep domestic cattle, it is sufficient to leave it in some quiet part of the garden, or elsewhere in the Green World, where the forces of the Green World can work on it and break it down, until it is eventually absorbed into the earth once more.

Technical Points

The festival of Imbolg is very much a family and indoor affair, and is not suited to individual Working, or any sort of outdoor Working. It is also very much a women's ritual, and not suited to being Worked by men alone. If the house or room in which the ritual is being performed does not have a fireplace in which to burn Brighid's Wand, then it is acceptable to bury it as close to the house as possible. The effect is the same if the intention is the same. Not everyone will have celebrated the previous Lughnassadh, and therefore, not everyone will have a corn-doll to use during the Imbolg ritual. If you do not already have a suitable doll, then simply make a new one now. Once the first one has been made, and assuming you go on to celebrate the rest of the year's festivals, you will have a new corn-doll for next year's Imbolg, and the one you make this year can go to feed the cattle or the earth, after next year's ritual is over.

Chapter Thirteen

The Festival of Bealtaine

Of all the ancient Celtic festivals, Bealtaine is probably the one which is most widely celebrated throughout the world. Most of the celebrations today take the guise of May Day parades and carnivals, the festival's true origins having been widely forgotten. In Ireland and Scotland, the old-style celebrations continue, and traces of the original Celtic way of celebrating the festival can still be found. The festival is reckoned to fall on the first day of May, which has become a set date in the festival calendar, but like all of the festivals, this would not originally have been the case.

Bealtaine is an agricultural and pastoral celebration which would have been celebrated when the Green World dictated. Bealtaine marked the coming of summer, as the light half of the year grew, and the dark half waned for another season. It celebrated the time when the trees, plants, and crops came into full greenery and bloom, and when the cows were returned to the fields from their winter quarters and started to give their fullest of the all-important milk.

Clearly, these conditions would have varied greatly from region to region, so the actual night and day of Bealtaine would have been recognised at different times in different places by the ordinary people. The druidical order, however, for political reasons, agreed to a set day each year on which to celebrate the festival. This would have been the same day throughout the land, although not necessarily the same date each year. The fixing of this set date was so that all the fires in Ireland could be extinguished the night before; then, as dawn approached, a great fire lit at Tara, the spiritual centre of Ireland. From this fire all the other fires in the land were lit.

One of the later Christian legends of St. Patrick mentions this custom, and tells us that St. Patrick lit his own fire on the Hill of Slane, near to Tara, immediately before the druidical fire was ignited. When the High King Laoghaire asked his druids what this meant, they told him that the fire which had just been lit would never be extinguished, and that their old order had now been superseded. This is clearly a piece of Christian propaganda, but it does show the importance which must have been placed on the Bealtaine fire at Tara, even at the comparatively late time of the coming of Christianity to Ireland.

Today, the first of May is generally accepted as being the fixed date for Bealtaine, and this has given rise to many customs known as May Day celebrations. Most of these latter-day festivals still contain a good deal of ancient (and sometimes obvious) symbolism connected with both the coming of summer and the fertility needed for the future well-being of the people. Unfortunately, this ancient magical festival has been overshadowed by modern political connotations. In recent years, May Day has become no more than a political rally, and an occasion for the display of military might by some Communist countries. This aspect, coincidentally, reflects an ancient Celtic element of the festival, as it was at Bealtaine that the young men of the clan were given arms, and new weapons were named and dedicated. Oaths, too, were sworn on weapons at this time.

The meaning of the word Bealtaine has been argued for centuries, with very diverse translations and spellings being advanced. All commentators on this topic agree that the last part of the word, *taine* or *teine,* means "fire." Today, in both Scottish and Irish Gaelic, this is still the word for fire. The first syllable, *beal,* is not so clearly defined. Early writers on Irish legends and customs were of the school of thought that the Celts were of an Indo-European race which had migrated from East to West, eventually reaching Ireland, and that they shared a common root tongue, usually called Aryan or Indo-European. All the Celtic languages, according to this theory, could be traced back to this original language, and the meanings of obscure or archaic words could be found there as well.

This meant that Celtic religious beliefs and magical practices must also have a common root, as would the Celtic pantheon. Using this theory, many commentators have argued that the root meaning of Bealtaine is "Baal's Fire"—Baal being a Phoenician god, and the celebration of Bealtaine being, therefore, Phoenician or Mediterranean in origin. A similar theory is that the festival is named after the Celtic god Bel (also known as Beli, or Belinus), and again would mean "Bel's Fire." This god, in the guise of Donn, was considered by the Irish Celts to be the Father of All, insofar as he was associated with death.

Belinus was recognised more by the Celts of Switzerland, Germany, and Belgium, than he was by those of Ireland, where his name does not occur at all. This explanation of the meaning of Bealtaine is really not satisfactory from the Irish Celtic point of view. The idea of an East-to-West migration is now being reconsidered, in light of various scientific and archaeological finds, and seems less likely, as does the notion of an Indo-European root language. This calls into question the above theories as to the origins and meanings of the word Bealtaine.

A more plausible meaning of *beal* is in the Gaelic for "shining" or "brilliant." This shining or brilliance is no ordinary effect of light, but refers to a particular sort of light which emanates from the Otherworld. Many legends describe Otherworld beings as "shining." An old name for the fairy folk is "the Shining Ones" or "the Luminescent Ones." In the legends, such Otherworld beings are often described in language which contains many references to precious metal, as in the appearance of Elatha, an Otherworld warrior, to Eriu, the goddess of the sovereignty of Ireland, in the legend the Battle of Moytura:

He had golden-yellow hair down to his shoulders, and a cloak
with bands of gold thread around it. His shirt had embroidery of
gold thread. On his breast was a brooch of gold with the lustre
of a precious stone on it. Two shining silver spears and in them
two smooth riveted shafts of bronze. Five circlets of gold around
his neck. A gold hilted sword with inlayings of silver and studs
of gold.[1]

The description of shimmering brilliance would instantly have
told a Celtic listener that an Otherworld visitor was being described. It
is in this sense that the word *beal* should be understood when considering the meaning of Bealtaine, which can now be translated as
"Otherworld Fire" or "Brilliant Fire." The fact that the High King's own
druid was responsible for lighting the Bealtaine fire, and that every
other fire in Ireland was lit from this one, also indicates that it was no
ordinary bonfire, but one of the utmost importance, not only to the
druids, but to the ordinary people as well. The fire which was lit at
Bealtaine was split into two separate bonfires, close to each other, and
the beasts of the field were driven between them to be purified before
they were released to their summer pastures. The common people, too,
would leap over the great fires in an act of self-purification.

The whole festival was one of great merriment and rejoicing,
unlike its counterpart, the festival of Samhain, which was celebrated
six months prior, and was a dark and sombre affair. Being the beginning of summer, and the time when much fruitfulness was expected
from the beasts, the crops, the rivers, and the sea—as well as from the
people themselves—it was also the time when the High King was symbolically mated with the sovereignty of the land in order to ensure the
fertility of everything which was on and within the very land itself. This
idea has survived today in the crowning of a May Queen at most local
May Day celebrations in many European towns and villages. The symbolism has been greatly watered down over the centuries, due mainly

---

[1] "Cath Maige Tuired," translated by E.A. Gray, published by Irish Texts Society.

to the influence of the early Christian church. (I wonder how many boys, girls, mothers, fathers, and local clergy realise they are carrying on a very ancient pagan fertility rite as they parade along the local village green during their May Day celebrations!)

The common people would also take the opportunity to ensure their own fertility—and not just symbolically. It was this aspect of the festival which caused a great deal of consternation to the later Christian church, which could not accept such apparently licentious behaviour from newly converted Christians. This wrangling between allowing the people freedom to celebrate the old festivals, but at the same time cutting out the pagan aspects and substituting Christian values and morals, has continued until very modern times, when even the English May Pole, an obvious fertility symbol, was vigorously attacked by the Church.

This time of fertility is reflected in the legends, where major events are often described as happening at Bealtaine. According to the legends, three of the five invasions of Ireland—the invasions by Partholon, the Tuatha De Danann, and the Sons of Mil—are all specifically described as occurring at Bealtaine. A fourth, the invasion of the people of Neimheadh, can be assumed to have occurred at this time, as the "Fire of Mide," mentioned in this legend was probably the archetypical Bealtaine fire. Each of these separate invasions brought new growth and prosperity to Ireland, and this clearly links them with the fertility aspect of Bealtaine.

The very magical aspect of the festival can be seen from the descriptions we have of how the fire was actually lit. All fires in Ireland were extinguished on the eve of Bealtaine, and, therefore, the Bealtaine fire itself had to be started by the use of a fire "drill." Nine men were used to keep the fire drill moving until enough heat was generated by the friction to get the fire going. Nine different types of wood were used, which had been collected from nine trees by nine men. This constant reference to the number nine immediately tells us that something of the utmost importance and highest magical order is being described. Nine represents three times the three levels of being, a very magical state indeed. The use of different woods from different trees is also significant, as trees have a very special meaning and purpose in the Irish magical system.[2]

It is interesting to note an old rhyme, which was repeated until very recent times in parts of Munster, which reflects a vague memory of ancient tree lore. The rhyme was chanted as May Boughs, bunches of leafy young branches, were brought into the house. Note the mention of a ford in the last line, one of the important in-between places:

Cuileann agus coll

Holly and hazel

Trom agus carthen

Elder and rowan

Agus fuinseog gheal

and bright ash

O bheal an atha

from beside the ford[3]

Along with the decorating of homes, another custom which is still popular is to wash in the dew on May morning before the sun comes up. Nowadays this is usually performed by young ladies, who wash their faces in the glistening dew, as an aid to retaining their youthful beauty. Originally, the whole village would have turned out, sometimes completely naked, to have a thorough roll in the dew as an aid

---

[2] This will be discussed fully in my forthcoming work on this complicated subject.
[3] Reprinted from *The Year in Ireland* by Kevin Danaher, Mercier Press.

to health and vigour. The dew was also carefully collected, either by knocking it off the grass and flowers directly into jars, or by soaking linen sheets in it and wringing them out afterwards. This dew was then kept in sunlight to purify it even further, and was considered to be an excellent remedy for just about every ailment imaginable. The exact origins of this notion of the efficacy of dew are not known, but it is probably connected with the old Bealtaine fertility aspect, the dew being the semen of the Sky-Father fertilising the Earth-Mother, and also with the fact that Bealtaine heralded the start of the warm, dry season, which naturally brought with it increase and plenty.

One final point which should be noted, but is often forgotten or overlooked, is that the feelings and emotions experienced on the day of the festival are expected to stay with the celebrant until the next festival. Likewise, any promises made or contracts signed at this time are particularly binding. Bealtaine was the time of the old Hiring Fairs, when farmers and landowners hired their workers for the summer ahead. It was also the time of year when couples could approach the Brehons, or lawyers, to plead for divorce.

It was for the very sensible reason that everyone should be able to enjoy themselves to the full during festivals, that the Brehon Laws made it illegal for anyone to attempt to settle debts or even old scores on Bealtaine, for fear such actions would mar the general atmosphere of relaxation and enjoyment. It was also a day when outlaws and people on the run were free from prosecution or capture. This emphasis on pure enjoyment for enjoyment's sake is sometimes lacking in people who attempt to revive these old festivals, in their older forms, for no better reason than a vague sense of heritage, or for fear that such things may become lost and forgotten. There is no point in attempting such a revival if only the mere mechanics are gone through. The spirit of the event must be appreciated, too. In short— enjoy yourself!

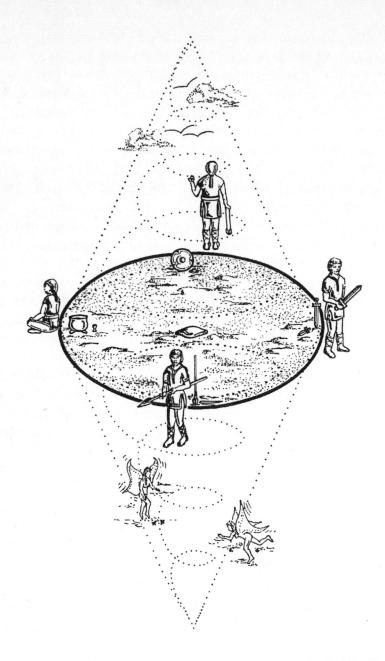

The Ritual Circle of the Festival of Bealtaine

RITUAL WORK

The Bealtaine Ritual

This festival marks the start of summer, the bright time of the year, and should reflect this image accordingly. Now with the advent of the longer, lighter, summer months, it is time to put all carefully planned and prepared schemes and ideas into effect. This is the time for self-cleansing, for sweeping away the cobwebs of winter and spring, and for preparing yourself for the hard work of the summer days ahead. This festival marks the start of a return to full group Working, or if you are not a member of a group, a time for Working outwardly, and for the benefit of those other than yourself.

It is, by tradition, a time for arming the new young warriors of the clan. This tradition is carried on among magical groups today by dedicating or consecrating new Magical Weapons and equipment during the modern Bealtaine ritual. It is also the time of year for acknowledging the Sovereignty of the Land, which becomes more and more evident with the new life and colour bursting forth all around. It is the time for each and every member of the group to recognise his or her status as High King, and to unite that with the Sovereignty of the Land, bearing in mind all it implies. It is a time of fertility. Finally, Bealtaine is a time for fixing contracts, setting targets, and acknowledging debts and responsibilities. Once the business side of things has been completed, it is time for games and music, for competitions, feasting, and drinking.

Preparation

Bealtaine is a daytime, open-air festival, and a good deal of preparation is necessary to locate a suitable site, tidy it up, prepare a safe bonfire, and make sure of all the necessary magical equipment, including musical instruments, gaming materials, food, and drink. Make sure any new Magical Weapons or other equipment are ready for dedication and consecration during the ritual. If in a group situation, ensure beforehand that everybody knows who is responsible for what during the ritual. If necessary, go through the whole thing in a dry run before the ritual proper, in case there is any doubt in anyone's mind as to what they are supposed to do or when they are supposed to do it.

Spend some time tuning into the feelings and emotions of the Green World around your chosen site, as you will be calling upon this aspect during the ritual. If for any reason things do not feel right or comfortable in this place, then do not use it. No matter how attractive a place it may be, or how secluded or suitable it may appear, if it does not feel right, then it is not right. It is just as important to pay attention to your intuition and feelings as it is to look upon the whole thing from a practical point of view.

You will be testing your own eligibility for the position of High King during this ritual, so it is a good idea to spend several days prior to Bealtaine thinking over exactly what this means, and asking yourself honestly and openly if you are really ready or worthy of this position. It is important to be able to enter into the Bealtaine ritual with confidence, and a certain amount of eagerness. Although this may appear to affect only the men taking part, this is not the case. As will be seen when we come to look at the ritual itself, the women members of the group have an equally important part to play in this recognition of High Kingship. Considering that part of this involves a mating process, when two become one, it is clear that anything affecting one, must likewise affect the other.

Finally, by tradition, Bealtaine is a time for extending invitations to other groups and individuals who are sympathetic to your beliefs and practices. It is not necessarily true that the more people Working a ritual the better, but the celebrations after the Working can be much more enjoyable if you have the opportunity to entertain guests and chat over various magical and occult matters with fellow Workers. Quite a lot of preparation will be needed if you are going to invite others to participate in your ritual. Consider this point well before the day of Bealtaine. You may, of course, find yourself being invited to someone else's ritual, in which case you will need to decide whether to go it alone, with your own planned festival, or abandon any such plans and participate in a ritual someone else has planned and prepared. Again, as always, listen to your intuition in such things, and simply do what feels right.

Equipment Needed for the Ritual

Robes, four Greater Magical Weapons, four Lesser Magical Weapons, any new Weapons or equipment to be dedicated, matches, sufficient materials for a large bonfire, a large, flat stone, gaming equipment, musical instruments, and plenty of food and drink.

Place and Timing

This festival should be celebrated when the weather has cleared sufficiently to allow the cows to be turned out to the summer pastures. As with the festival of Imbolg, it is unlikely that many today will be keeping cows over the winter to help them make an authentic choice of the correct day for Bealtaine. Therefore, keeping the practical aspect of this system of magic firmly in mind, it is perfectly acceptable to celebrate Bealtaine on the first of May. The ritual should be started so that noon falls about halfway through the Working. Note that it is a daytime festival, unlike the rest of these main festivals, which start with the preceding evening and carry on into the following day.

The best site is an open area in a wood or forest preferably of hardwood trees; but any open, flat, outdoor site, big enough to hold all the participants comfortably, will do. Remember that an important part of the ritual is the bonfire, which by tradition, is a big one. This will need to be taken into careful consideration when choosing a suitable site. Any place with thick, dry grass is not advisable. Similarly, any heavily wooded areas are likewise dangerous, and should be avoided. As with all of these outdoor festivals, the visiting of potential sites, and the eventual choosing of one, is in itself a magical and worthwhile act.

It is not advisable to pick an existing site, such as a stone circle or previously recognised or well-known place of power, such as the many ancient burial mounds and prehistoric cairns which cover the countryside. A lot of these are either in government care, or are on private land, making legal access to them difficult or impossible—a point which must be taken into consideration. Such places also can be accidentally damaged during the Bealtaine ritual, no matter how careful you think you are. In order to avoid possible retributions later, and to give yourself a clear mind and free conscience as the Working is going ahead, keep away from such places. Let your intuition pick out a virgin site for your private use. None of these ancient standing stones, burial chambers, or stone circles were Celtic anyway, as they predate the Celts of Ireland by some two thousand years in most cases, and play no part in the Irish Celtic magical tradition.

The Ritual Itself

All participants should gather together in robes with their four Lesser Magical Weapons. Spend a quiet moment or two tuning into the Green World forces of the Working area and thinking over what is about to happen. When everyone is ready and in a suitable frame of mind, the person leading the ritual should take the large, flat stone, which is symbolic of the Lia Fail, and place it on the ground in what will be the centre of the Working area. Lay the four Greater Magical Weapons upon it, along with any new Weapon or equipment is be dedicated later. All present gather round and stand in a loose circle facing in toward the Lia Fail.

Take the Sword, go to the Eastern Quarter and draw out on the ground, in a clockwise direction, a circle big enough to contain everyone, and for everyone to move freely within. The rest of the group should be visualising a great protective barrier being put up all around them by the action of the Sword being drawn along the ground. When you get back to your starting place in the East, hold the Sword aloft and say:

Mighty Uiscias, teacher of the great Nuadhu of the Silver Arm

in the magical city of Findias, come forth and watch over us

and protect us with your mighty Sword this Bealtaine Day.

Thrust the Sword hard into the earth. All present should visualise a great warrior figure carrying a gleaming, enormous sword stepping toward the Working area, as if coming out of a swirling mist. As he approaches the Eastern perimeter of your circle, he turns and faces outward, holding his huge sword at the ready, and watches for anyone or anything who may try to approach your Working area. Go to the Lia Fail, take up the Spear, and go to the Southern Quarter. Hold the Spear level, point outward as if to repel an approaching enemy, and say aloud:

Mighty Esras, teacher of the powerful Lugh of the Long Arm

in the magical city of Gorias, come forth and watch over us

and protect us with your mighty Spear this Bealtaine Day.

Stab the Spear hard into the earth and visualise another great, larger-than-life warrior coming out of the Otherworld mist toward the Southern perimeter of your circle. He, too, turns his back to you, faces out, and levels his enormous spear in readiness to repel all unwelcome visitors. Go to the Lia Fail, take the Cauldron to the Western Quarter, hold it out before you as if offering it to someone, and say aloud:

Mighty Semias, teacher of the Good God, the Daghdha,

in the magical city of Murias, come forth and watch over us

and protect us this Bealtaine Day.

Place the Cauldron just inside the line drawn on the ground by the Sword, and visualise a great figure stepping toward you through the Otherworld swirls. See him stop, turn around, and squat down next to the great cauldron he has been carrying as if ready to greet and feed a friend, but also ready to spring up and repel an enemy. Go back to the Lia Fail, take up the Shield, and go to the Northern Quarter. Place the Shield on your left arm, hold it aloft, and say aloud:

Mighty Morfesa, teacher of us all and instructor to the High King

in the magical city of Falias, come forth and watch over us

and protect us this Bealtaine Day.

See through the mists a huge figure coming toward you. In one hand, he carries a hefty leather sling, and in the other a handful of boulders, which appear as pebbles next to his great stature. He turns as he nears the circle perimeter, and faces out, sling poised and ready to hurl a death-dealing stone at anyone foolish enough to approach this now well-protected magical circle. Take your personal Lesser Magical Weapons, and starting in the East with your Knife, go to the edge of your Working area, just behind the Sword stuck in the ground. Holding your Knife aloft, say:

Mighty powers of the East, mighty powers of Air which blow

and flow and clear away the rubbish and unwanted things which

cling to us all, protect me and aid me in this our Bealtaine Working.

As you say these words, feel a great hurricane wind blowing and surging and pushing right through you. As it does, feel lighter, and sense that things you have been carrying unnecessarily on an emotional level have been carried off by the purifying and cleansing Air. When you feel this purifying has stopped, leave your Knife on the ground behind the Sword. Go next to the Southern Quarter, hold aloft your Wand, and say:

Mighty powers of the South, mighty powers of Fire which burn

and consume all that is dead and no longer needed, protect me

and aid me in this our Bealtaine Working.

See and feel great flames leaping forward, which totally engulf you. Feel their heat and strength burning away all the incorrect thoughts, feelings, emotions, and attitudes which have been clogging up your mind for too long. When the burning has ceased, leave your Wand on the ground behind the Spear. Go next to the Western Quarter, hold aloft your Cup, and say:

Mighty powers of the West, mighty powers of Water which wash

and cleanse and carry away the dirt and blockages which stop

the flow of my own being, protect me and aid me in this our

Bealtaine Working.

See and feel huge waves surging forward, totally swamping you from head to foot. Feel the cold water flow, not only over you, but through and inside you. Feel all the dirt and blocked-up areas being purged and cleansed, and the freshness and comfort this brings with it. Once you feel you have a had a thorough cleansing, leave your Cup on the ground behind the Cauldron. Go next to the Northern Quarter, hold aloft your Stone, and say:

Mighty powers of the North, mighty powers of Earth which shake

and shudder and break down all that has become decayed and out-

dated, protect me and aid me in this our Bealtaine Working.

Feel the ground beneath your feet start to shudder and shake, as if a great earthquake is about to unleash its tremendous force. Feel as if pieces of you are being shaken off and absorbed into the earth where they are rapidly broken down and reused to build things which are needed. When the shaking has stopped, place your Stone on the ground behind the Shield. Once you have completed this circuit of the Working area, return to the Lia Fail, and the next participant should carry out the same procedure. If possible, alternate between men and women, as all members of the group work their way around the circle, placing their personal Lesser Weapons, and calling forth their own protection.

The next stage is different for the men and the women within the circle, although ultimately they are both Working toward the same end. If you are a man, once you have completed the circuit with your Lesser Magical Weapons, you should stand by the Lia Fail, and when ready, carefully and deliberately step onto this important stone. As you do so, realise the significance of this apparently simple act. By standing upon the Lia Fail in front of the rest of the group, you are making a public declaration that you feel fit and able to hold the position of High King, with all the weighty responsibilities it involves. As you stand on the Lia Fail, close your eyes and see a band of brilliant white light circling the perimeter of the Working area in a clockwise direction. As you become aware of this light, see it start to rotate upward and slightly inward, thereby creating a cone of white light spiraling up into the sky high above you. Realise that you are literally and symbolically the centre of this area of light, which is your own newly created kingdom.

Being the High King of this new kingdom, you can do what you like with it, and all the people within it, who are now your subjects. Think on this for a moment. How do you react to suddenly being given total power and total control over your immediate surroundings and your friends and relations? How do you relate to those friends surrounding you in the circle? Are they inferior? Superior? No different? Do you see any of them differently from the way you used to see them? Do you feel threatened? What about the responsibility involved in looking after these people and the very land itself? Do you want that? Could you cope with it? What if someone decides to challenge your right to be on the Lia Fail? How would you deal with that?

There are probably many more questions and doubts which will spring to mind as you consider your position on the Lia Fail and your own ability and worthiness to take on the role of High King. Once you have sorted out these questions and doubts in your mind as best you can, be aware of a shaft of brilliant white light starting to descend from the point of the cone of light high above you. See and feel it make its way down from on high, and start to burn its way right through your skull, through your head, down through your throat and heart, and right on through your genitals and legs, until it reaches your feet upon the stone. When it reaches the Lia Fail beneath your feet, it cannot go any farther, and an ear-piercing screech is heard as it turns and doubles back upon itself, and starts to flow back up through you, on up toward its source in the very point of the cone high above you. Let this circuit of light flow through you for as long as you feel comfortable with it. Once you feel you have had enough, or the time feels right to move, open your eyes and step down from the Lia Fail, and move over to a vacant part of the circle. Sit on the ground, and feel the throbbing life force of the Green World in the soil beneath you reaching up to the light, which is still flowing within you. See that light within you flow freely out of your body and into the soil. Feel the two uniting and reinforcing each other.

There is absolutely no obligation for anyone to stand on the Lia Fail, should he feel within himself that he is not yet ready or worthy of such a defiant act. No pressure must ever be brought to bear on anyone at this stage, who listens to his intuition, and decides that he is not ready to face up to his own High Kingship. There is no shame in this; it takes a stronger man to be able to deny the Lia Fail, under such close scrutiny from his fellow group members, than it does to stand upon the Stone and go with the flow.

If you are a woman, start your circuit of the circle perimeter, with your Lesser Magical Weapons, at the exact moment the first man stands upon the Lia Fail. When you have completed your circuit, pick a part of the Working area away from the Lia Fail and sit on the ground, thereby making maximum contact with the earth. The second man should now start his circuit with his Magical Weapons, prior to standing on the Lia Fail. While sitting on the ground, close your eyes and see a circle of light rotating counterclockwise around the perimeter of the Working area. As it becomes clearer to your visual imagination, see it start to spin faster and move down into the very earth itself. Be aware of it spinning down and down, and getting smaller and smaller, until it forms a spinning cone of light whose point is deep within the earth, and whose centre is you, sitting on the surface of the earth. Feel and see a flow of light start to concentrate in the point of the cone deep below you, and move steadily upward toward you.

As it reaches the surface of the ground, it flows on up and into you, filling every part of your body with a slow, deep, pulsing sensation, which gives you a beautiful feeling of warmth, nourishment, love, security, and comfort, all at the same time. Realise that you have become rooted to the spot, like a plant, and that you are entirely dependent upon the life-giving flow which pulses and throbs within you. Realise, also, that this flow is taking from you, as well as giving to you. You are feeding the flow by your contact with the Air, Fire, and Water above you. It is this symbiotic relationship which keeps you both alive and in love with each other.

As you think on this, see the flow bend around within your body, and sink back down to its source deep below you. A great circuit is now formed, with the point of the cone of light at one end deep within the earth, and your own body at the other, sitting on the surface of the earth. Once the flow is moving smoothly, consider the fact that very soon you are going to have to stand up and move away from this spot. How do you feel about that? You know that you will be able to take a certain amount of the flow with you, but how do you feel about sharing it with others, especially the men, who have not experienced it? Are you willing to be the provider? Will you feel you should demand payment for providing this nourishing link with the earth, or are you willing to give it freely to all who ask? What are you willing to give to the earth in the days and weeks to come, by way of return payment for the flow, which will remain in your body? When you have thought over these points, and any others which may occur to you, slowly and deliberately stand up and break the circuit of the flow within you and the earth. Move away to somewhere else within the Working area, and let another woman sit where you have been. The next man will be ready to stand on the Lia Fail at this point, and the next woman ready to commence her circuit.

Stand for a moment, and behold all the life force, in the form of the plants and trees and grasses which surround you. Feel the air on your face, the heat of the sun on your body, the dampness of the water around you, and realise that it is you who channels these things into the earth, which needs them as much as you do. If you have a male partner within the circle, who has completed his turn on the Lia Fail, go to him and share this feeling of the flow of the life forces of the earth within you. Let him give you a feeling of the flow of the spiritual forces of the Lia Fail, which he will be channeling at that point. Unite in whatever way feels right for you, physically, mentally, and spiritually: experience each other totally.

Just as the men have the option not to stand on the Lia Fail if they do not feel ready, so, too, do the women have the option not to commune with the sovereignty of the earth if they do not feel prepared for this important action. Again, no pressure must ever be brought to bear on any who wisely choose to decline this communication.

It is at this point that any new Weapons or equipment can be dedicated and consecrated for further magical use. This should be carried out by the person who is going to use the Weapon or equipment, and should be performed at the Quarter relevant to the Weapon, or at the Lia Fail if the object is not a specific Magical Weapon. The actual wording of the dedication or consecration is up to the individual concerned. In the case of a Weapon, it should obviously call upon the appropriate powers of the Quarter, Element, Teacher, City, and deity, as given in the Opening of the Quarters ceremony above. Once this dedication is over, the Weapon or equipment should be left at the Quarter, or the Lia Fail, as appropriate.

After everyone within the circle has had the opportunity to either stand on the Lia Fail or experience the flow of the earth forces, and all dedications or consecrations have been completed, then any matters relating to group Work for the months ahead, or the structure of the group, can be discussed by those present, and plans laid for the general Work and well-being of the group and the individuals within it. Once such discussions have been concluded, each member in turn (alternating from man to woman to man) should go counterclockwise around the Working area and pick up their personal Lesser Magical Weapons, making a short statement of thanks to the powers of each Quarter for their help and protection during the ritual. Once all the Magical Weapons have been removed, the person in charge of the ritual should go to the Northern Quarter, pick up the Shield from the ground, and say aloud:

Great Morfesa, we thank you for coming and protecting us

during this our Bealtaine Working. Go now and return to your city

of Falias with our thanks and gratitude.

See the great warrior start to walk forward, away from the circle, and slowly disappear into the Otherworld mist. Replace the Shield at the Lia Fail and go to the Western Quarter. Take up the Cauldron, and say aloud:

Great Semias, we thank you for coming and protecting us

during this our Bealtaine Working. Go now and return to your city

of Murias with our thanks and gratitude.

Return the Cauldron to the Lia Fail, go to the Southern Quarter, take the Spear out of the ground, and say:

Great Esras, we thank you for coming and protecting us

during this our Bealtaine Working. Go now and return to your city

of Gorias with our thanks and gratitude.

Return the Spear to the Lia Fail, proceed to the Eastern Quarter, pull the Sword out of the ground, and say:

Great Uiscias, we thank you for coming and protecting us

during this our Bealtaine Working. Go now and return to your city

of Findias with our thanks and gratitude.

Before you return the Sword to the Lia Fail, go round the perimeter of the Working area once again, this time in a counterclockwise direction, and redraw the circle on the ground. Once you are back at your starting point in the East, return the Sword to the other Greater Magical Weapons at the Lia Fail, announce loudly and proudly that summer has now arrived, and that the feasting, drinking, and games should commence. Light the bonfire which you have prepared and let the celebratory part of the ritual begin with a total emphasis on fun and enjoyment without inhibition or retribution. This part of the ritual will probably go on into the night (if you have planned it well enough) and is a great relief, after the very intense magical part of the ritual. If guests are there from other groups or as individuals, this is a great time to get to know each other, and to cement new friendships and partnerships.

Technical Points

This is clearly very much a group Working, and an open-air Working. It is possible to perform it satisfactorily on your own if you have to, by carrying out all of the main parts, as detailed above, and then following the part for a man or woman, depending upon what physical sex you are. It will not be possible to feel, on the physical level, the experience of your partner, but this part can be experienced by the use of the visual imagination in an Otherworld journey. The celebratory part will also have to be quite different, but how that is actually carried out will depend entirely upon the tastes and preferences of the individual.

If you are organising this Working on behalf of a group, it is a good idea to arrange that partners are performing the Lia Fail and the earth-contact parts of the ritual at the same time, so that they can connect with each other immediately after the personal part of their Working is completed. Try to keep a smooth flow of a man on the Lia Fail, woman circling, woman on the ground, man circling, and so on, as this helps the Polarities stabilise, and also gives a satisfying shape and visual aspect to the ritual.

If for any reason it is not possible or practical to use a large, flat stone as the Lia Fail, then the Shield can be taken from the Northern Quarter, once all the Quarters have been opened, and placed in the middle of the Working area. Remember to put it back at the Northern Quarter when you come to the closing stages of the circle Working.

Always remember in any outdoor Working, to leave your Working and play areas clean, tidy, and devoid of any rubbish or damage, once you have completely finished the celebrations. If the festival involves the use of a bonfire, as this Bealtaine festival does, be sure that it is thoroughly extinguished, and any hot ashes are covered over with fresh earth before leaving the site. It is amazing how long the embers of large bonfires remain hot; if any doubt remains as to the safety of the extinguished fire, go back the next day and double-check. This is all part of a healthy and disciplined attitude to magical Work and the Green World. Never be sloppy or careless, and always respect other people's property and the well-being of the environment.

Chapter Fourteen

The Festival of Lughnassadh

The Festival of Lughnassadh was widely celebrated throughout the Celtic world, yet surprisingly few people are familiar with it today. Its importance is indicated in a short passage from *Lebar na hUidhre*, the *Book of the Dun Cow*, the oldest non-ecclesiastical book in Ireland, which states:

> For these were the two principal gatherings that the men of Ireland had: Tara's Feast at every Samhain and at each Lughnassadh the Convention of Taillte. All precept and all enactments which in either of these festivals were ordained by the men of Ireland, during the whole space of that year none might infringe.[1]

Taillte is the present-day Teltown. This name appears with various spellings throughout the legends dealing with Lughnassadh. The date given for its celebration is August first, but as with all the Celtic

---

[1] From *Keating's History of Ireland* by P.S. Dinneen, Irish Texts Society.

festivals, it is an agricultural time-marker, and would have been celebrated only when Green World conditions dictated the time was
right. The agricultural event it marked was harvest time, and the
occasion of the weaning of the lambs and calves from their mothers.
As such, it was carried into later Christian times and celebrated under
a variety of names, its original pagan source having been forgotten.
The most common Christian name for the festival is Lammas, a word
derived from the Anglo-Saxon, *hlafmaesse*, which means "loaf-mass"
or "bread-mass," so named because a mass or feast was commemo-
rated as a thanksgiving for the first fruits of the corn harvest. This
manner of celebrating was carried on in Scotland until recent times.
An account of the festival, as recorded by Alexander Carmichael in
his extremely important work, *Carmina Gadelica*, is as follows:

> The day the people began to reap the corn was a day of com-
> motion and ceremonial in the townland. The whole family
> repaired to the field dressed in their best attire to hail the God of
> harvest. Laying his bonnet on the ground, the father of the fam-
> ily took up his sickle and, facing the sun, he cut a handful of corn.
> Putting the handful of corn three times sunwise round his head,
> the man raised the "Iolach Buana" reaping salutation. The whole
> family took up the strain and praised the God of harvest, who
> gave them corn and bread, food and flocks, wool and clothing,
> health and strength, and peace and plenty. When the reaping
> was finished the people had a trial called "cur nan corran," cast-
> ing the sickles, and "deuchain chorran," trial of hooks. This con-
> sisted, amongst other things, of throwing the sickles high up in
> the air, and observing how they came down, how each struck the
> earth, and how it lay on the ground. From these observations the
> people augured who was to remain single, and who was to be
> married, who was to be sick and who was to die, before the next
> reaping came around.

One of the old reaping blessings, translated from the Gaelic by Carmichael, contains elements of both Christian and pagan belief:

On Tuesday at the feast of the rise of the Sun

And the back of the ear of the corn to the East

I will go forth with my sickle under my arm

And I will reap the cut, the first act.

I will let my sickle down

While the fruitful ear is in my grasp

I will raise mine eye upwards

I will turn me on my heel quickly.

Rightway as travels the Sun

From the direction of the East to the West

From the direction of the North with motion slow

To the very core of the direction of the South.

I will give thanks to the king of grace

For the growing crops of the ground

He will give food to ourselves and to the flocks

According as He disposeth to us.

It is interesting to note that this old rune recommends that the harvest be started on a Tuesday. In a passage from the Battle of Moytura, the god of the Tuatha De Danann, Lugh, asks the Fomhoire king, Breas, when is the best time to plough, to sow, and to reap. In reply, Breas says:

> On Tuesday their ploughing; on Tuesday their sowing the seed
>
> in the field; on Tuesday their reaping.[2]

There is clearly some ancient agricultural symbolism, and perhaps even ritual, hidden in this, which has been lost to us today. Likewise, it will be noted from the above that the sickle played an important part in the old celebrations of harvest carried out by the Scottish Western Islanders. This may be a remnant which has survived in a much watered-down form from the original Celtic festival, part of which involved the slaying of the king with an edged weapon. The agricultural celebration does not really give any indication of the more ancient reasons for the festival.

The word Lughnassadh is derived from the two words Lugh and *nassad*. Lugh is one of the more important gods of the Tuatha De Danann. The word nassad can mean "fair" or "assembly." Lughnassadh can thus be translated as "Assembly of Lugh." Various explanations are given for Lugh's having a fair or assembly at this time of year, and the most common explanation is, to quote from the old-Irish historian, Keating:

> Lugh Lamhfhada son of Cian took the kingship for forty years. It is this Lugh that first instituted the fair of Tailltin, as an annual commemoration of Tailtiu, the daughter of Maghmor, the king of Spain; and she was wife to Eochaidh mac Eirc, the last king of the Fir Bolg; she was afterwards wife to Eochaidh Gharbh, son of

---

[2] Reprinted from *Cath Maige Tuired* by E.A. Gray, Irish Texts Society.

Duach Dall and chief of the Tuatha De Danann. It is by this woman that Lugh Lamhfhada was fostered and educated, until he was fit to bear arms. It is as a commemoration of honour to her that Lugh instituted the games of the fair of Tailltin, a fortnight before Lammas and a fortnight after.[3]

The goddess Tailtiu is very closely linked with the land, and with the concept of sovereignty. It is through her that we first get a glimpse of the true significance of this festival. The fact that she is specifically described as Lugh's foster-mother is also significant, as the giving of children in fosterage was an important social convention and an important magical act. Perhaps the most important legend concerning Tailtiu is one which relates how she spent a year clearing a great plain, now Co. Meath, in order to make the land more fertile for her people. The effort involved in carrying out this huge magical task was so great that she eventually died. Here we have a very clear statement of self-sacrifice to the fertility of the land and of becoming a part of the land itself. Lugh buried his foster-mother in a huge chambered cairn, on the plain which she had cleared, and he ordered games to be started in her honour. The games themselves consisted of a variety of sports and feats of strength, and primarily, horse racing.

Another fair is noted as having taken place at the same time at Cruachan, in celebration of two other Irish heroes, Ailill and Meadhbh, but very little is known of this fair. A third fair was held triennially at Carman, Wexford, at the same time, and seems to have been very similar to the Lughnassadh fair at Tailltin. All of these places are known pre-Christian burial grounds, and this fact, coupled with the legend of Tailtiu's death, gives the fairs a very funereal touch. It may seem odd to us to have such cheerful and rowdy celebrations at a burial ground on the occasion of a death; however, if we remember that the death

---

[3] From *Keating's History of Ireland*, translated by P.S. Dinneen, published by the Irish Texts Society.

in question was in fact the goddess sacrificing herself to increase the fertility and yield of the land, then the emphasis shifts from death and mourning to life and celebration. On a more mundane level, we should consider the ancient Celtic outlook on death and the Otherworld, and remember that these were far-removed from the depressing, gloomy views taken by modern humankind.

The connection with the Otherworld is obvious to any student of Celtic mythology, just by examining Tailltiu's full name, and her father's name, Maghmor, king of Spain. Maghmor (moy-more) literally means "Great Plain," and this was an allusion to the Otherworld, as are references to Spain, which should not be confused with the modern Iberian country. Her two husbands are also significant. Her first, Eochaidh mac Eirc (yochi mak erk), was of the Fir Bolg race, and her second, Eochaidh Gharbh (yochi garv), was of the Tuatha De Danann. The Fir Bolg represent the purely physical level of being, and the Tuatha De Danann represent the purely spiritual. Her husbands, therefore, represent the transition from a purely physical existence to a purely spiritual one. The first name, Eochaidh, means "horse," and this could explain the emphasis on horses and horse racing during these festivals.

According to Keating, and the conclusions drawn from the characters' names, Lughnassadh is a feast celebrating the self-sacrifice of Tailtiu to give greater abundance and yield to Ireland, and the continuation of life after physical death. There is another legend which sheds quite a different light on the festival's original meaning and purpose. This obscure legend is found in a manuscript in the Royal Irish Academy, referred to as D iv 2, folio 82b, the relevant part of which is as follows:

The Refuse of the Great Feast, that is Taillne. It is here that Lug Scimaig proceeded to make the great feast for Lugh mac Ethlenn for his entertainment after the battle of Magh Tuired; for this was his wedding of the kingship, since the Tuatha De Danann made the aforesaid Lugh king after the death of Nuadhu. As to the place where the refuse was thrown, a great knoll was made of it; this was henceforth its name, The Knoll of the Great Feast, or The Refuse of the Great Banquet, that is to say, Taillne.[4]

This story is significant, as it introduces the concept of the king wedding the land, the most important of the Celtic magical tenets. The ritual at this important occasion involved the use of a horse. This leads us to reconsider the meaning of the word nassad and we can begin to see that "fair" or "assembly" may not be the correct translation. This meaning was, in fact, given to the word at a comparatively late date by Cormac, in his Glossary of the ninth century, and later reintroduced by Keating. This meaning, however, cannot be found in any manuscript predating the ninth century. It may well be that Cormac was simply guessing as to its meaning, based on how he found this ancient word used in a purely oral context. The word probably stems from the same root as the Latin word *nexus* which means "tying" or "binding together," a legal obligation. A word found quite frequently in Irish manuscripts, also from the same root, is *ar-nass*, which means "the betrothing of a daughter." Another word of the same origin is *nassa*, which means "a girl already betrothed."

These meanings, together with the fragment of the above legend, would seem to indicate that the real meaning of nassad has to do with brides and weddings. The original meaning of Lughnassadh may be "Lugh's Wedding," or even "Lugh's Bride (or Bride to Be)." This makes a lot more sense, bearing in mind the importance of the king wedding the land, and also explains the very jolly, festive atmosphere surrounding the games. Many more legends exist which contain references to Lugh's wedding the land. Many Irish folklorists have noted that the festival of Lammas was a popular time for young couples to betroth, and that Teltown was a popular place to go to to announce their engagement.

The apparent shift from what was originally a celebration of Lugh's wedding to the later celebration of the first fruits of harvest is

[4] From *A Social History of Ancient Ireland* by P.W. Joyce, Longmans.

not all that surprising. One of the reasons Lugh, or the High King, wed the land was to ensure abundance and plenty, both for the people and the earth itself. This was also reflected in the other two levels of existence—the mental and the spiritual. The one most likely to inspire the common people to celebrate was the physical level, where the hard evidence of a successful mating could clearly be seen. There is also speculation that the celebration of Lughnassadh, falling as it did two weeks before August first, may have been connected with the Summer Solstice, the longest day of the year. While there is no evidence that the Celts celebrated the solstices and equinoxes, it is likely that they recognised the importance of the increasing daylight from an agricultural point of view. Lugh was also very much a solar deity, and it would have been appropriate to allocate some recognition of the longest day of the year at this important agricultural time.

Modern farming techniques have removed the mystery and joy of watching long-buried seeds begin to show above the surface of the soil, and grow, nourished by the sun, until ready for harvesting and eating. We can no longer celebrate the festival of Lughnassadh with the same intensity of feeling with which the Celts did, but there is no reason to prevent us from celebrating on the mental and spiritual levels, for there the cultivation and nourishment is entirely our own. It is up to each individual to reap what he or she will on these levels, according to individual lifestyle, outlook, and philosophy. If a good "crop" can be nurtured on these two levels, and hopefully the third as well, then celebrate and perform your own festival of Lughnassadh, your own Wedding-to-the-Land-Feast.

RITUAL WORK

The Lughnassadh Ritual

The reason for this festival and ritual is as a harvest celebration, on the physical level. It is also an acknowledgement of work in the Otherworld carried out over the past three months between the High King and the Sovereignty of the Land to produce the fruits and grains which are now evident. It is the time of year when your magical Work should be showing fruitful signs, and starting to become real in your day-to-day world. (This is another reason why at Samhain you should think very carefully over what you are going to write on your card. The objectives you have for the year to come should be realistic and attainable.)

You should also reflect on how the cooperation in the physical world between the High King and the Sovereignty of the Land relates to you personally. If you are a man, consider how you have acted, especially toward the Green World, since Bealtaine. If you are a woman, consider how you have reacted to your own spirituality, and your own powers of giving. Are you satisfied? Could you have done better? What are you going to do about it now?

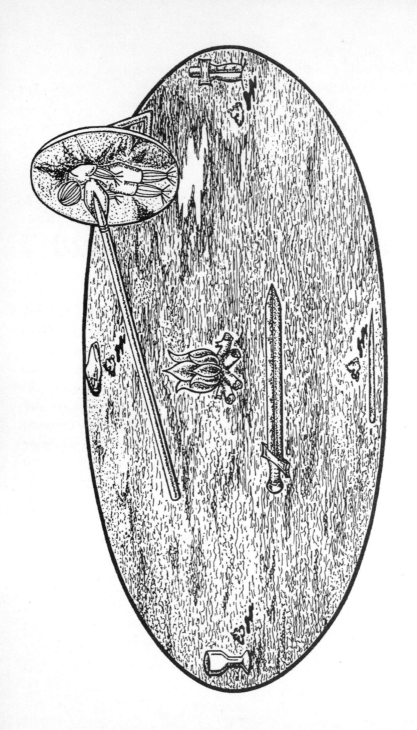

Ritual Working Area for the Festival of Lughnassadh

Part of the Working is to preserve the spirit of the Green World—of the growing things—and to keep it safe over the dark months of winter until the spring, when it can be released safely to once more fertilise and activate the sleeping earth forces. The effects of this ritual carry on well past the day of its performance, as do all of the rituals and Workings you will be performing.

Preparation

This is another outdoor ritual, and choosing and preparing a suitable site is once again necessary. Using the same site you used at Bealtaine and Samhain will help you to build a link with the forces of the Green World at that particular location. It also helps you to notice the many changes which occur throughout the year in the Green World, as each time you visit the place it will have taken on a totally different appearance and feel. A bonfire is an integral part of the Lughnassadh ritual, so careful preparation will be needed for this aspect, as it was at Bealtaine. This bonfire, however, will be needed at nighttime, and perhaps for several hours, so gather a good supply of dry logs.

This Working requires an important change in mental attitude and emotions. Although it has a joyous and celebratory aspect to it, the main theme of this ritual is death and sacrifice. Consequently, a funereal air tends to take over at some points in the ritual itself. Prepare mentally and emotionally to cushion what could be an upsetting experience.

Some time before the eve of the ritual, cut and construct two corn-dolls—one to represent the High King, the other to represent the Sovereignty of the Land. The latter one will eventually become the corn-doll that is used during the Imbolg celebration. Gathering the corn needed for these two dolls is a significant magical act in itself, and should be handled as such. If corn is not available, then dolls can be made from reeds, or even long, stiff grasses. The important point is that they should be made from plants, and not from human-made fibres. The dolls do not need to be elaborate, but they should be clothed and decorated in such a way as to easily distinguish the High-King doll from the Sovereignty-of-the-Land doll. Remember that one corn-doll will need to be stored until Imbolg, and then hung in the house for a full year, so it needs to be put together well enough to last for at least eighteen months.

Equipment Needed for the Ritual

Robes (dark ones if possible), four Lesser Magical Weapons, Spear, Sword, a large cup or chalice, two corn-dolls, a wooden board or target, candles, matches, bonfire fuel, newly baked loaf, red wine, food, and drink.

Place and Timing

You will need an outdoor area big enough to accommodate a large Working area with bonfire. This can be the same site as used for earlier rituals. The preparation should start toward dusk on the eve of Lugh-nassadh. The ritual itself should be started shortly before midnight. The original timing of the festival would have been to coincide with the reaping of the last sheaf at the end of the harvest, but as very few of us today grow and reap our own grain, and as natural growing cycles have been severely altered by the use of artificial fertilisers, starting the festival on the evening of the thirty-first of July is quite acceptable.

The Ritual Itself

Strictly speaking, the ritual starts with the cutting of the corn to be used to make the corn-dolls. This act should be carried out with due reverence, and in the correct frame of mind. If you are part of a group, then the whole group should participate in the gathering of the corn to make the dolls. Put on your robes and build and light the bonfire in the middle of what will be your Working area. Leave on the ground next to the bonfire everything other than the food and drink you have brought to eat later, which can be stored away from the Working area.

It may be some hours between lighting the bonfire and commencing the ritual proper, depending upon how light the evening is, how cold the air is, and so forth. The time can be spent discussing any important or impending group Work, making plans for the fast-approaching dark half of the year and, especially relevant to Lughnassadh, examining partnerships and relationships.

This is the traditional time for new engagements to be announced, and for existing marriages to be reinforced and publicly stated. Any such business can be carried out as the evening grows darker, and the time approaches for the ritual to commence in full. Remember to keep an eye on the bonfire and keep it well-fuelled. Toward midnight, collect everything you are going to need during the Working. Set up the board or target as close as possible to what will be the perimeter of your Working area. Spend a moment or two stilling your mind and preparing mentally and emotionally for the ritual which is about to begin.

Take the Sword from the centre and go to the Northern Quarter. Draw out on the ground, in a clockwise direction, the full extent of your Working area. Make this as big as is practical. Return the Sword to the centre, next to the bonfire, and take up your Lesser Magical Weapons. Go to the Northern Quarter and open that Quarter as you did during the Bealtaine ritual. Go around to all the Quarters, in a clockwise direction, calling upon each appropriate guardian and Element for help and protection (refer to the Bealtaine Working in Chapter Thirteen). Leave each Lesser Magical Weapon at its Quarter, and return to the centre when you have finished. As each individual goes around, one by one opening their own Quarters and calling for protection and assistance, the rest of the group should visualise each guardian coming forth, and should keep in mind the solemnity of this Working.

The men then take the newly baked loaf and carry it in a group around each Quarter, as if in a triumphant procession carrying the spoils of battle and displaying them to a waiting crowd. The bread represents the powers of the Elements combining with the Sovereignty of the Land and with the High King. Stop at each Quarter, and thank the appropriate Element for playing its part in producing the grain that was grown and cut down to be milled and baked into this loaf. Think about this whole process beforehand, and identify the various stages involved in the growing of the grain, the harvesting, the preparing, and baking of the flour. Think about how the element of Earth has played a very obvious

and important part in this process; how Fire warmed and fed the growing grain, and baked it in the oven; how Water gave life to the grain while
in the soil; how Air blew away the unwanted parts of the grain during
the threshing process, and expanded within the grain in the oven to form
the loaf. Construct an appropriate rune, or rhyme, for each Element,
describing what part it played and thanking it for so doing. Before going
on to the next Quarter with this powerful symbol, a small piece of the
bread should be broken off and left at that Quarter. Once all the Quarters
have been visited, and all the runes and thanks spoken, return with what
is left of the loaf to the centre.

The women then take up the wine in a suitably sized cup or chalice, and go in procession around the Quarters, thanking the Elements for
playing their parts in producing the grapes and other ingredients which
went into making the wine. This wine is the blood produced by the uniting of the Elements, the Sovereignty of the Land, and the High King. A
small amount of wine should be poured onto the earth at each Quarter,
before moving on to the next one. Once all the Quarters have been visited, and all the appropriate words said and feelings expressed, return
again to the centre. Each woman should then take a turn at, first, drinking from the cup, and then offering it to one of the men. He should take
a sip from the cup, which the woman is still holding, break a piece of
bread, take a bite, and offer the rest to the woman.

Once she has taken the bread, she should then pass the cup to the
next woman, who will repeat the process with the next man, and so on,
until everyone has drunk of the wine and eaten of the bread. Any words
which may arise spontaneously in the mind during this sharing should
be spoken. Try to realise the significance and importance of this sharing
of bread and wine as it is taking place. Try to perform this very important part of the ritual with solemnity, and at a slow, steady pace. Realise
as you eat the bread and drink the wine that you are taking within your
own body the full potential of the Four Elements, who have worked so
hard together to produce them. Realise, on a higher level, that you are
also taking into your own body the physical-level manifestation of the
spiritual aspects of both the High King and the Goddess of Sovereignty.

These are weighty considerations, and should be thought over well, both before the ritual and as it is actually taking place.

Once all have eaten and drunk, and the empty wine chalice has been returned to the centre of the Working area, take the corn-doll representing the High King and place him on or next to the target, which should be set up in one corner of your Working area (which is why it was suggested that you make your Working area as large as possible). Go back to the centre and stand in silence, looking upon your High King and relating his powers and abilities to your own. Think over how he has acted during the preceding year. Was it a good year? Was it a fruitful one?

Realise that the High King, from this point of view, is really your own Higher Self. Any faults or criticisms you have about the past year are really directed at yourself, and indicate areas upon which further Work will be necessary. Realise also, on a practical level, that the physical High King only rules as long as the people let him. The ordinary people, you and I, have the right to take that kingship from him, and even to kill him, if need be, in order to ensure the fertility of the land. This is what you are about to do. Think over his role in fertilising the land and ensuring it produces the grain necessary to keep us all alive. Consider the fact that this has now happened, and that this High King has fulfilled his function.

In silence, and with respect and dignity, take the Spear from beside the bonfire, steady yourself, and throw it as hard as you can at the High King, killing him, and pinning him to the board on which he rests. Go forward, remove the Spear, and hand it to the next person, man or woman, standing by the bonfire. He or she then throws the Spear at the High King as hard as he or she can, and repeats the process, until all present have thrown the Spear, and accepted equal responsibility for sacrificing the High King. Once all have taken their throw, and the Spear has been returned to the centre for the final time, spend a moment or two gazing upon the broken and twisted body of the High King. Realise how gladly we accept the fruits of the field, without thinking about how the grain is put through a similarly destructive process to give us our daily bread.

Take the body of the High King and throw it on top of the bonfire. Stand in silence and watch as the remains burn away to nothing. Realise that what has taken place is a necessary thing, and an event which is occurring all the time in the Green World around you. Realise that, just as everything in the Green World is eventually reborn, so, too, will the High King be made alive, vital, and fertile at the Bealtaine ritual of the following year. Once there is nothing left of the High King, take the corn-doll representing the Sovereignty of the Land, and place her beside the target. Take the Spear (which only a moment ago was used as an instrument of death) and lay it on the ground in front of her, to show that she is to be honoured and protected.

Each person can now go back around the Quarters, starting in the North and moving counterclockwise, thanking the appropriate guardian for coming forth and helping (again, refer to the text of the Bealtaine ritual in Chapter Thirteen). Each person picks up his or her Lesser Magical Weapons, and then, once all have proceeded around the Quarters and are back in the centre, take the Sword and retrace on the ground the circle describing the perimeter of your Working area. As always when closing, do this in a counterclockwise direction.

The rest of the night should be spent in a good traditional funeral wake, with feasting, drinking, singing, and general merrymaking, all the time under the watchful eye of the corn-doll of the Sovereignty of the Land. The final act of this Lughnassadh ritual is to put the corn-doll somewhere in the house, where it will be safe and free from disturbance. Leave her there until she is needed at Imbolg. Realise that, at this stage, she represents the sleeping spirit of the life forces of the Green World, which are preparing to go under the ground for the dark winter months until they are called forth once again in the spring.

Technical Points

The bonfire can be lit any time during the evening before the actual Working begins, for purely practical reasons—to give light and heat during what may be a dark and cold night. Remember that the earlier you light it, the more fuel you will need.

It is ideal for everyone taking part in the ritual to have had some practice in spear throwing. If this is not possible, or if the physical size of your Working area makes throwing the Spear impractical, substitute holding the spear for actually throwing it, and pushing it into the heart of the corn-doll without the need to let go. It also may not be practical to start the ritual at midnight, and this, of course, is not vital. You should always be practical and realistic in these matters.

I have deliberately not given you any words as examples of what to say when passing around the bread and wine. Such words are important, and can only be composed by the participants according to how they are relating to what is happening within themselves at that time. If, at any other point, anyone feels like making a relevant statement or rune, then he or she should do so. It is always better to say spontaneously what pops into your mind or heart than to stick to pre-scripted words composed by a third party, which may not feel right at the actual time of saying them.

As with the other rituals given in this book, this ritual can be Worked alone, but if at all possible, it should be Worked in the company of like-minded friends or relations, as this adds so much to it. Do not let restrictions of numbers put you off, though; go ahead even if you are alone. It is the act of performing the ritual and the intention behind it which is important, and not how colourful or busy it looks.

Finally, it should be noted that some people can become very upset during the ritual when it comes to the part involving the slaying of the High King. It is a good idea for all those who are going to participate in the Working to sit down together some time beforehand and discuss fully what is going to happen and what it all means, in order to prepare for this. Even with this wise precaution taken, some people may become upset when it comes to throwing the Spear. This is because, during any magical ritual, your mental and spiritual levels come much farther into consciousness than normal, and you find yourself in a very heightened and aware state. Any symbolic acts performed while in this state will be much more powerful and meaningful. It is no easy task to ask someone to kill in cold blood, which is what this boils down to, although on a symbolic level here. If someone does react emotionally, it is actually a good thing and should not be discouraged. Often people who react like this find that as soon as they have thrown the Spear, there is an enormous release of emotional tension, and they suddenly feel much better. They

realise the full significance of what they have done and just how necessary it was. If this happens, then the person involved knows conclusively
that the Working, at least from their point of view, has been powerful
and successful.

Section Six

Magical Weapons and Working Areas

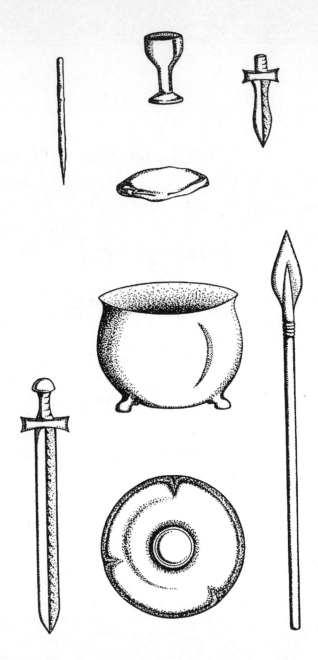

Lesser and Greater Magical Weapons

Chapter Fifteen

How to Choose
and Dedicate
Your Own Weapons

Much has been said throughout this book about Magical Weapons and their use during ritual. This section will take a brief look at how to choose your Weapons, and how to prepare them for use. Perhaps it would be more accurate to say we shall take a look at how your Weapons will *choose you*, for that is closer to the way it works. First, it is necessary to clearly define in your mind just what these Weapons are, and for what they are to be used.

Some people refer to these basic instruments of magical Working as Magical Tools, preferring not to use the word Weapon, due to its implications of violence and aggression. I prefer the word Weapon, because this is clearly what these various objects are. The instruments used under the Celtic system were developed and devised by warriors. You should not let your modern understanding of war and warriors influence the way you look upon the ancient Celtic warriors; there is simply no comparison. How you choose to refer to your own instruments, however, is entirely up to you. The important thing is that you relate to them on all three levels.

Note that when I refer to the Weapons, I always use capital letters. This is to show that I am not referring to the ordinary, everyday objects which bear the same names, and to show respect while indicating that I am writing about something greater than simple arms or pieces of crafted metal. The respect with which you treat these important tools is vital to building a good Working relationship with the forces and energies you will eventually channel through them.

The basic Magical Weapons used under this tradition are split into two groups—the Lesser Magical Weapons and the Greater Magical Weapons. The Lesser group consists of the Knife, Wand, Chalice, and Stone; these are your personal Weapons. The Greater Weapons consist of the Sword, Spear, Cauldron, and Shield, and belong to a group, or an individual Working within a group. It can be seen that the Greater Weapons are larger versions of the Lesser Weapons.

Choosing your own Lesser Magical Weapons is a deceptively simple act, which should carry with it a great deal of thought, dedication, feeling, and intuition. Thought comes into play as soon as you decide to collect your Magical Weapons. At that moment, you will set in motion a chain of events which may take months to reach its conclusion. You should be aware of this. Although you will not have actively performed any magical act at that particular instant, you *will* have created the desire within yourself to find and dedicate your own Magical Weapons. This is a powerful magical act, as is any act of creation. From that moment forward, it is important to always think upon your (as yet unfound) Magical Weapons as a part of you. Do not think of them as some remote, unidentified objects which you hope to stumble across one day. Think of them more as objects which you have temporarily mislaid, and which you are now consciously seeking. This will have the effect of attracting the correct Magical Weapons to you, and of forming a strong emotional link with them, before they are even recognised. This emotional link will be very important.

Dedication in finding your Magical Weapons occurs when you become despondent or depressed because your search seems unsuccessful. You may lose confidence in your ability to find them, and start to believe you are going about things in the wrong way. There is always a certain amount of testing in these Magical Workings. The test of finding your Magical Weapons is patience. The newcomer to these magical arts is always wanting to learn more, do more, and experience more. One of the first things which must be learned is patience, and allowing things to take their own time.

It is true that some people may find their Magical Weapons very quickly, and never experience the test of patience, but this is very rare. From the moment you formulate the desire to collect a set of Magical Weapons, you are on trial. You are being monitored by those beings who control the power behind these instruments, and they will only make them available to you if they see within you a genuine desire to obtain and use them properly. This is dedication. Think about this and your motives for wanting a set of Magical Weapons. (Is it so you have some impressive looking objects to show off to your friends? Or is it so you have a set of powerful tools which you can eventually learn to use for the betterment of yourself and everything else on the planet?)

Feeling and intuition come into play once you come across potential Magical Weapons. I say "potential" because not every knife you find will be suitable for magical Working, and not every cup will be acceptable as a Magical Chalice. There are certain physical attributes each object must have before it should even be considered as a likely candidate. Again, the main test is feeling and intuition. If an object looks perfect for the job, or has been found in just the right way, but it does not feel right, or your intuition says there is something unidentifiably wrong with it, then it should be discarded. The final and ultimate test in choosing Magical Weapons must always be the way you feel toward them. This is why I said that, as soon as you decide to collect a set of Magical Weapons, you should look upon them as already being yours, but temporarily mislaid somewhere. If you look for them with this attitude, then as soon as you find them, you will know instinctively that they are yours.

So, just how do you find them? There are many different ways, and as always, no one way is right, and no one way is wrong. The way I shall suggest is the way I was taught to find mine, and is a way I have seen used successfully many times. First of all, I would suggest that it is a good idea to concentrate on one Weapon at a time. This helps you focus your thoughts and feelings exclusively on one object until it is found, as opposed to looking here and there for four or eight objects simultaneously. The best order in which to look for them is Stone, Wand, Knife, and Cup. This can be followed later by Shield, Spear, Sword, and Cauldron, if you are needing a set of Greater Magical Weapons. The reason I suggest this particular order is that the Stone represents this world, the basis upon which everything else will eventually be built. It is only by understanding the forces, stresses, and strains of this world, that you will be able to come to an understanding of the higher forces, stresses, and strains of the Otherworld. By seeking out your Stone first, you are seeking out the powers and energies of this world, and are literally being forced to take a closer look at the very earth upon which you walk.

The Wand represents the Will of the magician, and this is always the most important part of any Working—the Will to carry it through despite the difficulties. One unexpected difficulty you may come up against is people's attitudes toward you when you start looking for your Wand. Why do you want such an object? What do you mean, you are "just looking for a straight piece of wood to use"? Use for what? This interest in your actions may sound a bit unlikely, but when you start to concentrate on anything in a magical way, it can become so engrossing that you do not realise you are bringing yourself to the attention of others. It will take a lot of will power to carry this part of your quest through successfully without resorting to lies to avoid awkward questions, and to keep going even when all avenues seem to have been exhausted. This may help you to understand the much-misunderstood subject of occult secrecy, but it is no more than common sense: If your actions are likely to cause unwanted curiosity in others, then be discreet, and do not talk about what you are doing.

The Knife represents the power of the magician, your ability to wield the forces invoked during magical Workings. This can be achieved once you understand the powers of this world, and once you have developed sufficient will power to deal with these forces safely and effectively. This stresses the need to look for your Stone and *then* your Wand, and to understand exactly what they represent before you go on to find your other Magical Weapons. Again, be discreet when looking for your Knife, as it will not be so easy to explain why you should suddenly want such an object. This discretion will be a good test of your power to handle these mundane situations. This is the real energy of the Knife. Learn to use it before you even find it.

The Cup is the symbol of sharing the common good. All magical Workings, no matter how personal they may seem to be, will eventually be shared with someone or something else, either of this world or of the Otherworld. If a magical act is only of advantage to the magician, then it is a totally selfish act. The powers and energies of this world and the Otherworld are given freely and equally to all who know how to recognise them and handle them. To turn this free giving into a selfish act is an abuse of these natural energies. The Cup symbolises the completion of the Work and the sharing of its fruits. Keep this in mind as you search for your lost Cup. Look for it with love, and with the intention of passing it around and sharing its contents with all and sundry. This will attract it to you all the quicker, and will help to establish in your mind exactly what it should be used for, before you have the chance to put it into practice.

The Greater Magical Weapons represent exactly the same things, but on a higher, or group level. It is not everyone who will be suited to group Working, and it is not everyone who will feel the need to collect the Greater Magical Weapons. If you are a member of a group, you may not need such Weapons, as they may already be held by the group. As always, let your intuition decide. Just remember, if you do decide to collect a set of Greater Magical Weapons, they should be used as group Weapons, and not left to gather dust in a cupboard. There is a responsibility when you take stewardship of a set of Magical Weapons—Lesser or Greater—they must be looked after, cared for, loved, and above all, used.

Finding Your Magical Weapons

Your Stone should be flat, six or so inches in diameter, and not too heavy to carry, but wide enough for you to rest your feet on during meditations or Otherworld journeys. If at all possible, it should be taken from a ford in a river or from between the upper and lower reaches of the tide on a beach. Both of these places are important in-between areas, which are referred to so often in the legends. Similarly, it should be looked for at dawn or dusk, the in-between times of the day and night, and to make things perfect, at either Bealtaine or Samhain, the in-between times of the year. Look at as many stones as you can. Pick them up. Feel them. Study them. Consider how you like them as objects. Let your intuition tell you which is the right one for you. Once you have identified it, do not look for others "just in case" there may be a better one lying a little farther ahead. To do so is to deny your own intuition—not a good start in such an important venture!

Your Wand should be sought out in much the same manner, except woodlands are the places to look. A good and practical Wand should be relatively short, about eight or nine inches, straight, and come from a rowan, hazel, yew, or ash tree. At this stage, the type of tree chosen does not really matter. Fallen wood is suitable, if it has not rotted so far as to be soft and crumbly. There is no harm in taking a short piece off the tip of a branch of a living tree, if no alternative can be found. Should you choose to do this, however, it is vital that you spend some time close to the tree, explaining to it what you are about to do and why you are doing it. If you keep in mind the Celtic belief that everything on the planet is inextricably linked with everything else, you will realise that there is nothing harmful, malicious, cruel, or unacceptable about such an act. You are, in essence, cutting a piece from your own body. The fact that the piece of wood is eventually going to be used to direct and control the forces of the Green World should also be explained to the tree. No harm will be done if this is carried out with the correct motives, and with due respect and explanation.

Once you have found your Wand, you may carve it if you wish, or simply leave it as a natural-looking piece of wood. Should you choose to carve it, I would suggest that you do not include astrological signs, Egyptian hieroglyphs, non-Celtic god or goddess names, or anything which is not of the Celtic tradition. All of the rituals and exercises described in this book are from the pure tradition, and it is not a good idea to introduce symbols, names, or signs from other traditions. It should also be kept in mind that your Wand will be held aloft, carried around circles, and waved in the air as the occasion demands. It is for this reason that I suggest you keep your Wand short. It will be far more manageable, and far safer than attempting to manipulate a great, long pole which may look impressive, but which is totally impractical and can utterly ruin the flow of a good ritual.

Your magical Knife cannot be found among the growing things of the Green World, so you must resort to looking in more mundane places. Traditionally, your Knife and your Sword should be won by combat, but today it is quite acceptable to pay for a suitable Knife with money which you have earned honestly. To earn money, you must give up your own time and effort in the service of someone else—quite an acceptable sacrifice to make. A good Knife should be of the dagger type, with a double-edged blade, which should be without engraving or marking. It is a good idea to obtain a new Knife which has never been used before. You may come across some perfectly splendid Knives in antique stores, but the problem with old and used Knives is that you do not know their histories and cannot tell how they have been used. A virgin Knife is far preferable to an older Knife with a dubious background. It should also be a real Knife, capable of cutting solid objects, as opposed to a symbolic Knife, which does not have an edge and which cannot be used in practice.

Your Cup should be of silver or silver plate, and be of the chalice type (with a straight stem and bulb-type opening), again without engravings or markings unless you choose to impose your own. Traditionally, the Cup is given in love, and if you have such a Cup given by a loved one, this would be ideal. The giving-in-love aspect can be equated with the giving of your own time and effort to earn money with which to buy a suitable Cup. Remember that the Cup symbolises the completion of this part of the Work. A hasty decision should not be made as to a suitable container. Let your intuition decide. You will be surprised at just how easily and how quickly suitable Magical Weapons become available, once you set your mind and heart to look for them, despite earlier upsets and disappointments.

The above comments apply equally to the Greater Magical Weapons. If you are capable of making any of these larger implements as a joint venture within the group then do so. To have each member of the group contribute a part to each Weapon will give them both more power and a much more personal aspect for the group as a whole. If making them is not practical or possible, then a group effort to buy suitable Weapons is perfectly acceptable.

Whereas the Stone and Wand can be found in the Green World, it is not feasible to find a Shield or a Spear there. The group will have to resort to the likes of military dealers or the manufacturers of replica weaponry. Again, try to avoid pieces whose history is unknown or which bear any sort of engraving or insignia. Take your time, for the correct Magical Weapons will eventually turn up.

Cleansing and Consecrating Your Weapons

Once you have found your Magical Weapons, the next step is to cleanse and consecrate them to make them ready for use. The cleansing process is twofold: First, clean each Weapon on the physical level. Scrape off any dirt or encrustations sticking to your Stone. Remove the bark from your Wand, and smooth down any rough bits of wood at the ends. Polish your Knife, and remove any stains or tarnish. Clean your Cup thoroughly, and rub it until it shines. The second cleansing is carried out by the forces of the Green World—Earth, Water, Fire, and Air—and is on a higher level, removing dirt which is not physical. The process for the Lesser Magical Weapons is very simple, but demands a certain amount of time and attention.

Each Weapon must be handed over to the forces of the Green World for a period from dawn until dusk, or dusk until dawn. This is done by digging a hole in the earth large enough to accommodate all of your Lesser Magical Weapons. This should be in the place where you intend to do your outdoor rituals, or if such a place has not yet been decided, at some other wild spot where the hand of humankind has not left too noticeable a scar on the landscape. Starting at dusk, place each Weapon carefully and lovingly in the ground, and cover them over with the earth from the hole. Leave them there overnight. As they lie in the earth during the hours of darkness, you should imagine the powers of the Earth Working steadily to remove and break down any influences attached to them which could be harmful, or which are no longer necessary, and which should rightfully be returned to the earth, as all things eventually are. At dawn, you should carefully recover them for the next stage.

The next cleansing is by Fire, and will require a bit more effort on your part. Construct an open fire immediately after removing your Magical Weapons from the earth, and have it ready to receive them. This fire should be made from fallen wood, and from many different types of wood. Once it is lit, you should carefully pass each Weapon through the flames as often as possible, all the time visualising unwanted and outworn influences being burned away. How long this takes is up to you, and depends upon how large a fire you have constructed. Once you feel each Weapon has had due cleansing, or once the fire has burned out, each Weapon should be laid out on the ground in such a way that it receives maximum sunlight for the rest of the day. Leave them there until dusk. Again, spend this time visualising the burning and cleansing power of the sun removing all unwanted influences and energies.

Return at dusk and collect your Fire-cleansed Magical Weapons. Take them to a source of fresh, running water, and lay them in the bed of the stream so that the water flows the length of the Knife and

Wand, and into the mouth of your Cup. Again, spend the night imagining the flow of the water washing away that which is outworn and unnecessary, and purifying each Weapon with its cleansing action. Return at dawn and retrieve the well-washed Weapons.

The final act of cleansing is carried out by the powers of Air. This is done by hanging the Magical Weapons from a tree or bush so they swing freely, and are blown and tossed as the winds and breezes dictate. Leave them suspended thus until dusk, and all the while see in your mind's eye your Magical Weapons being cleansed of the final traces of anything unwanted or unneeded which may still be clinging to them. Retrieve them at dusk, and put them away in a place kept aside for them, until such time as you are called upon to use them in an act of magic.

The cleansing and consecrating of the Greater Magical Weapons is symbolically the same, but is carried out differently in practice. It would be impractical to bury, burn, immerse, and suspend such large objects as Shields, Spears, Swords, and Cauldrons, but you can simulate this process in a ritual situation. As with all rituals, it is the intention which is the important part, and not necessarily the means by which it is carried out. The intention of this ritual is to cleanse and consecrate your Greater Magical Weapons, and that is what should be kept in mind throughout the Working.

The exact form of the ritual is entirely up to each group, just as each group has its own way of Working. These Greater Magical Weapons symbolise the power of the group, and, therefore, it is apt they should be consecrated in the way the group feels best and most appropriate. I would suggest that, as a basis for such a Working, the following simple guidelines should be adhered to: All members of the group should be given the opportunity to hold each Greater Magical Weapon at least once. All members should be given the opportunity to use their own personal Lesser Magical Weapons to cleanse and consecrate each Greater Magical Weapon in whatever manner they deem appropriate. The person who is given custody of the Greater Magical Weapons by the group must let all members know where the

Weapons will be kept when not in use, and how they can be accessed. It is traditional for groups to give their group Weapons names. These names should be decided upon and agreed to by all members of the group, and should not be revealed to anyone outside the group.

If the above suggestions are followed with sincerity, integrity, and dedication, then you should have a Working set of Magical Weapons which will last you a lifetime, and which will become more powerful the more they are used. It goes without saying that these tools, whether Greater or Lesser, are not objects of curiosity, and should not be displayed to all and sundry; nor should they be used for mundane tasks such as chopping firewood, or as props in the local drama group's play. Treat them with respect on all three levels, and they will become the most valuable asset you have.

Chapter Sixteen

An Indoor Working Area

This chapter is for the benefit of those of you who are unable to perform these rituals and exercises outdoors. It is preferable to get into the habit of Working in the open whenever possible, but I acknowledge that there will be circumstances which make this practice impossible for some people. This should not deter you from persevering with your Workings, and the following guidance may be of benefit to you in these circumstances.

The main point behind any Working area—indoors or out—is that it is a special place, and should always be regarded as such. It should never be allowed to become just another part of the country-side or just another room in your home. It is your attitude toward these places, and how you approach them, which makes them special places of real power. The correct attitudes can be applied to a room in a house just as well as they can be applied to a sacred tree grove.

Those of you who are unable to use a wild, open, countryside site, but who have a garden, may be able to use it just as effectively. A great deal will depend upon the situation of the garden, whether it adjoins another garden, whether it is overlooked by neighbouring houses, and so forth. If you have a secluded garden, or even a secluded area of an otherwise open garden, then this could be put to good use for magical purposes. Use your common sense, though. There is absolutely no point in dressing up in robes and performing elaborate rituals in a garden which is in full view of the nearby road or the gaze of astonished neighbours. This will only serve to ostracise you from your community, and displays a distinct lack of discretion on your part. Care must be taken, even when using secluded gardens, especially if you intend to have a bonfire. Is that acceptable in your neighbourhood, or is it likely to bring complaints and questions from irate neighbours?

If your garden is completely open, it can still be used to learn about the powers of the Green World as you observe the plants, grasses, flowers, birds, and animals in it over a year. Note how the plants change shape and colour. See how different birds visit at different times. Watch what animals appear and when. If at all possible, grow your own vegetables and plant some trees. By nurturing your own food, you will be nurturing a close link with the growing powers of the Green World. This will teach you as much as any magical ritual or Working. It will also help you to understand how our forebears came to recognise the importance of the earth energies and powers. Once you have carefully placed your seeds in the ground and covered them over, you realise that the rest is out of your hands. If the seeds do not germinate and produce edible plants, you starve and die. Planting a few vegetables can help induce this same feeling of awe and wonder which our forebears felt. This is a good link with both the land and with the past, a link which has been lost by those who only buy food from the local store. As always, it is your attitude to these things which will make them come alive and be properly instructive.

For those of you who do not have access to such a garden, it will be necessary to set aside a room, or part of a room, within your home. This need not be elaborate nor unduly large, just a place which is big enough for you to stand upright, and move a few paces in all directions. It should have a good source of natural light, and be a place which can be closed off to the rest of the world. It is important to make sure that you are not interrupted halfway through a ritual. A room which can be locked or shut off in some way is best.

Similarly, telephones or doorbells should be either inaudible in this area, or disabled before Work commences.

The preparation of such a room or area is important, and should be carried out with the same solemnity and sense of purpose that you would assume when carrying out a full ritual. Preparation of the area is a ritual in itself, and a very important one. You will be creating a magical Working area which was not there before, and this act of creation should be seen and understood for what it is. Any such area should be carefully swept clean of all physical level dirt or debris and then left to settle for a while. During the cleaning process, keep your thoughts on what you are doing, and visualise the area or room being cleansed on all three levels. Do not regard this cleaning as simply another household chore, for it is much more than that. Once it has been completely cleaned and cleared of any mundane objects and furniture, spend some time sitting quietly and creating in your mind's eye an image of how this place will develop and grow over the seasons. Think about the many different acts you will carry out here over a full ritual year, and start to develop a sense of the importance of this special place.

Your next step is to fill your area with objects relating to the Irish Celtic tradition. You may have some favourite drawings or paintings depicting Celtic deities, for example. You may have some photographs of favourite or important places in Ireland or other Celtic countries. Place these on the walls in such a way that they become a focal point, but not necessarily a constant distraction. Any paintings or photographs you have taken yourself are good to use. Similarly, any pottery or other handicrafts you have made along Celtic themes will be most suitable. Think carefully on this point of decoration, for it is an important one. Try to incorporate plants and shrubs or anything else that is a living part of the Green World. It is a good idea to rotate and replace any plants over the seasons, with different species which are more appropriate for each season of the year. This will help you to keep in tune with the changes taking place in the Green World outside.

Music can be helpful in creating atmosphere, and the addition of a cassette deck or other form of music player would be a great help. A suggested selection of Celtic recording artists is given at the end of this book. Any of these artists, with their widely different musical styles, would help to create the correct atmosphere. Most classical music is suitable as well, since it seems to transcend the ordinary bounds of nations and countries. The choice as always is yours. Do what you feel is best.

While on the subject of music, it should be noted that although your everyday mundane thoughts and actions should be kept away from this special Working area, there is no harm at all in using it, on occasion—after the Samhain ritual, for example—to hold a *ceilidh* (kay-lay). A ceilidh is a traditional form of in-house entertainment still enjoyed in Ireland and Scotland. It takes the form of a group of friends or relatives playing their own music, telling their own stories, and generally making their own entertainment. Remember that an important aspect of the Celtic tradition is fun and enjoyment. Your Working area can be used for this type of entertainment, should the occasion arise.

It is good practice to keep your Magical Weapons in this place, and preferably in some sort of box or container where they will not be on constant display. This helps create a focus for the powers behind these Weapons, and helps you to focus on the importance of this place. As you use it over the months, you will find things start to attract themselves to it and become a part of it. Things like a feather found while out walking, a stone picked up from a beach, a plant given to you by a friend or loved one, a new picture or musical recording may naturally gravitate toward your special Working area, and can be incorporated into it and become an integral part of it. This will help you to place your individual stamp on the area, and help make it much more personal and important to you. It will also serve to make it a living, constantly changing place, just like everywhere else in the Green World. Change is important, and natural change, as opposed to enforced change, is a good thing to cultivate.

Should you find that you need to permanently leave your home, you must ensure that you dismantle your special Working area carefully and thoroughly, explaining all the time to the powers, energies, and beings which have come to focus there, exactly why you are having to do this. This need not be an unhappy affair, as it is only a reflection of something which is happening constantly in the Green World. It is, nonetheless, important for you to do this, as it helps clear away all previous associations with this particular area. This means that when you set up your next one in your new home, you will not still be mentally, emotionally, and spiritually tied to the old one. Such a tie would be confusing for the beings you will get to know and Work with over the years, who are not tied to physical places as we are. A clean, peaceful, and calm break is what should be achieved.

You should find that the focal point of a special magical area helps you to progress along the Celtic spiritual and magical Path all the quicker. Those of you who are unable to accomplish this, by reason of physical disability or by the sheer lack of space, need not despair. Such places and techniques are only aids to concentration. If you can concentrate on the Work at hand, and if you can adopt the attitudes described in this book, then you will have a sound enough footing upon which to start your own journey along the Celtic spiritual Path. Take that important first step—and don't look back.

Glossary

The following definitions are provided to clarify the words I use in this book, along with other mainly Irish words which are common, and likely to be found in other books on the Celts. A rough guide to pronunciation is given for the less-obvious words. Some of these may differ from more popularly held definitions, and some readers may disagree with some of them, but I give them to dispel any confusion arising from different interpretations of their use in this work.

Aided (oy-ded). A violent death. One of the main classes of legends. The titles of some fourteen of these tales are known, the most famous probably being Aided Con Culaind (oy-ded kon koolan), the Death of Cu Chulainn; Aided Chonchobair (oy-ded kon-ho-var), the Death of Conchobhar; and Aided Fhergusa (oy-ded far-eesh), the Death of Fearghus.

Aisling (ashling). A vision or dream. One of the main classes of legends. The best known is Aislinge in Maic Oic (ashling een mac oac), the Dream of Mac Oc, or, as it is more commonly known, the Dream of Aonghus.

Aithed (oy-ha). Elopement. Another of the main groups of story types. Similar to the group, Tochmarc, but in the case of an Aithed, it is the woman who encourages the elopement, whereas in a Tochmarc, it is the man. The names of twelve Aithedha are known, the most famous being Aithed Deirdrinne re macaib Uislenn (oy-ha deerdrin ra macav ooshlen), the Elopement of Deirdre with the son of Uisnech; Aithed Graine re Diarmait (oy-ha groyn-ya ra jeermit), the Elopement of Grainne with Diarmaid.

Ard Righ (art-ree). The High King. Physical level representative of the spiritual level of his people. The High King had to be without blemish on all three levels because of his immense significance, and was only accepted once he had undergone the test of the Lia Fail, which would cry out beneath the feet of the true candidate.

Baile (bah-li). Frenzy. One of the main classes of tales. Six such tales are known, the most famous and important being Baile Suibhne Geilt (bah-li Sweeney Gaylt), the Frenzy of Mad Sweeney.

Bealtaine (bal-tayn). One of the four major festivals of the Irish Celts. This festival heralded the start of summer and was celebrated at the beginning of the growing season, now standardised to the first of May.

Brehon Laws. The legal and judicial system of the Irish Celts, which is said to take its name from the old word for a judge, *breitheamh* (brehon-ahv). The Brehon Laws are the oldest and most intricate legal system known in Europe, covering every conceivable aspect of day-to-day life; it affected all members of Celtic society, from the peasantry to the High King himself. So intricate and diverse are these laws, that it is suspected they were meant to reflect life as it should have been, as opposed to how it actually was.

Buile. Frenzy. See Baile.

Cath (kah). A battle. One of the main classes of tales. Some twenty battle-tales are known, the most famous being Cath Maige Tured (kah moytura), the Battle of Moytura (for a full examination of the magical content of this legend, see my book *The Irish Celtic Magical Tradition*); Cath Maige Mucrame (kah moy mucrame), the Battle of Moy Mucrame.

Celts/Celtic. Originally the Celtic countries and peoples covered a vast area of Europe and parts of Asia, but for the purposes of this book, I am only concerned with the peoples and practices found in ancient and modern Ireland, and the West of Scotland. See the opening sections for a brief history of the Celtic people.

Compert. Conception. One of the main classes of tales. At least five conception tales are known, the most famous being Compert Con Culaind (kompert con coolin), the Conception of Cu Chulainn.

Druid. Member of the most important caste in Celtic Ireland. Not the keepers of the Celtic religion, as is usually assumed, but more lawmakers, advice-givers, and magical practitioners. There were also Druidesses in Ireland.

Echtra (ehtra). Adventure, journey to the Otherworld. One of the main classes of tales. Twenty-three different names of Echtra are known, but as with the other tale categories, not all of them have survived. Most of the great heroes have an Echtra named after them. The strangest is Echtra Nera (ehtra nayra), the Adventure of Neara.

Eamhain Abhlach (evain avaloch). One aspect of the Celtic Otherworld believed to be the present-day Isle of Arran in the Scottish Firth of Clyde. The word Abhlach is pronounced avaloch, and is the original form of the Arthurian Avalon, which of course equates with the same place.

Eamhain Macha (evain maha). Seat of the King of Ulster, the present-day Navan Fort near Armagh in Ulster. Scene of many of the great tales from the epic Ulster Cycle.

Eric. A fine or compensation, especially for killing someone, as defined by the Brehon Laws.

Falias. One of the four magical cities mentioned in The Battle of Moytura and the *Book of Invasions*, where the Tuatha De Danann received magical training before setting off for Ireland. The Lia Fail, the Stone of Destiny, which sat at Tara and cried aloud beneath the feet of the rightful High King, was brought from Falias.

Far-memory. The ability to recall the memory of the ancestors.

Feis (faysh). Feast, or to spend the night (with someone). One of the main classes of tales. The names of thirty-one Feis are known, the most celebrated being Feis Tige Bricrenn (faysh toya Breekrin), the Feast of Bricriu's House.

Fess. Feast. See Feis.

Fidchell (fee-hill). A board game, which seems to have been similar to chess, and was very popular among the Celts. It may have held some magical symbolism, for the word means "wood-knowledge" and it could have been connected in some way to the Tree Alphabet, and the lore of trees as known and used by the druids.

Filidh (feelee). A class of poets whose main function was to praise their patron and to remember and record his or her genealogy. An important person in Celtic society.

Findias. One of the four Otherworld cities where the Tuatha De Danann were taught their magical skills before arriving in Ireland. Nuadhu's sword was brought from this city.

Forbais (fore-baysh). Siege or night watch. See Forfess.

Forfess. Siege or night-watch. One of the main classes of tales. The names of nine such tales are known.

Fo Scel (fo shkayl). Lesser Tales. A classification for some of the many different tales a Bard or Druid was expected to remember. See also Prim Scel and Rim Scel.

Geis (gaysh), plural Geasa (gaysha). A prohibition or taboo placed upon someone, usually the High King, which defined what he or she could or could not do. A very important part of many legends and also in the real life of the ordinary Celt. Some geasa were connected with totem animals, some with certain aspects of hospitality, some with journeys and travelling but, whatever the geis concerned, should a person wittingly or unwittingly break it, then certain doom would follow.

Geantraighe (goyn-troy). One of the Three Strains of Music, this one being the Laughing Strain, which made whoever heard it, no matter how depressed or despondent they were, instantly merry and happy.

Glamour. The attraction and illusion of the Otherworld.

Glamoury. The ability to Work magically with Glamour.

Goltraighe (gol-troy). One of the Three Strains of Music, this one being the Weeping Strain, which made whoever heard it instantly start to weep and feel sorrow.

Gorias. One of the four Otherworld cities where the Tuatha De Danann received their magical training before coming to Ireland. From Gorias was brought the spear which Lugh had.

Green World. Equivalent to the more common term *World of Nature,* but including the mineral kingdom as well as the plant and animal kingdoms of this world. A very important, but often neglected, aspect of the Irish Celtic magical tradition.

Guide. A general term used to describe anyone or anything from the Otherworld who appears during an Otherworld journey and offers assistance. Some guides may appear regularly, and you may strike up a real bond of friendship with them, while others may only appear for one particular Working and never be encountered again. They should always be treated with respect and courtesy, and thanked for their assistance.

Imbolg (eem-bolk). One of the four main festivals of the Celts. This festival was celebrated when the ewes started to lactate at the start of the lambing season. The date has now been standardised to the first of February. Seen as the start of spring. Particularly associated with the goddess Brighid.

Immram. A sea voyage literally, to row a boat. One of the main classes of tales. Five titles under this heading are known to us. It is possible that several under the heading Longes—we know the names of eight such tales—may also rightly fall into the category of Immram.

Inner Level. Modern expression used to designate the realms of existence originally referred to as the Otherworld by the Celts. The realms you enter during Pathworkings or Otherworld journeys in which the physical senses play no part.

Irish System/Tradition. The magical, religious, and spiritual beliefs of the early Irish Celts, and the surviving traces and practices of such beliefs as I have defined them within this book.

Lay (lay). A poem, song or short piece of prose.

Lia Fail (lee-ah-foyl). The Stone of Destiny which had been brought from the Otherworld city of Falias, and which stood at Tara. Its function was to declare the true High King of Ireland by screaming aloud when the successful candidate stood upon it. The stone which stands at Tara today is probably not the original.

Longes (lawn-jess). Exile, banishment. One of the main classes of tales. We know the titles of eight such tales, the most famous being Longas mac nUislenn (longes mac ooshlin), the Exile of the Sons of Uisnech. Similar to the other tale-type known as Immram.

Lughnassadh (loo-nassa). One of the four main festivals of the Celts connected to the harvest time. Now standardised to the first of August. Associated with the god Lugh.

Magical Diary. A personal notebook kept to record details of Otherworld journeys or rituals carried out during your Practical Work. It is by keeping such a diary accurately and meticulously that you will be able to gauge your progress and learn in the years to come. The diary can also be used to record any coincidences which occur in your day-to-day life, or any thoughts, realisations, or ideas that may come to you at any time of day or night, which may be of importance later.

Magical Weapons. Also referred to as Magical Tools. There are two sets of Magical Weapons: the Greater Weapons, which are the Spear, Sword, Cauldron, and Shield; and the Lesser Weapons, which are the Wand, Knife, Cup, and Stone. These are the basic implements with which all ritual Work is carried out. The Greater Weapons are used in large, group Workings, usually outside, whereas the Lesser Weapons are used for small, personal Workings either inside or outside. See Chapter Sixteen for details of how to obtain and consecrate these Magical Weapons.

Murias. One of the four Otherworld cities where the Tuatha De Danann were taught their magical skills before they came to Ireland. The Daghdha's ever-full cauldron was brought from here.

Navan Fort. Present day site of Eamhain Macha, King Conchobhar Mac Neasa's royal palace.

Noinden (noyn-dane). A period of days and nights split into either four days and five nights or five days and four nights, which was of more magical significance than it was of practical use. The Curse of the Men of Ulster, in which they became as weak as a woman in labour, is also sometimes given this name.

Ogham (oh-um). Ancient form of writing consisting of various notches across the straight edge of a stick or standing stone. Although by tradition it is closely associated with magic, the only known authentic Ogham inscriptions are all dedications to dead warriors and the like. Said to have been invented by the god Oghma, the god of eloquence. The original Ogham may actually have been a very formalised way of asking and answering questions. Associated with the Tree Alphabet.

Ollamh (oll-ahv). Highest grade of poet in Ireland. Their training was very long and arduous, and by the end of it, they were expected to have memorised the hundreds of different main stories, plus hundreds more lesser stories. The word is still used in modern Irish to mean "professor."

Orgain (awr-gain). Murdering, plundering, or destruction. One of the main classes of tales. Forty-two different titles are known under this heading. The better known ones are Orgain Dinn Rig (orgain jin ree), the Destruction of Din Rig; Orgain Maic Da Tho (orgain mac dah-ho), the Destruction of Da Tho's Pig; Orgain Ratha Cruachan (orgain ra-ha Croo-ahan), the Destruction of Cruachan Fort.

Otherworld. The non-physical realms which interlock with this world, but which are not obvious to the physical senses. They can be experienced by using the techniques which are discussed in this book. The world of the deities and non-human beings who inhabit our universe. More often referred to as the Inner Levels nowadays.

Pathworking. The modern term for an Otherworld journey which uses a connected series of images in the visual imagination to help the individual experience or learn important points pertinent to the Irish system as a whole, and/or his or her personal relationship to it. Sometimes also called a guided meditation. The main technique used today by practitioners of most magical disciplines. Strictly speaking, the name Pathworking refers only to a specific technique used by followers of the Qabalistic tradition.

Prim Scel (preem-shkayl). Greater Tales. A classification used for some of the many tales the Bard or Druid was expected to remember. See also Fo Scel and Rim Scel.

Red Branch Cycle. An alternative name for the Ulster Cycle, deriving its name from Craobh Ruadh, the Red Branch (Knights).

Rim Scel (reem-shkayl). Secondary Tales. A short introductory tale to one of the main tales, which was used to explain how things came to be the way they are when the main tale opens. See also Fo Scel and Prim Scel.

Ritual. A predetermined series of movements and words which combine to produce an effect, at one or all of the three levels, either on the individual performing the ritual or on his or her surroundings.

Samhain (sow-in). One of the four major festivals of the Celts, which signified the end of summer and the start of the new year. A very magical time. Nowadays standardised to October 31 and November 1, and celebrated as Hallowe'en. A feast of the dead, and a time for much magic to be Worked for the forthcoming year.

Satire. A short poem pointing out a person's faults or bad characteristics designed to shame that person into changing.

Sidhe (shee). An all-encompassing term, which originally referred to the underground dwellings of the fairy people, but is used here to designate the fairies or non-human Otherworld inhabitants themselves.

Sluagad (shloo-ak). Military expedition. One of the main classes of tales. We know the names of five such tales but it is likely that there were originally many more.

Suantraighe (soon-troy). One of the Three Strains of Music, this one being the Sleeping Strain, which caused all who heard it to fall asleep. See also Geantraighe and Goltraighe.

Tain (toyn). A plundering expedition, usually in the form of a cattle raid. One of the main classes of tales. We know the names of at least fourteen of these raids. The most famous is the great Tain Bo Cuailnge (toyn boh Cooley), The Cattle Raid of Cooley.

Tara. The seat of the High King where the Lia Fail stood. Also given as Teamhair (tah-var). The spiritual centre of Ireland.

This World. The physical world in which we live our conscious lives, and in which we rely on our physical perceptions and senses for information relating to it. Opposite of the Otherworld.

Three Levels. The physical, mental (or emotional), and spiritual aspects of everyone and everything in both this world and the Otherworld, which interlock and combine to give us the universe and all it contains as we know it. The very hub of the Irish Celtic system. Sometimes called the Three Worlds.

Tir (cheer). Land or country. Most of the Otherworld locations visited by heroes during the Immrama tales are described as a series of lands or islands. When the word Tir is given in a place name, it is indicative of that place being in the Otherworld.

Tochmarc (toh-mark). Wooing. One of the main classes of tales. We know the names of fifteen Tochmarca, the most famous being Tochmarc Etaine (toh-mark etain), the Wooing of Etain, and Tochmarc nEmire la Coin Culaind (toh-mark emer lah con coolin), the Wooing of Emer by Cu Chulainn.

Tochomlod (toh-hom-lot). Setting forth, advancing. One of the main classes of tales dealing not so much with mythological happenings, but with the movements of tribes and peoples. We know the names of thirteen such tales.

Togail (toh-kal). Destruction. One of the main classes of tales. We know the names of fourteen of these tales, among them being Togail Bruidne Da Choca (toh-kal broona da hoh-ka), the Destruction of Da Choca's Hostel; and Togail Bruidne Da Derga (toh-kal broona da jarrik), the Destruction of Da Derga's (the Red God's) Hostel.

Torc (torc). A metal collar (usually gold) worn around the neck by Celtic warriors.

Toruidheacht (toh-roo-acht). A pursuit. One of the main classes of tales.

Troscad (trosh-kah). A hunger strike defined in the Brehon Laws as a way of compelling justice. The wronged party would sit outside the house of the accused and refuse to eat until his case was given a full hearing. While the faster was outside the accused was compelled to likewise fast, and so disputes were settled quickly. It is interesting to note that even in very recent years, members of the Republican groups in Ireland have used this same ancient method to demand justice from the British government, although usually with little success.

Bibliography

The Celts

Anderson, Joseph. *Scotland In Pagan Times*, 2 Vols. Edinburgh: Douglas, 1886.

Chadwick, Nora. *The Celts*. London: Pelican, 1971.

Cunliffe, B. *The Celtic World*. London: The Bodley Head, 1979.

Delaney, Frank. *The Celts*. London: BBC Publications, 1986.

Forman, W. & Kruta, V. *The Celts Of The West*. London: Orbis, 1985.

Harbison, Peter. *Pre-Christian Ireland*. London: Thames & Hudson, 1988.

Herm, Gerhardt. *The Celts*. London: Wiedenfield & Nicolson, 1976.

Hubert, H. *The Rise of the Celts*. London: Constable, 1987.

———. *The Greatness and Decline of the Celts*. London: Constable, 1987.

Joyce, P. W. *A Social History of Ancient Ireland*. Harlow: Longmans, 1903.

Keating, Geoffrey. *The History of Ireland*, 4 Vols. London: Irish Texts Society, 1902, 1908, 1914.

Kendrick, T. D. *The Druids*. Largs: Banton Press (Reprints), 1990.

Kruta, V., et al., ed. *The Celts*. New York: Rizzoli, 1991.

Mackenzie, Donald. *Scotland the Ancient Kingdom*. Glasgow: Blackie, 1930.

Mackenzie, W. C. *The Races of Ireland and Scotland*. Paisley: Gardner, 1915.

Markale, Jean. *Women of the Celts*. Paris: Inner Traditions, 1986.

Matthews, J. *Boadicea*. Dorset: Firebird Books, 1988.

Newark, Tim. *Celtic Warriors*. London: Blandford, 1986.

———. *Women Warlords*. London: Blandford, 1989.

Piggot, Stuart. *The Druids*. London: Thames & Hudson, 1985.

Powell, T.G.E. *The Celts*. London: Thames & Hudson, 1983.

Ross, Anne. *Pagan Celtic Britain*. London: RKP, 1967.

———. *The Life and Death of a Druid Prince*. London: Rider, 1989.

Rutherford, Ward. *The Druids*. Wellingborough: Aquarian Press, 1983.

Celtic Mythology

Bellingham, David. *An Introduction to Celtic Mythology*. London: The Apple Press, 1990.

Berresford Ellis, Peter. *A Dictionary of Irish Mythology*. London: Constable, 1987.

Book of Leinster Tain, London: Irish Texts Society, 1969.

Buile Suibhne Geilt, London: Irish Texts Society, 1913.

Caldecott, Moyra. *Women In Celtic Myth*. London: Arrow Books, 1988.

Cath Maige Mucraime, London: Irish Texts Society, 1975.

Cath Maige Tuired, London: Irish Texts Society, 1983.

Cross, T.P. and Slover, C.H. *Ancient Irish Tales*. Dublin: Figgis, 1936.

Delaney, Frank. *Legends of the Celts*. London: Hodder & Stoughton, 1989.

Dillon, Miles. *Cycles of the Irish Kings*. Oxford: Oxford University Press, 1946.

———. *Irish Sagas*. Dublin: Mercier, 1985.

Dillon, M. and Chadwick, N. *The Celtic Realms*. London: Wiedenfield and Nicolson, 1967.

Duanaire Finn, 3 Vols. London: Irish Texts Society, 1908, 1933, 1954.

Fled Bricrend, London: Irish Texts Society, 1899.

Gantz, J. *Early Irish Myths and Sagas*. London: Penguin, 1981.

Gregory, Lady Augusta. *Cuchulainn of Muirthemne*. Gerrards Cross: Smythe, 1984.

———. *Gods and Fighting Men*. Gerrards Cross: Smythe, 1979.

Hull, E. *The Cuchulainn Saga*. London, 1988.

Jackson, Kenneth. *A Celtic Miscellany*. London: RKP, 1951.

Joyce, P.W. *Old Celtic Romances*. London: Kegan Paul, 1879.

Kinsella, Thomas. *The Tain*. Oxford: Oxford University Press, 1986.

MacAlister, R.A.S., trans. *Lebor Gabala Erenn.*, 5 Vols. London: Irish Texts Society, 1938-56.

Maccana, P. *Celtic Mythology*. London: Hamlyn, 1975.

———. *The Learned Tales of Medieval Ireland*. Dublin: Institute for Advanced Studies, 1980.

Matthews, John. *Fionn Maccumhaill*. Dorset: Firebird Books, 1988.

———. *Taliesin: Shamanism and the Bardic Mysteries on Britain and Ireland*. Shaftesbury: Element Books, 1992.

Matthews, John and Matthews, Caitlin. *The Aquarian Guide to British and Irish Mythology*. Wellingborough: Aquarian Press, 1988.

Meyer, Kuno. *Death Tales of the Ulster Heroes*. Dublin: Hodges, 1906.

———. *The Voyage of Bran Son of Febal*. Dublin: Nutt, 1895.

Neeson, Eoin. *First Book of Irish Myths and Legends*. Dublin: Mercier, 1981.

———. *Second Book of Irish Myths and Legends*. Dublin: Mercier, 1982.

O'Grady, S. H. *Silva Gadelica*, 2 Vols. Dublin: Williams and Norgate, 1892.

O'Hogain, D. *Myth, Legend and Romance*. London: Ryan, 1990.

O'Rahilly, T. F. *Early Irish History and Mythology*. Dublin: Institute for Advanced Studies, 1946.

Rees, A. and Rees, B. *Celtic Heritage*. London: Thames and Hudson, 1974.

Rhys, J. *The Hibbert Lectures*. Dublin: Williams and Norgate, 1888.

Rolleston, T. W. *Celtic Myths and Legends*. London: Bracken Books, 1985.

Smyth, D. A. *Guide to Irish Mythology*. Dublin: Irish Academic Press, 1988.

Squire, Charles. *Celtic Myth and Legend*. Henley-on-Thames: Gresham, 1905.

Stewart, R. J. *Celtic Gods Celtic Goddesses*. London: Blandford, 1990.

———. *Cuchulainn*. Dorset: Firebird Books, 1988.

Toraidheacht Dhiarmada Agus Ghrainne. Dublin: Irish Texts Society, 1967.

Williamson, Robin. *The Craneskin Bag*. Edinburgh: Canongate, 1989.

Young, Ella. *Celtic Wonder Tales*. Edinburgh: Floris Books, 1983.

Magic and the Western Mystery Tradition

Ashcroft-Nowicki, Dolores. *First Steps in Ritual*. Wellingborough: Aquarian Press, 1982.

Blamires, Steve. *Irish Celtic Magical Tradition*. Wellingborough: Aquarian Press, 1992.

Carr-Gomm, Philip. *The Elements of the Druid Tradition*. Shaftesbury: Element Books, 1991.

———. *The Druid Way*. Shaftesbury: Element Books, 1993.

Green, Marian. *Magic for the Aquarian Age*. Wellingborough: Aquarian Press, 1983.

———. *Experiments in Aquarian Magic*. Wellingborough: Aquarian Press, 1985.

Hartley, Christine. *The Western Mystery Tradition*. Wellingborough: Aquarian Press, 1968.

Hope, Murry. *Practical Celtic Magic*. Wellingborough: Aquarian Press, 1987.

Knight, Gareth. *The Rose Cross and the Goddess*. Wellingborough: Aquarian Press, 1985.

———. *The Secret Tradition in Arthurian Legend*. Wellingborough: Aquarian Press, 1983.

Matthews, Caitlin. *The Elements of the Celtic Tradition*. Shaftesbury: Element Books, 1989.

———. *The Celtic Book of the Dead*. London: St. Martin's Press, 1993.

Matthews, Caitlin and Matthews, John. *The Western Way*, 2 Vols. London: Arkana, 1985.

Matthews, Caitlin and Jones, Prudence. *Voices from the Circle*. Wellingborough: Aquarian Press, 1989.

Matthews, John. *The Celtic Shaman*. Shaftesbury: Element Books, 1991.

Nichols, Ross. *The Book of Druidry*. Wellingborough: Aquarian Press, 1990.

Sharkey, John. *Celtic Mysteries*. London: Thames and Hudson, 1975.

Spence, Lewis. *Magic Arts in Celtic Britain*. Wellingborough: Aquarian Press, 1970.

Stewart, R. J. *The Underworld Initiation*. Wellingborough: Aquarian Press, 1988.

———. *Living Magical Arts*. London: Blandford Press, 1987.

———. *Advanced Magical Arts*. Shaftesbury: Element Books, 1988.

The Celtic Soul

As An Fhearann. Edinburgh: Mainstream Publishing, 1986.

Campbell, J. F. *Popular Tales of the West Highlands*, 4 Vols. Aldershot: Wildwood House, 1983.

Carmichael, Alex. *Carmina Gadelica*. Edinburgh: Floris Books, 1992.

Danaher, Kevin. *The Year in Ireland*. Dublin: Mercier, 1972.

Evans-Wentz, W. Y. *Fairy Faith in Celtic Countries*. London: Smythe, 1977.

Greene, David. *An Anthology of Irish Literature*, 2 Vols. New York: New York University Press, 1967.

Macleod, Fiona. *The Collected Works*, 7 Vols. London: Heinnemann, 1910.

Matthews, John. *A Celtic Reader*. Wellingborough: Aquarian Press, 1990.

McNeill, F. Marian. *The Silver Bough*, 4 Vols. Edinburgh: Maclellan, 1957.

Merry, Eleanor. *The Flaming Door*. Edinburgh: Floris Books, 1983.

Yeats, William Butler. All Poems and Prose.

Discography

Afterhours. Irish band who are often compared to Planxty (see below) with excellent musicians and singers.

Mary, Frances and the Black Family. Irish family of two sisters and three brothers who have recorded many, many albums as a family, solo and as members of other groups. All very good.

Blackeyed Biddy. A Scottish group who play traditional songs as well as their own compositions. Lively and good fun.

Capercaillie. A Scottish group who perform both ancient and original songs and tunes in Gaelic and English. Very popular. Well worth getting to know.

Fiona Davidson. Scottish harper, singer, storyteller, and Celtic bard. A very powerful performer who clearly knows her stuff, both from this world and from the Otherworld.

The Iron Horse. Scottish band playing contemporary Scottish songs and tunes with a very unique and interesting sound. One of my favourites!

Dougie MacLean. Scottish singer and songwriter who displays a passion not only for the Scottish people and their history but also for their present-day social and political problems.

Christy Moore. Irish singer and songwriter with a very deep passion for his people, country, and culture.

Moving Hearts. Sadly now-disbanded, but their recordings are still available. A unique group who fused traditional Irish music with contemporary jazz. Very influential. A good example of how the Celtic spirit of innovation and experimentation is still very much alive.

The Old Blind Dogs. Scottish group who are rapidly gaining a large following on both sides of the Atlantic. Excellent recordings and outstanding live performances.

Planxty. Another now-disbanded Irish group whose recordings are still available. A traditional group who gave excellent renditions of both instrumental and vocal material, contemporary and traditional.

Runrig. Scottish rock group who play first-class music and compose their own material in both English and Gaelic.

Sileas. Two Scottish harpers who sing and play the clarsach. They combine traditional material with more modern material to produce a very pleasant sound.

Alan Stivell. Very influential Breton harper and singer who has a strong feel and passion for his music and his people.

Sulis Music and Tapes. Produce many musical and magical tapes of a very high standard. Write to BCM Box 3721, London WC1N 3XX

The Tannahill Weavers. One of the stalwarts of the traditional Scottish music scene. They have recorded many fine albums and are always lively and entertaining on stage.

Whistlebinkies. One of the very few Scottish groups who play traditional Scottish music on the old instruments such as the clarsach, highland pipes, snare drum, bodhran, and wooden flute. The singer, Mick Broderick, also carries on the old Celtic storytelling tradition.

Robin Williamson. One of the very few modern-day Celtic bards who plays the harp, sings, writes much of his own material, and produces excellent story tapes as well as excellent music. Write to Robin Williamson Productions, BCM 4797, London, WC1N 3XX or P.O. Box 27522, Los Angeles, CA 90027, for full catalogue and details of live performances.

Journals and Societies

Archaeology Ireland, P.O. Box 69, Bray, Co. Wicklow, Eire. A quarterly journal keeping abreast of what is happening in the world of Irish archaeology. An informative and easy-to-read publication with a nice sense of humour. Worth subscribing to if you wish to mix magical experience with practical knowledge.

Cambrian Medieval Celtic Studies, Department of Welsh, University of Wales, Aberystwyth, SY23 2AX, Wales. An excellent if somewhat academic journal covering many obscure areas of the Celtic tradition from all of the Celtic countries.

Emania, Journal of the Navan Fort Research Group, Department of Archaeology, Queen's University, Belfast, BT7 1NN, Northern Ireland. A very accessible journal detailing the ongoing research work at Navan Fort, home of King Conchobhar mac Neasa and the Knights of the Red Branch, as well as study and analysis of the legends of the Ulster Cycle.

Irish Texts Society, c/o The Royal Bank of Scotland, Drummonds Branch, 49 Charing Cross, Admiralty Arch, London SW1A 2DX, England. The best translations of Irish legends available, all with extensive notes and glossaries.

Order of Bards, Ovates and Druids, P.O. Box 1333, Lewes, East Sussex, BN7 3ZG, England, provides a first-class correspondence course as an introduction to the vast and complex druidic system.

Pagan Life, Newsletter of the Irish Pagan Movement, The Bridge House, Clonegal, Enniscorthy, Co. Wexford, Eire. A journal dedicated to the Irish tradition, which also sponsors festivals in the Celtic style.

PAS Newsletter, Pictish Arts Society, School of Scottish Studies, 27 George Square, Edinburgh, EH8 9LD, Scotland. A society dedicated to the study of the Picts of the northeast of Scotland. They produce an excellent journal as well as putting on many talks, lectures, and field trips throughout the year.

Seanchas, Journal of the Celtic Research and Folklore Society, Isle of Arran, Scotland. A society dedicated to the Irish Celtic tradition, which produces a quarterly journal for members as well as putting on talks, lectures, and storytelling sessions.

Shadow, Journal of the Traditional Cosmology Society, School of Scottish Studies, 27 George Square, Edinburgh, EH8 9LD, Scotland. Covers the traditions of not only the Celts, but all other cosmologies and traditional belief systems throughout the world.

Index

Stay in Touch. . .

Llewellyn publishes hundreds of books on your favorite subjects

On the following pages you will find listed some books now available on related subjects. Your local bookstore stocks most of these and will stock new Llewellyn titles as they become available. We urge your patronage.

Order by Phone

Call toll-free within the U.S. and Canada, **1–800–THE MOON.**
In Minnesota call **(612) 291–1970.**
We accept Visa, MasterCard, and American Express.

Order by Mail

Send the full price of your order (MN residents add 7% sales tax) in U.S. funds to:
> **Llewellyn Worldwide**
> **P.O. Box 64383, Dept. K069-8**
> **St. Paul, MN 55164–0383, U.S.A.**

Postage and Handling

- ◆ $4.00 for orders $15.00 and under
- ◆ $5.00 for orders over $15.00
- ◆ No charge for orders over $100.00

We ship UPS in the continental United States. We cannot ship to P.O. boxes. Orders shipped to Alaska, Hawaii, Canada, Mexico, and Puerto Rico will be sent first-class mail.

International orders: Airmail—add freight equal to price of each book to the total price of order, plus $5.00 for each non-book item (audiotapes, etc.). Surface mail—Add $1.00 per item.

Allow 4–6 weeks delivery on all orders. Postage and handling rates subject to change.

Group Discounts

We offer a 20% quantity discount to group leaders or agents. You must order a minimum of 5 copies of the same book to get our special quantity price.

Celtic Myth & Magic
Harness the Power of the Gods & Goddesses
by Edain McCoy

Tap into the mythic power of the Celtic goddesses, gods, heroes and heroines to aid your spiritual quests and magickal goals. *Celtic Myth & Magic* explains how to use creative ritual and pathworking to align yourself with the energy of these archetypes, whose potent images live deep within your psyche.

Celtic Myth & Magic begins with an overview of 49 different types of Celtic Paganism followed today, then gives specific instructions for evoking and invoking the energy of the Celtic pantheon to channel it toward magickal and spiritual goals and into esbat, sabbat and life transition rituals. Three detailed pathworking texts will take you on an inner journey where you'll join forces with the archetypal images of Cuchulain, Queen Maeve and Merlin the Magician to bring their energies directly into your life. The last half of the book clearly details the energies of over 300 Celtic deities and mythic figures so you can evoke or invoke the appropriate deity to attain a specific goal.

This inspiring, well-researched book will help solitary Pagans who seek to expand the boundaries of their practice to form working partnerships with the divine.

1–56718–661–0, 7 x 10, 464 pp., softbound $19.95

By Oak, Ash & Thorn
Modern Celtic Shamanism
by D. J. Conway

Many spiritual seekers are interested in shamanism because it is a spiritual path that can be followed in conjunction with any religion or other spiritual belief without conflict. Shamanism has not only been practiced by Native American and African cultures—for centuries, it was practiced by the Europeans, including the Celts.

By Oak, Ash and Thorn presents a workable, modern form of Celtic shamanism that will help anyone raise his or her spiritual awareness. Here, in simple, practical terms, you will learn to follow specific exercises and apply techniques that will develop your spiritual awareness and ties with the natural world: shape-shifting, divination by the Celtic Ogham alphabet, Celtic shamanic tools, traveling to and using magick in the three realms of the Celtic otherworlds, empowering the self, journeying through meditation and more.

Shamanism begins as a personal revelation and inner healing, then evolves into a striving to bring balance and healing into the Earth itself. This book will ensure that Celtic shamanism will take its place among the spiritual practices that help us lead fuller lives.

1–56718–166-X, 6 x 9, 288 pp., illus., softcover $12.95

Faery Wicca, Book One
Theory & Magick • A Book of Shadows & Lights
by Kisma K. Stepanich

Many books have been written on Wicca, but never until now has there been a book on the tradition of Irish Faery Wicca. If you have been drawn to the kingdom of Faery and want to gain a comprehensive understanding of this old folk faith, *Faery Wicca, Book One* offers you a thorough apprenticeship in the beliefs, history and practice of this rich and fulfilling tradition.

First, you'll explore the Irish history of Faery Wicca, its esoteric beliefs and its survival and evolution into its modern form; the Celtic pantheon; the Celtic division of the year; and the fairies of the Tuatha De Danann and their descendants. Each enlightening and informative lesson ends with a journal exercise and list of suggested readings.

The second part of *Faery Wicca, Book One* describes in detail magickal applications of the basic material presented in the first half: Faery Wicca ceremonies and rituals; utilizing magickal Faery tools, symbols and alphabets; creating sacred space; contacting and working with Faery allies; and guided visualizations and exercises suitable for beginners.

1–56718–694–7, 7 x 10, 320 pp., illus., softcover $17.50

Faery Wicca, Book Two
The Shamanic Practices of the Cunning Arts
by Kisma Stepanich

Faery Wicca, Book Two continues the studies undertaken in *Faery Wicca, Book One,* with a deepening focus on the tradition's shamanic practices, including energy work, the Body Temple, healing techniques and developing Second-Sight; meditation techniques; journeys into the Otherworld; contacting Faery Guardians, Allies, Guides and Companions; herbcraft and spellcasting; different forms of Faery divination; rites of passages; the four minor holidays; and a closing statement on the shamanic technique known as "remembering."

The Oral Faery Tradition's teachings are not about little winged creatures. They are about the primal earth and the power therein, the circles of existence, Ancient Gods, the ancestors and the continuum. *Faery Wicca, Book Two* is not a how-to book but a study that provides extensive background information and mystery teachings for both novices and adepts alike.

1-56718-695-5, 7 x 10, 320 pp., illus., softcover $17.50